Mystical Hermetic &
Christian Dialogues

Beyond the Nag Hammadi Canon

*Egyptian Wisdom, the Divine Mind,
and the Ascent of the Soul*

A Modern Translation
Adapted for the Contemporary Reader

Various Hermetic & Early Christian Writers

Translated by Tim Zengerink

Table of Contents

Preface - Message to the Reader

What If You Could Help Rebuild the Greatest Library in Human History?

Thousands of years ago, the Library of Alexandria stood as the crown jewel of human achievement — a sanctuary where the collected wisdom of every known civilization was gathered, preserved, and shared freely.

And then, it was lost.

Through fire, conquest, and the slow erosion of time, humanity lost not just books — but ideas, dreams, discoveries, and stories that could have changed the world forever.

Today, the Library of Alexandria lives again — and you are invited to be a part of its restoration.

Our mission is simple yet profound:

To rebuild the greatest library the world has ever known, and to translate all timeless works into every language and dialect, so that no seeker of knowledge is ever left behind again.

By joining our movement to rebuild the modern Library of Alexandria, you become part of an unprecedented mission:

- **Unlimited Access to the Greatest Audiobooks & eBooks Ever Written:**

  Instantly explore thousands of legendary works—Plato, Shakespeare, Jane Austen, Leo Tolstoy, and countless more. All instantly available to read or listen, placing a complete literary universe at your fingertips.

- **Beautiful Paperback & Deluxe Editions at Printing Cost**

  Own any title as an elegant paperback, deluxe hardcover, or stunning collectible boxset—offered to you at true printing cost, delivered straight to your door. Build your personal Library of Alexandria, crafted for beauty, built for durability, and worthy of proud display.

- **Fresh Translations for Modern Readers—in Every Language & Dialect**

  Enjoy timeless masterpieces reimagined in clear, contemporary language—no more outdated phrases or obscure references. Alongside the original versions, we're tirelessly translating these classics into every language and dialect imaginable, ensuring accessibility and understanding across cultures and generations.

- **Join a Global Renaissance of Literature & Knowledge**

  You directly support expanding our library, publishing deluxe editions at true cost, translating works into all global languages, and bringing humanity's greatest stories to people everywhere. By joining today, you're not just preserving a legacy of masterpieces; you set in motion a powerful wave of literary accessibility.

Become a Torchbearer of Knowledge.

Join us for free now at **LibraryofAlexandria.com**

Together, we will ensure that the light of human wisdom never fades again.

With gratitude and a shared love of knowledge,
The Modern Library of Alexandria Team

Visit:

www.libraryofalexandria.com

Or scan the code below:

Introduction

The Convergence of Traditions:
Egyptian, Greek, and Christian

The collection presented in this volume brings together a rich tapestry of mystical writings that straddle the boundaries between Egyptian Hermetic philosophy, Hellenistic thought, and early Christian theology. These works, though historically fragmented and theologically diverse, converge around a central aim: the transformation of the soul and its reunification with the divine source. They are not mere religious texts or philosophical treatises—they are roadmaps for inner ascent, metaphysical dialogues meant to provoke, enlighten, and awaken.

Hermeticism, named after the legendary figure Hermes Trismegistus, emerged as a spiritual-philosophical tradition in Greco-Roman Egypt, synthesizing elements of ancient Egyptian religion, Platonic and Stoic metaphysics, and Jewish thought. It is both initiatory and contemplative, aimed not at institutional theology but at experiential gnosis—divine knowledge obtained through inner vision and mystical union. The Nag Hammadi library, discovered in 1945 near the town of the same name in Egypt, included among its many texts a number of Hermetic and Christian writings that are now recognized as some of the most profound documents of early spiritual exploration.

The Hermetic writings included here—such as The Discourse on the Eighth and Ninth and The Prayer of Thanksgiving—are emblematic of this tradition. They guide the soul upward through layers of reality, each governed by a celestial intelligence, until it reaches the realm of pure Mind, the ineffable One. This journey, though cast in mythical and philosophical terms, is deeply psychological and transformative. It demands the purification of thought, the shedding of illusion, and the embrace of the divine light within.

In parallel, early Christian mystics—particularly those influenced by Jewish apocalypticism, Hellenistic Judaism, and Alexandrian Platonism—were also articulating their own visions of spiritual ascent. Some of the Christian texts that found their way into the Nag Hammadi codices, such as The Gospel of Thomas and The Sophia of Jesus Christ, resonate powerfully with Hermetic themes. The divine spark within, the ignorance that blinds humanity, and the call to awakening all echo across both traditions. It is within this shared space—what might be called a mystical interfaith dialogue—that the texts in this volume dwell.

The Journey of the Soul: Ascent, Transformation, and Return

The Hermetic worldview envisions the cosmos as a structured hierarchy, a ladder stretching from the material to the immaterial, from the corruptible to the eternal. At the base lies the realm of matter and multiplicity, where the soul, ensnared by sense perception and bodily attachment, forgets its divine origin. But above it stretches the noetic cosmos—spheres of stars, planets, and intelligences that can be transcended through spiritual refinement and gnosis.

In The Discourse on the Eighth and Ninth, the master leads the disciple through a ritual of ascent. As the text unfolds, the disciple experiences a vision of cosmic harmony, praising the intelligences that govern the heavens and declaring their union with the divine source. The journey culminates in a mysterious silence, a paradoxical union with the One that transcends speech and thought. This is not merely an allegory—it is a mystical initiation into the direct experience of transcendence. The initiate moves from knowledge (episteme) to insight (gnosis), from intellect to illumination.

This same structure of ascent appears in early Christian texts, particularly those with Gnostic leanings. In works such as The Sophia of Jesus Christ, salvation is described as the restoration of divine knowledge lost through the soul's descent into the material world. Ignorance, not sin, is the primary affliction, and awakening—through the teachings of the Savior—is the cure. Thus, salvation is not transactional but transformational: the soul remembers who it truly is and reclaims its birthright.

The Prayer of Thanksgiving, likely used as a liturgical conclusion to Hermetic initiations, celebrates the awe and joy of this realization. It is a hymn of unity, where the barriers between self and divinity dissolve. In both Hermetic and Christian mystical traditions, such unity is the goal. It is not enough to believe; one must become. The journey is not just upward, but inward.

The Legacy and Relevance of
the Hermetic-Christian Dialogue

Why do these ancient texts matter today? In an era marked by religious conflict, institutional rigidity, and spiritual longing, they offer a third path—a contemplative, experiential approach to divinity that transcends doctrinal boundaries. They remind us that mysticism is not the property of any one tradition but the beating heart of them all. Whether couched in the language of Hermes or Christ, the call is the same: awaken, ascend, and unite.

Moreover, these writings challenge modern assumptions about the early Christian world. They reveal a time of rich diversity, where ideas flowed between cultures and boundaries were fluid. The early followers of Jesus did not yet have a fixed canon or creed. They experimented, searched, and sometimes crossed paths with sages of other traditions. This syncretism is not a flaw but a feature—evidence of a vibrant and evolving spiritual ecosystem.

The Hermetic dialogues included in this volume are not static texts; they are invitations. To read them is to engage in a process of initiation. They ask us not merely to understand, but to awaken. To see ourselves not as passive recipients of religious tradition, but as active participants in the soul's journey toward the Divine Mind. They ask us to remember that within each human being lies a divine spark—waiting to rise through the spheres and return to its Source.

May the texts you are about to encounter stir your mind, ignite your spirit, and open new pathways of divine remembrance. This is not just a book. It is a doorway. Step through it.

Discourses

Epictetus

Book 1

Chapter 1
On the Things That are in Our Power and Not in Our Power

Out of all the abilities we have, none of them can truly look at itself. Because of that, they also can't approve or disapprove of themselves. For example, how much can grammar think about itself? It can only judge what is written and spoken. And how about music? It can judge melodies. But can either grammar or music think about themselves? Not at all. When you need to write something to a friend, grammar can tell you which words to use, but it won't tell you whether you should write or not. The same goes for music: it can guide you on musical sounds, but it won't tell you if now is the right time to sing or play the flute, or if you should do neither. So, which ability will tell you these things? The one that can think about both itself and everything else. And what is this ability? It's our ability to reason. This is the only ability we have that can examine itself, figure out what it is, what power it has, and how valuable it is. It also looks at all our other abilities. For what else tells us that gold is beautiful? The gold doesn't say it itself. It's the ability that judges appearances. What else judges music, grammar, and other abilities, shows their uses, and points out when to use them? Nothing else does.

So, as it should be, the best and highest ability we have is the only thing the gods put in our control—using appearances correctly. But all other things are not under our control. Why is that? I think that if the gods could have, they would have put these other things in our control too, but they couldn't. Since we live on earth and are tied to our bodies and companions, how could we not be limited by these external things?

9

But what does Zeus say? "Epictetus, if it were possible, I would have made your small body and your little property free and not subject to any obstacles. But now, understand this: your body isn't yours, it's like finely molded clay. And since I couldn't give you what I wanted, I gave you a small part of us—the ability to pursue or avoid things, to desire or dislike things, and to use the appearances of things. If you take care of this ability and see it as your only possession, you'll never be stopped, never face obstacles, you won't complain, blame, or flatter anyone."

"Do these seem like small things to you?" I hope not. "Be satisfied with them, then, and pray to the gods." But now, when we can focus on one thing and attach ourselves to it, we prefer to focus on many things—our body, property, brother, friend, child, and even our slave. Since we're tied to so many things, they weigh us down and pull us down. This is why, when the weather isn't right for sailing, we worry and keep checking which way the wind is blowing. "It's blowing from the north." What does that matter to us? "When will the west wind blow?" It will blow when it wants to or when Aeolus, the god of the winds, decides. We don't control the winds, Aeolus does. What should we do then? Make the best use of what's in our control and accept the rest as they are. What is their nature? Whatever God wishes.

"Must I be the only one to lose my head?" Would you want everyone to lose their heads just to comfort you? Will you not stretch out your neck like Lateranus did when Nero ordered his beheading? After he stretched out his neck and received a weak blow that made him pull back for a moment, he stretched it out again. And earlier, when Nero's freedman Epaphroditus visited him and asked why he offended the emperor, he said, "If I want to explain, I'll tell your master."

What should a man be ready to say in such circumstances? Nothing but, "What's mine and what's not mine? What's allowed to me and what's not?" I must die. Must I die in sorrow? I must be put in chains. Must I also feel sad? I must go into exile. Does anyone stop me from going with a smile, cheerfulness, and peace? "Tell me the secret you hold." I won't, because that's my choice. "But I'll put you in chains." My leg, you mean. "I'll throw you into prison." You mean my body. "I'll cut off your head." Did I ever tell you my head couldn't be cut off? These are the things philosophers should think about, write about daily, and practice.

Thrasea used to say, "I'd rather be killed today than exiled tomorrow." What did Rufus reply? "If you think death is worse, how foolish is your choice? But if you think it's easier, who gave you the choice? Will you not learn to be content with what is given to you?"

What did Agrippinus say? He said, "I am not an obstacle to myself." When he heard his trial was happening in the Senate, he said, "I hope it turns out well. But it's the fifth hour,"—this was his exercise time before his cold bath—"let's go exercise." Afterward, someone told him, "You've been condemned." He asked, "To exile or death?" "To exile," the man replied. "What about my property?" "It's not taken from you." "Then let's go to Aricia and have dinner," Agrippinus said.

This is what it means to study what one ought to study: to make desire and aversion free from obstacles and from everything a person would avoid. I must die. If now, I'm ready. If later, then I'll eat dinner because it's time, and after that, I'll die. How? Like someone giving up something that belongs to someone else.

Chapter 2
How a Man on Every Occasion Can Maintain His Proper Character

Being rational is tolerable for us; what's irrational is not. Blows aren't naturally unbearable. How so? See how Spartans endure whipping when they've learned it's reasonable. Hanging yourself isn't unbearable. When you believe it's rational, you go and hang yourself. In short, we'll find that nothing pains humans as much as what's irrational, and nothing attracts them as much as what's rational.

But what's rational or irrational appears differently to different people, just like what's good or bad, profitable or not. That's why we need discipline, to learn how to adapt our ideas of rationality and irrationality to different situations in line with nature. To judge what's rational and irrational, we not only consider external things but also what suits each person. For one person, it's rational to hold a chamber pot for another, thinking that if he doesn't, he'll be punished and won't get food. But if he does, he won't suffer anything bad. But for another person, it's intolerable to hold a chamber pot, even more so to let someone else do it for him. So if you ask me whether you should hold the chamber pot or not, I'd say that getting food is better than not, and being whipped is worse than not being whipped. So if you judge by these things, go and hold the chamber pot. But you might say, "That's not worthy of me." Then it's you who must bring that into the decision, not me. You know yourself, how much you're worth to yourself, and at what price you sell yourself because people sell themselves at different prices.

That's why when Florus wondered if he should perform in Nero's spectacles, Agrippinus told him to go ahead. When Florus asked why Agrippinus wasn't going, Agrippinus replied, "Because I don't even consider such things." Those who begin to deliberate about such matters and weigh the value of external things are close to forgetting their own character. Why do you ask me if life is better than death? I say life. Pain or pleasure? I say pleasure. But if not acting in a tragedy will get me beheaded, then act in it. But I won't. Why? Because you see yourself as just one thread in the tunic, so you need to fit in with the others, just as a thread doesn't aim to stand out. But I want to be the purple thread, the small part that's bright and makes the rest look graceful and beautiful. Why do you tell me to be like everyone else? If I do, how can I still be purple?

Priscus Helvidius understood this and acted accordingly. When Vespasian commanded him not to go into the Senate, he replied, "You can stop me from being a senator, but as long as I am, I must go in." "Well, go in, but say nothing," said the emperor. "Don't ask my opinion, and I'll be silent," Priscus replied. "But I have to ask your opinion," said Vespasian. "And I must say what I think is right," said Priscus. "But if you do, I'll put you to death." "When did I ever tell you I was immortal? You'll do your part, and I'll do mine. It's your part to kill, and mine to die, but not in fear. Your part is to banish me, and mine is to leave without sorrow."

What good did Priscus do, being just one person? What good does the purple thread do in the toga? It stands out as purple and serves as a fine example to everything else. But in such cases, another person would have thanked Caesar for sparing him. But such a man Vespasian wouldn't have even stopped from entering the Senate because he knew he'd either sit there quietly like an empty vessel or say what Caesar wanted, and perhaps even more.

There was also an athlete who faced death unless he allowed a part of his body to be cut off. His philosopher brother came to him and asked, "What are you going to do, brother? Shall we have it cut off and then return to the gym?" But the athlete chose to keep his dignity and died. When someone asked Epictetus how he did it, whether as an athlete or philosopher, Epictetus replied, "He acted as a man, a man who had been proclaimed a champion in the Olympic Games and had trained hard for it, not just someone practicing in a small gym." Another person might let his head be cut off if it meant he could keep living. But some people have such a strong sense of character that they incorporate it into everything they do and every decision they make.

"Come on, Epictetus, shave your head." If I'm a philosopher, I would say, "I won't shave my head." "But I'll cut your head off if you don't." If it helps you, go ahead.

Someone once asked, "How can each of us know what suits our character?" Epictetus replied, "How does a bull know when a lion attacks? It knows its own strength and steps forward to defend the herd. It's clear that with power comes the understanding of it, and those who have power won't be unaware of it. A bull isn't made in a day, and neither is a brave person. We must train ourselves in the winter to be ready for the summer campaign, and not rush into things that don't concern us.

Think carefully about the price at which you sell your will. If nothing else, at least don't sell it for too little. But what is great and superior might belong to Socrates and those like him. "Why then, if we are naturally like that, aren't more of us like him?" Is it true that all horses become fast or all dogs become skilled at tracking? "Then, since I'm naturally slow, should I not try at all?" Of course not. I'm not better than Socrates, but if I'm not worse, that's enough for me. I'll never be as strong as Milo, but I still take care of my body. I'll never be as rich as Croesus, but I don't neglect my property. In short, we don't ignore taking care of anything just because we might not reach the highest level.

This is the approach we must take in life, understanding our limitations, but always striving to be the best we can within them. Even if we can't reach the level of greatness that others have, we should still aim to be the best version of ourselves.

Chapter 3
How a Man Should Act Based on the Belief that God is the Father of Everyone

If someone truly believes that we are all children of God, and that God is the father of both humans and gods, then he would never think poorly of himself. Imagine if Caesar adopted you; you would likely become very proud. So, if you know that you are the child of Zeus, wouldn't you feel proud too? However, we don't always think this way. Since humans are made of both a body, like animals, and reason and intelligence, like the gods, many people focus more on their body, which is mortal, rather than on their mind, which is divine and eternal.

Those who think that they are meant for honesty, humility, and proper use of their mind will not think lowly of themselves. But many people do the opposite. They might say, "What am I? A poor, miserable person with a weak body." It's true that your body is weak, but you have something much better than that—your mind. So why do you focus on your weak body and neglect your mind, which is stronger?

Because some of us focus more on our bodies, we start to act like animals—some become like wolves, untrustworthy and harmful; some become like lions, wild and untamed; and most of us become like foxes, or even worse animals. What else is a person who spreads lies or acts with malice but a fox, or something even worse? So, be careful not to become one of these unfortunate creatures.

Chapter 4
On Progress or Improvement

When someone is making progress, they learn from philosophers that "desire" means wanting good things, and "aversion" means staying away from bad things. They also learn that happiness and calmness can only be reached if they get what they desire and avoid what they don't want. So, such a person removes desire from themselves completely and puts it off for later. But they only avoid things that are within their control. If they try to avoid something that's outside of their control, they know that sometimes they'll end up facing what they wanted to avoid, and this will make them unhappy. Now, if virtue brings good fortune, calmness, and happiness, then moving towards virtue is the same as moving towards these things. It's always true that wherever perfecting something takes us, progress is getting closer to that point.

So why do we admit that virtue is what I've described but still seek progress in other things and show off about it? What does virtue produce? It produces calmness. So, who is really improving? Is it the person who has read many books by Chrysippus? But does virtue mean understanding Chrysippus? If it does, then progress is nothing more than knowing a lot about Chrysippus. But now we say that virtue produces one thing, and getting closer to it is something else—namely, progress or improvement. Someone might say, "This person can already read Chrysippus by themselves." Indeed, you are making great progress. But what kind of progress? Why do you make fun of the person? Why do you distract them from realizing their own misfortunes? Won't you show them what virtue does so they can see where to look for improvement? Look for it there, wretched person, where your work lies. And where is your work? It's in desire and aversion—so you won't be disappointed in your desires, and you won't fall into what you want to avoid. It's in your pursuit and avoidance—so you don't make mistakes. It's in agreeing or not agreeing with things—so you won't be deceived. The first and most important things are those I've mentioned. But if you're trembling and crying to avoid what you fear, tell me how you're improving.

Do you then show me your improvement in these things? If I were talking to an athlete, I'd say, "Show me your shoulders"; and they might say, "Here are my weights." You and your weights deal with that. I'd reply, "I want to see the result of using those weights." So, when you say: "Take this book on active powers and see how I've studied it." I reply, "Slave, I'm not asking about that, but how you practice pursuit and avoidance, desire and aversion, how you plan and prepare yourself—whether it's in line with nature or not. If it is in line, give me proof, and I'll say you're making progress. But if it's not, go away, and not only explain your books but write such books yourself. And what will you gain by it? Don't you know that the whole book costs only five denarii? Is the person explaining it worth more than five denarii? Never look for the actual thing in one place and progress toward it in another."

So, where is progress? If any of you, turning away from external things, focuses on their own will to work on it and improve it through effort, so it becomes in line with nature—strong, free, unrestricted, unhindered, trustworthy, modest; and if they've learned that anyone who desires or avoids things they can't control can neither be trustworthy nor free, but must change with those things and be tossed around by them like a ship in a storm, and must submit to others who have the power to give or prevent what they desire or want to avoid— finally, when they get up in the morning, if they observe and follow these rules, bathe like a trustworthy person, eat like a modest person; in the same way, if in every situation that arises, they work out their main principles like a runner does with running, and a singer does with their voice—this is the person who is truly making progress, and this is the person who hasn't traveled in vain. But if they've put all their effort into reading books and work only on that, and have traveled for that, I tell them to go back home immediately and not to neglect their responsibilities there; because the reason they've traveled is meaningless. But the other thing is something—to study how a person can remove complaining and groaning from their life, and saying, "Woe is me," and "Poor me," and to remove bad luck and disappointment, and to learn what death is, and exile, and prison, and poison, so they can say when they're in chains, "Dear Crito, if it is the will of the gods, let it be so," and not say, "Poor me, an old man; have I lived to see this?" Who says this? Do you think I'll name some unknown person of low status? Doesn't Priam say this? Doesn't Oedipus say this? No, all kings say it! What else is a tragedy but the troubles of people who value external things, shown in this kind of drama? But if someone must learn through fiction that no external things, which are beyond our control, affect us, I would like this fiction, through which I could live happily and peacefully. But you must decide for yourselves what you want.

What, then, does Chrysippus teach us? The answer is, "to know that these things are true, from which happiness comes and peace arises. Take my books, and you'll learn how true and natural these things are that make me free from troubles." Oh, great good fortune! Oh, the great benefactor who shows us the way! Everyone has built temples and altars for Triptolemus because he gave us food through farming. But to the person who discovered the truth and brought it to light and shared it with everyone, not just the truth about how to live, but how to live well, who of you has built an altar, or a temple, or dedicated a statue, or who thanks God for this? Because the gods gave us the vine or wheat, we sacrifice to them: but because they produced in the human mind the wisdom to show us the truth about happiness, shall we not thank God for this?

18

Chapter 5
Against the Academics

Epictetus said that if someone argues against obvious truths, it's not easy to convince them to change their mind. But this isn't because the person is strong or because the teacher is weak; it's because when someone remains stubborn like a rock, even after being proven wrong, how can we reason with them?

There are two types of stubbornness: one affects understanding, and the other affects a person's sense of shame. When a person decides not to agree with what is clearly true or refuses to stop arguing against it, they become stubborn in their understanding. Most of us are afraid of physical pain and would do anything to avoid it, but we don't care as much about hurting our souls. And when it comes to the soul, if someone is in such a state that they can't understand anything or grasp any ideas, we think they're in a bad condition. But if someone's sense of shame and modesty is gone, we sometimes mistakenly call that strength.

Do you understand that you're awake? "I don't," the person replies, "because I don't even understand when I'm dreaming that I'm awake." Is there no difference between these two states? "None at all," he replies. Should I keep arguing with this person? What can I do to make him realize he's become numb to the truth? He does understand, but he pretends that he doesn't. He's worse off than a dead person because he doesn't see the contradiction: he's in a bad condition. Another person might see the contradiction but doesn't care and doesn't try to improve: he's in an even worse condition. His modesty and sense of shame are gone, and while his ability to reason hasn't been completely lost, it has become like an animal's. Should I call this strength of mind? Certainly not, unless we also consider it strength when people do or say anything that comes into their head without self-control.

Chapter 6
On Providence

Epictetus said that from everything that exists or happens in the world, it is easy to praise Providence if a person has these two qualities: the ability to see how everything fits together and a thankful attitude. If a person doesn't have these two qualities, one person won't see the purpose of the things that exist and happen, and another won't be thankful for them, even if they do understand them. For instance, if God had created colors but hadn't given us the ability to see them, what would their use be? None at all. On the other hand, if He had given us the ability to see but hadn't created objects to be seen, what use would that be? None at all. Now, if He had made both vision and objects, but hadn't created light, what use would they be? Again, none at all. So, who made these things fit together so perfectly? And who made the knife to fit into its case and the case to fit the knife? Was it no one? And indeed, from the very structure of things that have reached their completion, we can tell that the work is certainly the act of some creator, and it hasn't been made without a purpose. So, if each of these things shows evidence of a creator, don't visible things, the ability to see, and light also show evidence of Him? And the existence of male and female, and the desire each has for union, and the ability to use the parts of the body that were made for this—don't these also reveal the work of a creator? If they don't, let's think about how our understanding works: when we encounter physical objects, we simply receive impressions from them, but we also choose certain things from them, ignore others, add, combine, and move from some things to others that are similar. Isn't this enough to make some people realize there's a creator and not forget about Him? If it isn't, let them explain to us what makes each thing, or how it's possible that things so wonderful and purposeful could exist by chance and by their own movement.

Are these things found only in humans? Many things are indeed found only in us, things that the rational animal particularly needed. But you'll find many things we share with irrational animals. Do these animals understand what happens? No, they don't. For using things is one thing, and understanding them is another. God needed irrational animals to use the appearances of things, but He needed us to understand how to use them. So it's enough for them to eat, drink, sleep, reproduce, and do all the other things that they do. But for us, to whom He has also given the ability to understand, these things are not enough. If we don't act in a proper and orderly way, in line with the nature and purpose of each thing, we'll never achieve our true purpose. Where the natures of living beings are different, their actions and purposes are also different. So for those animals whose nature is only to use things, just using them is enough. But for an animal that also has the power to understand how to use things, unless there is the proper exercise of understanding, it will never achieve its true purpose. So God made each animal with a purpose: one to be eaten, another to help with farming, another to provide milk, and another for some similar use. For these purposes, what need is there to understand appearances and be able to distinguish them? But God created humans to be spectators of God and His works, and not just spectators, but also interpreters. For this reason, it is shameful for humans to start and end where irrational animals do. Instead, we should start where they do and end where nature intended us to end: in contemplation and understanding, living in harmony with nature. So be careful not to die without having been spectators of these things.

But you would take a journey to Olympia to see the work of Phidias, and you would think it a misfortune to die without having seen such things. But when you don't need to take a journey, and the works of God are right in front of you wherever you are, won't you want to see and understand them? Won't you realize what you are, what you were born for, and what purpose your ability to see serves? But you might say, "There are some unpleasant and troublesome things in life." Aren't there unpleasant things at Olympia? Don't you get sunburned? Don't you get pushed around by crowds? Don't you have uncomfortable places to bathe? Don't you get wet when it rains? Don't you deal with a lot of noise, clamor, and other unpleasant things? But I suppose that balancing all these things with the magnificence of the spectacle makes you bear and endure them. Well, then, haven't you received abilities that will help you bear everything that happens? Haven't you received greatness of soul? Haven't you received courage? Haven't you received endurance? So why should I worry about anything that might happen if I have greatness of soul? What can disturb me, upset me, or seem painful? Shouldn't I use the abilities I've been given for their intended purpose, instead of complaining about what happens?

"Yes, but my nose runs," you say. So why do you have hands? Isn't it so you can wipe your nose? "But is it reasonable that there should be runny noses in the world?" Isn't it better to wipe your nose than to complain about it? What do you think Hercules would have been if there hadn't been a lion, a hydra, a stag, a boar, or certain unjust and evil people that he had to drive away and defeat? What would he have done if those challenges didn't exist? It's obvious that he would have wrapped himself in a blanket and slept. In that case, he wouldn't have been Hercules, because he would have spent his life in luxury and ease. Even if he had been strong, what good would that have been if he didn't face challenges? What use would his strength, his arms, his endurance, and his noble spirit have been if he hadn't been tested and exercised by those challenges?

"So, should a person create challenges for themselves, like bringing a lion or a boar or a hydra into their country?" That would be foolish and crazy. But since challenges do exist, they are useful for showing what kind of person we are and for exercising our strengths. So when you recognize these things, look at the abilities you have, and when you've looked at them, say: "Bring now, Zeus, any challenge you want, for I have been given the means and powers by You to honor myself through whatever happens." But instead of doing this, you sit around, trembling with fear that something bad will happen, and you weep, lament, and groan about what does happen, and then you blame the gods. What else can come from such weakness but impiety?

And yet, God has not only given us the abilities to handle everything that happens without being crushed or broken by it, but like a good king and a true father, He has given us these abilities freely, without any hindrance, completely under our control, and without reserving any power for Himself to stop or obstruct us. You, who have received these powers freely and as your own, don't use them. You don't even recognize what you've been given or who gave it to you. Some of you are blind to the giver and don't acknowledge your benefactor, while others, out of weakness, blame God. But I will show you that you have the abilities for greatness of soul and courage. But what abilities do you have for blaming and accusing others? Show those to me.

Chapter 7
On the Use of Sophistical Arguments, Hypotheticals, and Similar Things

Epictetus said that dealing with tricky and hypothetical arguments, as well as those based on questions and answers, is important for understanding our duties in life, even though most people don't realize this. In every situation, we try to find out how a wise and good person should handle things properly. So, let people either say that a serious person won't get involved in debates, or that if he does, he won't care about avoiding rash or careless behavior when questioning and answering. But if they don't agree with either of these points, then they must admit that we need to look into the topics that involve questioning and answering.

What is the goal of reasoning? It is to establish true statements, remove false ones, and avoid agreeing with unclear ideas. Is it enough, then, to have just learned this? "Yes, it's enough," someone might say. But is it also enough for someone who doesn't want to make a mistake with money to only know that they should accept real coins and reject fake ones? "No, it's not enough." What else is needed? The ability to test and tell the difference between real and fake coins. Similarly, in reasoning, just knowing the goal isn't enough; you also need the ability to examine and tell the difference between what's true, what's false, and what's unclear. "Yes, that's necessary."

What else is important in reasoning? "You need to accept what follows logically from what you've agreed to." Is it enough just to know this? No, it's not. You need to learn how one thing leads to another, and when one thing follows from one thing or several things together. Think about whether it's necessary for someone who wants to be good at reasoning to develop the ability to prove the points he's discussing and understand the arguments of others. He should also avoid being tricked by people who use false reasoning as if they were proving something. This is why practicing and exercising with logical arguments has become important and necessary.

But sometimes we agree on the starting points, or assumptions, of an argument, and something follows from them that isn't true, but it still logically follows. What should I do in that case? Should I accept the false conclusion? How can I do that? Should I say that I didn't really agree to the assumption? "But you can't do that either." Should I say that the conclusion doesn't follow from what we agreed on? "But you can't do that either." So what should be done in this situation? Think of it this way: borrowing money doesn't make someone a debtor forever; they remain in debt only if they don't repay the money. Similarly, you're not forced to accept the conclusion just because you agreed to the assumptions—you have to stick with what you agreed to. If the assumptions stay the same as when you agreed to them, then you must accept the conclusion. But if the assumptions change in any way, you must withdraw your agreement and reject the conclusion that doesn't follow from the original agreement.

So, we should carefully examine these kinds of assumptions and pay attention to how they change during questioning, answering, or drawing conclusions. This is important to avoid being confused or tricked by false reasoning, especially when we don't see what the real conclusion should be. Why should we examine this? So that we don't get involved in discussions in a careless or confusing way.

The same applies to hypotheses and hypothetical arguments. Sometimes it's necessary to accept a hypothesis as a starting point for the argument that follows. Should we allow every hypothesis that's proposed, or not? If not, which ones should we allow? And if someone has accepted a hypothesis, must they always stick to it? Or can they sometimes withdraw from it while still accepting the logical consequences and avoiding contradictions? Yes, but what if someone says, "If you accept this hypothesis, I'll lead you to an impossible conclusion"? Should a wise person avoid engaging with such a person and refuse to discuss it with them? But who else but a wise person can use reasoning, is skilled in questioning and answering, and can't be tricked or deceived by false reasoning? Shouldn't he take care when he enters into an argument, making sure he doesn't do so rashly or carelessly? And if he doesn't take care, how can he be the kind of person we think he is? Without some practice and preparation, how can he maintain a consistent and logical argument? If this isn't the case, then all these discussions are unnecessary and go against our idea of what it means to be a good and serious person.

So, why are we still lazy, negligent, and slow to take action, and why do we look for excuses not to work hard or be careful in developing our reasoning? "If I make a mistake in these matters, it's not like I've killed my father!" someone might say. But where was there a father involved in this situation that you could kill? What, then, have you done? The only mistake possible here is the one you've already made. This is what I told Rufus when he blamed me for not finding the one thing missing in a certain argument: "I suppose," I said, "that I've burned down the Capitol." "Fool," he replied, "was the thing missing here the Capitol?" Are the only crimes burning down the Capitol or killing your father? But to use the appearances presented to you recklessly, foolishly, and carelessly, to not understand arguments, demonstrations, or sophisms, or, in short, to not see in questioning and answering what is consistent with what you've agreed to or not—is there no error in that?

Chapter 8
The Abilities of the Untrained Are Not Reliable

Epictetus said that just as we can change things that are equal to one another in many ways, we can also change the forms of arguments and reasoning. Here's an example: "If you borrowed money and didn't repay it, you owe me the money. You didn't borrow money and didn't repay it; so, you don't owe me the money." To be able to do this skillfully is especially important for a philosopher because if an enthymeme is an incomplete form of reasoning, it's clear that someone who is trained in complete reasoning must also be good at the incomplete kind.

"Then why don't we practice this more often?" someone might ask. I would reply that right now, even though we don't practice these things and aren't distracted from studying morality, we still don't make much progress in becoming better people. So, what should we expect if we add this practice? Especially since it would not only distract us from more important things but could also make us conceited and arrogant. The power of arguing and persuasion is great, and if someone practices it a lot and adds some flair with language, it can easily lead to arrogance, especially if the person isn't well-trained. Any skill gained by someone who is untrained and weak can bring the danger of making them proud and boastful. How could you convince a young person who is good at these things that they shouldn't let the skill control them, but instead, they should control the skill? Doesn't he just dismiss all advice and show off, refusing to listen to anyone who tries to correct him or remind him of what he's neglecting?

"But wasn't Plato a philosopher?" someone might ask. "And wasn't Hippocrates a doctor? But look at how Hippocrates speaks." Does Hippocrates speak like that because he's a doctor? Why are you mixing up things that just happened to be part of the same person? If Plato was handsome and strong, should I also try to become handsome and strong, as if that were necessary for philosophy, just because a certain philosopher was both handsome and a philosopher? Shouldn't you choose to see and understand what makes a person a philosopher and what other qualities they might have? If I were a philosopher, should you also become lame just because I am?

What then? Am I taking away the abilities you have? Not at all; just as I wouldn't take away your ability to see. But if you ask me what the true good of a person is, I can only tell you that it's a certain state of the will in response to what we perceive.

Chapter 9
How Understanding Our Connection to God Leads to Important Outcomes

Epictetus said that if what philosophers say about our connection to God is true, then what should we do other than what Socrates did? When someone asks you where you're from, don't say that you're from Athens or Corinth, but instead say that you're a citizen of the world. Why do you say you're an Athenian? Why not just say you're from the small corner of the earth where your body was born? Isn't it obvious that you call yourself an Athenian or Corinthian because those cities are larger and include not only your small birthplace and family but also the entire country your ancestors came from?

So, if someone understands how the world is run and learns that the greatest and most important community is the one made up of both humans and God, and that from God come not only our father and grandfather but all living beings—especially rational beings, who are naturally connected to God through reason—why shouldn't that person call themselves a citizen of the world and a child of God? And why should they be afraid of anything that happens among humans? If being related to Caesar or some other powerful person in Rome is enough to make us feel safe, respected, and free from fear, then wouldn't having God as your creator, father, and protector free us from sorrow and fear?

But someone might ask, "How will I get food if I have nothing?"

Think about slaves and runaways—what do they rely on when they leave their masters? Do they rely on land, slaves, or silver? No, they rely on nothing but themselves, and yet they still find food. So, should a philosopher who travels to foreign places rely on others instead of taking care of themselves? Should they be less capable than animals, which are self-sufficient, always finding the food and way of life that suits them and is in harmony with nature?

I believe that an elder should be here, not just to stop you from having low thoughts or talking poorly about yourselves, but to make sure that none of us young people, after realizing our connection to God and seeing that we are tied to our bodies and the things we own, decide to throw off these burdens as if they were too painful to bear and leave to return to our divine family. This should be the task of a true teacher, if they are doing their job. You should go to them and say, "Epictetus, we can no longer stand being tied to this weak body, feeding it, giving it drink, resting it, and cleaning it, and doing what others want because of it. Aren't these things unimportant to us? Isn't death nothing to fear? Aren't we, in a way, children of God? Didn't we come from Him? Let us go back to where we came from. Let us finally be free from these chains that bind us and weigh us down. Here, there are robbers, thieves, courts, and tyrants who think they have power over us through our bodies and possessions. Let us show them that they have no power over us." And I would say, "Friends, wait for God. When He gives the signal and releases you from this duty, then go to Him. But for now, endure living in the place where He has put you. Your time here is short and easy to bear if you think about it the right way. What tyrant, thief, or court can scare those who don't care about their bodies or possessions? So wait, and don't leave without a good reason."

This is the kind of thing a teacher should say to serious students. But what happens now? The teacher is like a lifeless body, and you are lifeless too. After eating well today, you sit down and worry about tomorrow, wondering how you'll find something to eat. Poor soul, if you have food, you'll have it; if you don't, you'll leave this life. The door is open. Why do you grieve? Where is there room for tears? Why should you flatter anyone? Why should one person envy another?

Why admire the rich or powerful, even if they are strong and bad-tempered? What can they do to us? We won't care about what they can do, and what we do care about, they can't touch. How did Socrates behave in situations like this? He acted like a person who knew he was related to the gods. When he was on trial, he said to his judges, "If you tell me that you'll let me go if I stop speaking as I do, and stop bothering the young and the old with my words, I'll tell you that you're being ridiculous. You think that if one of our military leaders assigns me a post, it's my duty to stay there and be ready to die a thousand times before I leave it. But if God assigns me a place and a way of life, you think I should leave it?" Socrates spoke like a man who truly believed he was connected to the gods. But we think of ourselves as nothing more than stomachs, intestines, and shameful parts. We are afraid, we desire, we flatter those who can help us with these things, and we fear them too.

One time, a man asked me to write to Rome for him. He was someone who, according to most people, had fallen on hard times. He used to be wealthy and important, but he had lost everything and was living here. I wrote on his behalf in a humble way, but when he read the letter, he gave it back to me and said, "I asked for your help, not your pity. Nothing bad has happened to me."

Similarly, Musonius Rufus used to test me by saying, "This or that will happen to you because of your master." And I would reply that these are just normal events in life. He would ask, "Why should I ask someone else for something when I can get it from you?" Because, in truth, what a person has within themselves, it's unnecessary and foolish to seek from others. Should I, who can find greatness of soul and a noble spirit within myself, seek land, money, or a government position from you? I hope not; I wouldn't be so ignorant of my own abilities. But when someone is cowardly and weak, what else can be done for them except to write letters on their behalf, as you would for a dead body: "Please allow us to take care of the body of so-and-so and give us a little bit of blood to work with." For such a person is, in fact, just a body and some blood, nothing more. But if they were anything more, they would know that no person can make another person miserable.

Chapter 10
Against Those Who Eagerly Seek Power and Status in Rome

Epictetus said that if we put as much effort into our own work as the old men in Rome do in their duties, we might actually achieve something. I know a man who is older than me, who is now in charge of the corn supply in Rome. I remember when he passed through here on his way back from exile, talking about his past and saying that after his return, he would focus only on spending the rest of his life in peace and quiet. "After all," he said, "how little of life do I have left?" I replied, "You won't do that. As soon as you catch the scent of Rome, you'll forget everything you've said. And if you get a chance to enter the imperial palace, you'll eagerly go in and thank God for it." He responded, "If you ever see me setting even one foot in the palace, think what you will of me." So what happened? Before he even entered the city, he received letters from Caesar, and as soon as he got them, he forgot everything he had said and continued to add one responsibility after another. I wish I were by his side now to remind him of what he said when he passed through here and to show him that I'm better at predicting human behavior than he is.

So, am I saying that humans are meant to do nothing? Of course not. But why aren't we active in the right ways? For instance, when my day starts, I remind myself of what I need to teach my students. But then I think, "Why should I care how someone else learns? The first thing I should do is get some sleep." And really, how does what others do compare to what we do? If you observe what they do, you'll see. What do they spend their day doing? They keep accounts, discuss among themselves, and give and take advice about small things like a bit of grain, a piece of land, and minor profits. Is it the same thing to receive a request like, "I beg you to allow me to export a small amount of corn," as it is to receive one like, "I beg you to learn from Chrysippus what the order of the world is, what role the rational being plays in it, and to consider who you are and what the nature of good and bad is"? Are these things the same? Do they require the same level of care? Is it equally shameful to neglect one as it is the other?

So, are we the only ones who are lazy and love sleep? No, in fact, you young men are even more so. We older folks, when we see young people having fun, want to join in and play with them. And if I saw you being active and serious, I would be even more eager to join you in your pursuits.

Chapter 11
On Family Affection

When a magistrate visited Epictetus, he asked him several questions and inquired if he had children and a wife. The man replied that he did. Epictetus then asked how he felt about his situation. The man said, "Miserable." Epictetus asked, "In what way?" because people don't marry and have children to be miserable but to be happy. The man replied, "I'm so miserable about my children that when my little daughter was sick and in danger, I couldn't bear to stay with her. I left home until someone told me she had recovered."

Epictetus asked, "Do you think you acted rightly?" The man responded, "I acted naturally." Epictetus said, "Convince me that what you did was natural, and I'll convince you that everything natural is also right." The man replied, "This is how most fathers act."

Epictetus didn't deny that, but he pointed out that just because something is common doesn't mean it's right. For example, just because tumors are common doesn't mean they're good for the body. Similarly, just because most people do wrong doesn't mean doing wrong is natural. Epictetus asked the man to show him how his behavior was natural. The man said, "I can't, but can you show me how it wasn't natural and wasn't right?"

Epictetus then said, "If we were discussing colors, what would we use to tell the difference between white and black?" The man answered, "Our sight." "And if we were talking about hot and cold, or hard and soft, what would we use?" The man replied, "Our touch." Epictetus continued, "So, since we're discussing what is natural and what is done rightly or wrongly, what should we use to judge this?" The man said, "I don't know." Epictetus responded, "Not knowing how to judge colors or smells isn't a big problem, but if someone doesn't know how to judge what is good and bad, and what is natural and what is against nature, isn't that a serious problem?" The man agreed that it was.

Epictetus then asked, "Do all things that seem good to some people seem good to everyone? For example, when it comes to food, do Jews, Syrians, Egyptians, and Romans all have the same opinions?" The man replied, "No, it's not possible." Epictetus pointed out that if the Egyptians' opinions are correct, then the others must be wrong, and if the Jews are correct, then the others must be wrong. The man agreed. Epictetus then explained that ignorance leads to a lack of learning and training in what is necessary. The man agreed again.

So Epictetus said, "Now that you know this, will you focus on nothing else but learning the standard for what is natural and using it to judge everything?" The man agreed. Epictetus then asked, "Does loving your family seem natural and good to you?" The man said, "Yes, certainly." "Is this love natural and good, and is it not also good to act reasonably?" The man agreed that it was. "Is reason ever in conflict with love?" Epictetus asked. The man said, "I don't think so." Epictetus pointed out that if one thing is natural, the opposite must be unnatural. The man agreed.

Epictetus continued, "So, if we find something that is both loving and reasonable, we can say it's right and good." The man agreed. "So, was it reasonable to leave your sick child?" Epictetus asked. The man admitted that it wasn't reasonable. Epictetus then asked if it was loving. The man said, "Let's think about it." Epictetus then asked if the mother loved the child and whether she should have left too. The man replied, "No, she shouldn't have." "What about the nurse? Does she love the child?" The man said, "Yes, she does." "Should the nurse have left?" Epictetus asked. The man replied, "No, by no means." "What about the child's teacher? Should he have left?" The man agreed that he shouldn't have.

Epictetus concluded, "So, should the child have been left alone, without help, because of the great love of her parents and caregivers? Should she have died in the hands of those who didn't care for her?" The man admitted that this would be wrong. Epictetus pointed out that it's unfair and unreasonable to think that just because you have affection, you can do something that you wouldn't allow others with the same affection to do. It's absurd.

Epictetus then asked, "If you were sick, would you want your family and friends to love you so much that they'd leave you alone and deserted?" The man replied, "No, by no means." "Would you want to be so loved that through their excessive affection, you'd always be left alone in sickness? Or would you rather pray to be loved by your enemies so they'd leave you?" The man agreed that this would be ridiculous. Epictetus concluded, "So, your behavior wasn't really loving at all."

Epictetus then asked if nothing moved the man to leave his child. The man admitted that something must have, but he wasn't sure what it was. Epictetus explained that it's important to understand that the cause of all our actions—whether we do something or not, say something or not, feel happy or sad, avoid something or pursue something—is our own will. It's not the event itself but our will to do or not do something. The man agreed.

Epictetus explained that it wasn't the death of Patroclus that caused Achilles to mourn, but his own will to do so. Another person might not have reacted the same way. In the same way, it was the man's will that made him run away from his sick child. If he had willed to stay, he would have stayed. And now, if he chooses to go to Rome, it's because he wills to do so, and if he changes his mind, he won't go.

Epictetus then asked if he had convinced the man. The man replied that he was convinced. Epictetus continued, "So, from now on, when we do something wrong, we'll blame nothing else but our own will. We'll work to fix our will just as we would work to remove tumors or abscesses from the body. And we'll understand that when we do something right, it's also because of our will. We won't blame others for our problems—neither slaves, neighbors, spouses, nor children—because if we don't think something is a problem, we won't act as if it is. And whether we think something is a problem or not is up to us, not external events." The man agreed.

Epictetus concluded, "So from now on, we'll focus on examining our opinions and nothing else—not land, not slaves, not horses or dogs—just our opinions." The man agreed. Epictetus then pointed out that the man would need to become a dedicated student of philosophy, someone whom others might ridicule if he truly intended to examine his own opinions. And he would know that this work isn't something that can be done in an hour or a day.

Chapter 12
On Contentment

When it comes to the gods, people have different beliefs. Some say that gods don't exist. Others say they exist but are inactive and don't care about anything. A third group says gods exist and care, but only about big, heavenly things, not about anything on earth. A fourth group says gods care about both earthly and heavenly things, but only in a general way, not about individual things. Finally, there's a fifth group, which includes people like Ulysses and Socrates, who say, "I do nothing without your knowledge."

The first thing we need to do is to figure out which of these beliefs is true. If there are no gods, why should we follow them? If gods exist but don't care about anything, then why should we follow them? But if gods do exist and care about things, and if they communicate with us, then we should consider how to follow them. A wise and good person, after thinking about all this, will submit their mind to the one who rules everything, just like good citizens follow the laws of their country. Someone learning should approach their teacher with this intention: "How can I follow the gods in everything, be content with how they manage things, and become truly free?" For a person is free if everything happens according to their will and no one can stop them.

But what is freedom? Is it madness? Certainly not. Freedom and madness don't go together. "But," you might say, "I want everything to happen just as I like, in whatever way I like." That's madness. Don't you know that freedom is something noble and valuable? But wanting things to happen without thinking isn't noble; it's foolish. Think about writing. Do I wish to write someone's name however I want? No, I learn to write it correctly. The same goes for music and every other skill. If we didn't learn to do things properly, knowledge would be worthless. So, when it comes to the greatest and most important thing—freedom—should I be allowed to want whatever I want without thinking? Of course not. Learning means learning to wish for things to happen as they do happen. And how do things happen? They happen according to the plan set by the one who rules everything. This ruler has created summer and winter, plenty and scarcity, virtue and vice, and all opposites for the harmony of the whole. To each of us, this ruler has given a body, body parts, possessions, and companions.

Remembering this plan, we should approach learning, not to change the way things are—because we can't, and it wouldn't be better if we could—but so that we can keep our minds in harmony with the way things happen. Can we avoid interacting with others? How could we? And if we live with others, can we change them? Who has the power to do that? So, what's left? How can we interact with others in a way that lets them do what they think is right, while we still stay true to nature? You may not want to endure it and might be discontent. When you're alone, you call it solitude. When you're with others, you call them cheats and thieves. You complain about your parents, children, siblings, and neighbors. But when you're alone, you should call it peace and freedom, and see yourself as like the gods. When you're with others, you shouldn't see it as a crowd or trouble, but as a festival and gathering, and accept everything with contentment.

What happens to those who don't accept things? They remain as they are. If someone is unhappy being alone, let them be alone. If someone is unhappy with their parents, let them be a bad child and grieve. If someone is unhappy with their children, let them be a bad parent. "Throw him in prison," you might say. But what is prison? It's just being somewhere against your will. If you're somewhere against your will, you're already in prison. But Socrates wasn't in prison because he was there willingly.

"Must my leg then be injured?" you might ask. Are you really going to complain about the world because of one injured leg? Won't you willingly give it up for the good of the whole? Will you be upset with what Zeus has planned, which he and the Fates decided when you were born? Don't you realize how small a part of the whole you are? I mean physically. In terms of intelligence, you're not less than the gods, because intelligence isn't measured by size but by thought.

Won't you choose to place your value in what makes you equal to the gods? "But I'm unhappy because of my parents." Did you get to choose your parents? Did you get to say, "Let this man and this woman come together so I can be born"? No, it was necessary for your parents to exist first and then for you to be born. What kind of parents? The ones you got. Now that they're your parents, is there no solution for you? If you didn't know how to use your eyes, you'd be miserable if you closed them when there were colors to see. But you have greatness of soul and nobility of spirit to handle everything that happens, and you don't know it. Doesn't that make you more unfortunate? You have the power to deal with whatever happens, but you turn away from that power right when you need it most. Shouldn't you thank the gods that they've made you above the things that aren't in your control and responsible only for what is in your control? As for your parents, the gods have freed you from responsibility, just like with your siblings, body, possessions, death, and life. What are you responsible for? Only for how you use your perceptions. So why do you burden yourself with things you're not responsible for? You're just making trouble for yourself.

Chapter 13
How to Live in a Way That Pleases the Gods

When someone asked how a person could eat in a way that pleases the gods, Epictetus replied, "If you can eat justly, contentedly, calmly, temperately, and with order, won't that be pleasing to the gods?" But if you ask for warm water and the servant doesn't hear you, or if he hears you but brings only lukewarm water, or if he's not even around, and you don't get upset or angry, isn't that pleasing to the gods?

"How then should a person deal with such a servant?" you might ask. Epictetus replied, "You, who are also a servant, won't you bear with your own brother, who shares the same father, Zeus, and comes from the same divine origin? But if you've been placed in a higher position, will you immediately act like a tyrant? Won't you remember who you are and whom you rule? They are your family, your brothers by nature, the children of Zeus."

"But I bought them, and they didn't buy me," you might say. Epictetus responded, "Look at where your thoughts are focused—on earthly things, on these worthless human laws. But you're not looking toward the laws of the gods."

Chapter 14
That God Watches Over Everyone

When someone asked Epictetus how a person could believe that all their actions are watched by God, he replied, "Do you believe that everything is connected in one big whole?" The person said, "Yes, I do." Epictetus continued, "Do you also believe that things on earth are connected to things in heaven?" The person agreed. "Then how do things like plants follow God's command so precisely? When He tells them to flower, they flower. When He tells them to grow, they grow. When He tells them to produce fruit, they do so. When He tells the fruit to ripen, it ripens. And when He commands the fruit to fall, it falls. When He tells the leaves to drop, they drop. And when He tells the plants to rest, they rest. How else could there be such big changes on earth, like the phases of the moon or the changing of the seasons?"

"But if plants and our bodies are so closely connected with everything in the universe, isn't it even more true of our souls? Our souls are connected to God as parts of Him, and doesn't God notice every movement of these parts as if they were His own? Now, can you think about divine things and human affairs at the same time? Can you sense and understand many things at once, agree with some, disagree with others, and sometimes wait to decide? Can you keep so many thoughts in your mind and, being moved by them, remember similar thoughts? Can you hold on to many skills and memories of countless things? If you can do all this, can't God oversee everything, be present with everything, and get a sense of everything? The sun can light up such a large part of the world, leaving only the part that is in the earth's shadow. The sun is just a small part of the universe compared to the whole. So can't the one who made the sun and controls its movement also see everything?"

"But I can't understand all these things at once," the person might reply. Epictetus responded, "Who said you have the same power as Zeus? But even so, He has placed a guardian spirit with each of us, a personal guide who never sleeps and is never fooled. Who could take better care of us? So, when you close your doors and sit in darkness, never say you are alone because you are not. God is within you, and your guardian spirit is within you. They don't need light to see what you are doing. To this God, you should swear an oath, just as soldiers swear an oath to Caesar. But while soldiers are paid to swear that they will put Caesar's safety above all things, you, who have received so many great blessings, won't you swear? Or if you do, won't you keep your oath? And what should you swear? Never to disobey, never to complain, never to blame anything God has given you, and never to do or suffer anything unwillingly. Is this oath like the soldier's oath? Soldiers swear not to put anyone above Caesar; in this oath, you swear to honor yourself above all."

Chapter 15
What Philosophy Teaches

When someone asked Epictetus how he could persuade his brother to stop being angry with him, Epictetus replied, "Philosophy doesn't promise to get you things from outside. If it did, it would be overstepping its bounds. Just as a carpenter's material is wood and a sculptor's material is copper, the material for the art of living is each person's life. 'What about my brother's life?' you might ask. That's his own business, not yours. But in your case, your brother's anger is one of those outside things, like a piece of land, like health, or like reputation. Philosophy doesn't promise you any of these things. Philosophy says, 'In every situation, I will keep the part of you that governs your actions in harmony with nature.' Whose governing part? 'The one in whom I live,' philosophy says.

"How can I stop my brother from being angry with me?" Bring him to me, and I will talk to him. But I have nothing to say to you about his anger.

When the person asking for advice said, 'I want to know how, even if my brother isn't reconciled with me, I can keep myself in a state that is in harmony with nature,' Epictetus replied, 'Nothing great is produced quickly, not even a grape or a fig. If you tell me now that you want a fig, I will tell you that it needs time: it must first flower, then grow fruit, and then ripen. So, if the fruit of a fig tree doesn't mature quickly, would you expect the fruit of a person's mind to mature so quickly and easily? Don't expect it, even if I tell you so.'"

Chapter 16
On Providence

Don't be surprised if other animals, unlike humans, have everything they need for their bodies—like food, drink, and even a place to sleep—without needing shoes, bedding, or clothes. But we, as humans, need all these extra things. Animals weren't made for their own sake but to serve others, so it wouldn't make sense for them to need more. Imagine how difficult it would be if we had to take care of ourselves and also worry about clothing and feeding cattle and donkeys. Think about how soldiers are always ready for their commander—fully equipped with shoes, clothes, and weapons. But it would be really hard for the commander to go around putting shoes and clothes on each of his thousand soldiers. In the same way, nature has made animals that serve us ready and prepared, needing no extra care. That's why even a small child with just a stick can easily lead a herd of cattle.

But instead of being thankful that we don't have to worry about animals as we do ourselves, we often complain about God not giving us everything we want. Yet, in the name of Zeus and the gods, any one of the things that exist would be enough to make a person realize the care and wisdom of God—at least a person who is modest and grateful. Don't just think about the big things, but consider this: grass produces milk, milk produces cheese, and skins produce wool. Who created or designed these things? No one, you might say. That's an incredible amount of shamelessness and foolishness!

Let's put aside the great works of nature and look at the smaller, less important things she does. Is there anything less useful than a beard? But even here, nature has used it in the best possible way. Hasn't she used it to distinguish males from females? Doesn't every man's nature immediately declare from a distance, "I am a man. Treat me as a man, speak to me as a man. Expect nothing else—see the signs?" In the case of women, just as nature made their voices softer, she also removed the beard from their faces. You might argue that the human race would have been better off without these marks of distinction, forcing each of us to announce, "I am a man." But isn't the beard a beautiful, dignified, and respectable sign? How much more attractive is it than a rooster's comb or a lion's mane? For this reason, we should respect the signs that God has given us. We shouldn't try to get rid of them or blur the differences between the sexes as much as we can.

Are these the only signs of God's care in us? What words could ever be enough to praise them and give them the recognition they deserve? If we truly understood, wouldn't we spend our time, both together and alone, singing hymns and praising the deity, and talking about His blessings? Shouldn't we, while digging, plowing, and eating, be singing this hymn to God? "Great is God, who has given us such tools to work the earth: great is God who has given us hands, the ability to swallow, a stomach, invisible growth, and the power to breathe even while we sleep." This is what we should sing on every occasion, and we should sing the greatest and most divine hymn of all for giving us the ability to understand these things and use them properly.

Well then, since most of you have become blind to this, shouldn't there be someone to fill this role and, on behalf of everyone, sing this hymn to God? What else can I do, a lame old man, but sing hymns to God? If I were a nightingale, I would do the work of a nightingale; if I were a swan, I would do the work of a swan. But now I am a rational being, so I must praise God. This is my job, and I will do it. I won't leave this duty as long as I'm allowed to keep it, and I encourage you to join in this same song with me.

Chapter 17
Why Logical Thinking Is Necessary

Since it is reason that helps us understand and improve everything else, it is important that we understand and improve reason itself. But how should we understand reason? Should we use reason itself, or something else? If we use something else, it must either be reason or something greater than reason, which is impossible. If we use reason to understand reason, who will understand that reasoning? If reason can understand itself, then the reasoning we started with can do the same. But if we keep needing something else to understand each step, the process will go on forever.

Someone might say, "Fixing our decisions is more important than studying logic." If you want to talk about that, I'm ready to listen. But if you tell me, "I don't know if your argument is true or false," and if I use a word you don't understand and you ask me to explain it, I won't continue without addressing that. That's why the Stoic philosophers put logic first, just like when we measure grain, we first define what the measurement is. If we don't first define what a measuring tool is, how can we measure or weigh anything accurately? In the same way, if we don't fully understand the standard of judgment for everything else, how can we ever truly understand anything else?

Someone might argue, "But a measuring tool is just a piece of wood and doesn't produce anything." That's true, but it helps us measure grain. They might also say, "Logic doesn't produce anything." We'll discuss that later, but even if we agree with that, we can still say that logic helps us examine and understand everything else, just like a scale helps us weigh things. And who says this? Not just Chrysippus, Zeno, and Cleanthes, but even Antisthenes, who said, "The beginning of education is examining words." Socrates said the same, and Xenophon wrote that Socrates began by asking, "What does this word mean?"

Is your great achievement understanding and interpreting Chrysippus? Who says that? What, then, is your achievement? It's understanding the will of nature. Do you understand it all by yourself? If so, what more do you need? If "all people make mistakes without meaning to," and you've learned the truth, then you must already be doing the right thing. But, by Zeus, I don't fully understand the will of nature. Who, then, interprets it? People say Chrysippus does. So, I try to understand what this interpreter of nature says. But if I don't understand him, I look for someone who can explain it to me, like reading something in a foreign language.

But should the interpreter be proud of his skill? There's no reason for pride, not even for Chrysippus if he only interprets the will of nature but doesn't follow it himself. How much less should his interpreter be proud? We don't need Chrysippus for his own sake, but to help us follow nature. Just like we don't need someone who reads omens for their own sake, but because we believe they can help us understand the signs from the gods. We don't admire the crow or raven, but the god who sends us signs through them.

So, I go to this interpreter, this philosopher, and ask him to explain the signs for me. He interprets them, saying, "You have a mind that is naturally free from obstacles and constraints. Let me show you how, starting with your ability to agree with the truth. Can anyone stop you from agreeing with what is true? No. Can anyone force you to accept something false? No. So, in this area, your mind is free from obstacles. Now, what about your desires and choices? Can one impulse overpower another? Can one desire or fear overpower another?"

Someone might say, "If someone threatens me with death, they force me to act." But it's not the threat itself that forces you; it's your decision that it's better to do what they want than to die. So, it's your own mind that compels you, not the external threat. If God had created that part of us, which is part of Himself, to be forced or constrained by anything, He wouldn't be God, nor would He be caring for us as He should. This is what I find in the signs: If you will it, you are free; if you will it, you won't blame anyone or complain. Everything will be according to your will and the will of God. This is why I go to this interpreter, not admiring him for his interpretation, but for the wisdom it reveals.

Chapter 18
Why We Should Not Get Angry at People's Mistakes

If what philosophers say is true, that in all people, thought and action come from a single source—our feelings—then it makes sense that when we agree with something, it's because we feel that it's true, and when we disagree, it's because we feel that it's not true. And, by Zeus, when we're unsure, it's because we feel uncertain. The same goes for when we're drawn toward something; it's because we feel it's good for us. It's impossible to think one thing is good and yet desire something else. And again, it's impossible to think one thing is fitting and yet be driven to do something else. If all this is true, why are we still angry with people who make mistakes? "They are thieves," someone might say, "and robbers." What do you mean by "thieves and robbers"? They've simply gone astray when it comes to understanding what is good and what is bad. Should we be angry with them or rather feel sorry for them? Just show them their mistake, and you'll see how quickly they'll stop making it. But if they don't realize their error, they have nothing better than their own opinion.

Should this thief or adulterer be put to death, you ask? Not at all. Instead, you should ask, "Should someone be put to death who is in a state of error and confusion about the greatest matters and is blind, not in seeing black and white, but in distinguishing between what is good and what is bad?" And if you put it this way, you'll realize how inhuman a thought it is that you're expressing. It's as if you're saying, "Shouldn't this blind person or this deaf person be put to death?" If losing the greatest thing—a good moral purpose—is the greatest harm that can happen to someone, and if a person is deprived of this very thing, then what reason do you have to be angry with them? If you must feel something that goes against nature because of another person's misfortune, feel pity for them instead of hating them. Drop this readiness to take offense and this spirit of hatred. Don't use the same words that angry people use, like "These cursed and awful fools!" Fine, but how did you suddenly become so wise that you're angry at fools? Why, then, do we get angry? Because we admire the things that these people take from us. If you stop admiring your clothes, you won't be angry at the person who steals them. If you stop admiring your wife's beauty, you won't be angry at her adulterer. Remember, a thief or an adulterer doesn't have any power over the things that are truly yours, only over things that belong to others and aren't under your control. If you give these things up and count them as nothing, who will you still have a reason to be angry with? But as long as you admire these things, be angry with yourself, not with the people I've mentioned. Think about it: you have fine clothes, and your neighbor doesn't. You have a window and want to show them off. He doesn't know where the true good of a person lies, but he believes it's in having fine clothes—the same belief you have. Shouldn't he come and take them? When you show a cake to hungry people and then eat it all by yourself, aren't you asking for them to try to snatch it from you? Stop tempting them, stop having a window, and stop showing off your clothes.

Something similar happened to me recently. I keep an iron lamp by my household gods, and when I heard a noise at the window, I ran downstairs. I found that the lamp had been stolen. I thought to myself that the person who stole it wasn't acting unreasonably. So, I said to myself, tomorrow you'll find a lamp made of clay. A person can only lose what they already have. "I lost my cloak." Yes, because you had a cloak. "I have a headache." You don't have pain in your horns, do you? So, why are you upset? Our losses and pains only relate to things we possess.

"But the tyrant will chain—" What? Your leg. "But he will cut off—" What? Your head. What, then, will he neither chain nor cut off? Your moral purpose. This is why the ancients advised us to "Know yourself." So, what comes next? By the gods, we should practice with small things and then move on to greater ones. "I have a headache." Well, don't say "Oh no!" "I have an earache." Don't say "Oh no!" I'm not saying you can't groan, just don't groan deep inside yourself. And if your servant is slow in bringing your bandage, don't shout and make a face and say, "Everybody hates me." Why wouldn't they hate someone like that? From now on, trust in these teachings and walk around with your head held high, free, not relying on the size of your body like an athlete, because you shouldn't aim to be invincible like a donkey.

Who, then, is the invincible person? The one who isn't shaken by anything outside their control. Then, I start thinking about each situation, just like I would with an athlete. "This person won the first round. What will he do in the second? What if it's scorching hot? What will he do at the Olympics?" It's the same with this situation. If you put a silver coin in front of someone, he might ignore it. Yes, but if you put a pretty girl in front of him, what then? Or if it's dark, what then? Or if you tempt him with a bit of fame, what then? Or insults, what then? Or praise, what then? Or death, what then? He can overcome all these things. But what if it's scorching hot—meaning, what if he's drunk? What if he's mad with sadness? What if he's asleep? The person who passes all these tests is what I call the invincible athlete.

Chapter 19
How to Conduct Oneself Around Tyrants

If a man has some kind of superiority, or even just thinks he does, even if he doesn't, it's unavoidable that this man, if he's uneducated, will become arrogant because of it. For example, the tyrant declares, "I am the mightiest in the world." Very well, but what can you actually do for me? Can you give me a desire that is free from any obstacles? How could you do that? Do you even have that yourself? Can you protect me from things I want to avoid? Do you have that ability yourself? Or can you make choices that are always correct? How can you claim to have that power? Come on, when you're on a ship, do you trust yourself, or do you trust the skilled navigator? And when you're in a chariot, do you trust anyone other than the skilled driver? How is it with other skills? It's the same. So, what does your power really amount to? "Everyone pays attention to me." Yes, and I pay attention to my little plate, wash it, and wipe it clean, and I hang up my oil flask on the wall. What does that mean? Are these things better than me? No, but they are useful to me, so I take care of them. Also, don't I pay attention to my donkey? Don't I wash its feet? Don't I brush it? Don't you know that everyone pays attention to themselves, and to you, just like they do to their donkey? Who pays attention to you as a person? Show them to me. Who wants to be like you? Who follows you with enthusiasm, like people followed Socrates? "But I can cut off your head." Well said! I forgot that I should treat you like I treat a fever or cholera and set up an altar to you, just like they have an altar to the God Fever in Rome.

So, what is it that really upsets and confuses people? Is it the tyrant and his guards? How can that be? No, far from it! It's not possible for something naturally free to be disturbed or blocked by anything but itself. It's a person's own judgments that upset them. For example, when the tyrant says, "I will chain your leg," the person who values their leg highly replies, "Please, have mercy on me," but the person who values their moral purpose says, "If it seems better to you, then chain it." "Don't you care?" "No, I don't care." "I will show you that I am your master." "How can you be my master? Zeus has set me free. Do you really think he would let his own son be made a slave? You are, however, master of my dead body. Take it." "So you mean that when you come near me, you won't pay attention to me?" "No, I pay attention only to myself. But if you want me to say that I pay attention to you too, I do, but only in the same way I pay attention to my pot."

This isn't just selfishness; it's the nature of human beings. Everything a person does is for themselves. Why, even the sun does everything for its own sake, and, for that matter, so does Zeus himself. But when Zeus wants to be the "Rain-bringer," "Fruit-giver," and "Father of men and gods," you can see that he can't achieve these things or earn these titles unless he's useful to everyone. And in general, he has made human nature so that we can't get any of our own true goods unless we contribute something to the common interest. So, it follows that it's no longer considered unsocial for a person to do everything for their own sake. What else would you expect? That a person should neglect themselves and their own interests? And in that case, how can there be room for one and the same principle of action for all, namely, that of appropriating things to their own needs?

What then? When people have ridiculous opinions about what lies outside the scope of their moral purpose, thinking it's good or bad, it's completely unavoidable for them to pay attention to the tyrant. I wish it were only tyrants and not their servants too! And yet how can a man suddenly become wise when Caesar puts him in charge of his chamber pot? How can we suddenly say, "Felicio has spoken wisely to me"? I wish he would lose his job as chamber pot manager so that you may think he's a fool again! Epaphroditus had a cobbler who was useless, so he sold him. Then, by some chance, the man was bought by someone in Caesar's household and became Caesar's cobbler. You should have seen how much Epaphroditus respected him then! "How is my good Felicio doing?" he used to ask. And if someone asked us, "What is your master doing?" we'd answer, "He's consulting Felicio about something." But didn't he sell him because he was useless? So, who suddenly made him wise? This is what it means to honor something outside the scope of moral purpose.

"He's been given a tribuneship," someone says. Everyone who meets him congratulates him; one person kisses his eyes, another kisses his neck, and his slaves kiss his hands. He goes home, and he finds lamps being lit. He climbs up to the Capitol and offers a sacrifice. But who ever offered a sacrifice to give thanks for having had the right desires or for making choices according to nature? Because we give thanks to the gods for the things we consider good.

Today, a man was talking to me about becoming a priest of Augustus. I said to him, "Man, drop it; you'll be spending a lot of money for nothing." "But," he says, "those who draw up deeds of sale will inscribe my name." "Do you really plan to be there when the deeds are read and say, 'That's my name they wrote'? And even if you could be there whenever someone reads them, what will you do if you die?" "My name will stay after me." "Inscribe it on a stone, and it will stay after you. But come on, who will remember you outside of Nicopolis?" "But I will wear a crown of gold." "If you desire a crown at all, take a crown of roses and put it on; you will look much more elegant in that."

Chapter 20
How Reason Reflects on Itself

Every art or skill focuses on certain things. Now, when the art or skill is similar to what it deals with, it naturally reflects on itself; but when it's different, it can't. For example, the skill of leather-working is about working with hides, but the skill itself is completely different from the hides, so it doesn't reflect on itself. Similarly, the skill of grammar deals with written language, but it isn't itself written language, right? Not at all. For this reason, it can't reflect on itself.

So, what purpose did nature give us reason for? For the proper use of the impressions we get from the outside world. But what is reason itself? It's something made up of certain kinds of impressions from the outside world. So, it naturally can reflect on itself. Now, what are the things that wisdom helps us to understand? Things that are good, bad, and neither good nor bad. So, what is wisdom itself? It's a good thing. And what is foolishness? It's a bad thing. Do you see, then, that wisdom naturally reflects on both itself and its opposite? Therefore, the first and most important task of a philosopher is to test the impressions they receive and figure out which ones to trust, and to apply none that hasn't been tested.

You all know how careful we are with money, where we feel we have something at stake. We've even invented a whole art for testing coins, and the tester uses many methods—sight, touch, smell, and finally hearing. He drops the coin and listens to the sound it makes, and he's not satisfied with just one test but listens to the sound repeatedly, like a musician catching a tune.

So, when it comes to things where we feel it's important not to make a mistake, we put a lot of effort into telling the difference between things that could lead us astray. But when it comes to our reasoning ability, we yawn and sleep, accepting any and every impression without questioning it, because the loss we suffer doesn't seem important to us.

Therefore, if you want to realize how careless you are about what's truly good and bad, and how much more you care about things that don't really matter, think about how you feel about physical blindness versus being mentally deceived. You'll see that your feelings about good and bad are far from where they should be. "Yes, but this requires a lot of preparation, hard work, and learning many things." Well, what did you expect? Do you think you can master the greatest skill with little effort? And yet the most important teaching of philosophers is very brief. If you want to know, read what Zeno says and you'll see.

What's so long about his statement: "To follow the gods is the purpose of life, and the essence of good is using impressions properly"? If you ask, "What, then, is God, what is an impression, and what is the nature of the individual and the universe?" you already have a long explanation. If Epicurus comes and says that the good lies in the body, again the explanation gets lengthy, and you have to learn what the main faculty within us is and what our true nature is. Just as it's unlikely that the good of a snail lies in its shell, is it likely that the good of a human lies in their flesh? But think about yourself, Epicurus; what higher faculty do you have? What is it within you that thinks things over, that examines everything, and that, after examining the body itself, decides that it's the most important thing? And why do you light a lamp, work so hard for us, and write so many books? Is it so we won't fail to know the truth? Who are we? And what are we to you? And so the explanation gets longer.

Chapter 21
To Those Who Wish to Be Admired

When a person knows their proper place in life, they don't chase after things that are beyond that place. Man, what exactly do you want to happen to you? As for me, I'm content if I can desire and avoid things in a way that follows nature, if I can make choices and refusals that align with how I'm meant to, and if I can use my purpose, plans, and decisions according to my nature. So, why do you walk around in front of us like you've swallowed a stick and can't bend? "It has always been my wish that people who meet me would admire me and say as they follow me, 'Oh, what a great philosopher!'" But who are these people you want to be admired by? Aren't they the same people you usually say are crazy? What then? Do you really want to be admired by people you think are mad?

Chapter 22
On Understanding What We Already Know

Preconceptions are ideas that all people have in common, and one person's preconception doesn't contradict another's. For example, who among us doesn't think that what is good is also something useful and worth choosing, and that in every situation, we should seek and strive for what's good? And who doesn't believe that doing what's right is admirable and proper? So, when do contradictions happen? They happen when we apply our preconceptions to specific situations. For instance, one person might say, "He acted bravely and did the right thing," while another might say, "No, he's just acting crazy." This is where conflicts between people begin. The conflict isn't about whether we should prioritize doing what's right and holy, but about whether a particular action, like eating pork, is holy or unholy.

This was also the reason for the conflict between Agamemnon and Achilles. Let's imagine bringing them here to ask them what they think. Agamemnon, don't you think we should do what is proper and noble? "Yes, we should." And you, Achilles, do you agree that we should do what's noble? "I completely agree with that." Well, then, apply your preconceptions to this specific situation. That's where the conflict starts. One says, "I shouldn't have to give Chryseis back to her father," while the other says, "Yes, you should." Clearly, one of them is applying the preconception of "what one ought to do" incorrectly. Then, the first one says, "Fine, if I have to give Chryseis back, then I should take something from one of you as compensation," and the other replies, "Are you going to take the woman I love?" "Yes, the woman you love," the first one answers. "So, should I be the only one who loses something?" "But should I be the only one who gets nothing?" And so, a conflict arises.

So, what does it mean to get an education? It means learning how to apply these natural preconceptions correctly to each situation, in a way that aligns with nature, and also to understand that some things are within our control, while others are not. What's within our control are our moral choices and all the actions that come from those choices. But things like our bodies, body parts, possessions, parents, siblings, children, and our country—basically everything we interact with—are not under our control. So, where should we place the idea of "good"? To which group of things should we apply it? Should we apply it to things that are within our control? But isn't health a good thing, and a healthy body, and life itself? And what about children, parents, or our country? And who would tolerate you if you denied that these are good things? So, let's say these things are good. But then, can a person be truly happy if they suffer injury or don't get what is good? It's not possible. And can they maintain good relationships with others? How could they? Because it's in my nature to look out for my own interest. If it's in my interest to have a farm, then it's in my interest to take it from my neighbor. If it's in my interest to have a cloak, then it's also in my interest to steal it from a bathhouse. This thinking is what causes wars, rebellions, tyrannies, and conspiracies.

And again, how will I be able to fulfill my duty toward Zeus? If I suffer injury and am unlucky, then he isn't paying attention to me. And then we hear people say, "Why should I care about him if he can't help us?" Or, "Why should I care about him if he wants me to be in this miserable state?" The next step is that I begin to hate him. So, why do we build temples for the gods and make statues of them, as if they were evil spirits—as if Zeus were a god of fever? And how can he still be called "Savior," "Rain-bringer," and "Fruit-giver"? In truth, if we think that what is good lies in these external things, all these problems follow.

What, then, should we do?—This is a question for someone who truly wants to understand life and is deeply thinking about it. Such a person might say to themselves, "I don't really know what is good and what is bad right now; am I not being irrational?" Yes, but if I decide that the good is within the things I can control, people will laugh at me. Some old man with many gold rings on his fingers will come along, shake his head, and say, "Listen to me, my child; of course, you should study philosophy, but you also need to be sensible. All this stuff is nonsense. You can learn a syllogism from the philosophers, but you know better than they do what you ought to do."

Why, then, do you criticize me if I know? What should I say to this person? If I stay quiet, he'll be furious with me. So, I must say, "Forgive me, just as you would forgive someone who is in love; I'm not in control of myself; I'm crazy."

Chapter 23
Against Epicurus

Even Epicurus understands that we are naturally social beings, but since he believes that our good lies in our physical bodies, he cannot say anything that contradicts this belief. So, he strongly insists that we should neither admire nor accept anything that isn't connected to the nature of what's truly good; and in this, he is correct. But how, then, can we still be social beings if love for our own children isn't a natural feeling? Why do you advise the wise person not to raise children? Why are you worried that they will suffer sorrow because of their children? Does sorrow come to them because of a household slave named Mouse? What difference does it make if little Mouse in their house starts to cry?

No, Epicurus knows that once a child is born, it is no longer within our power not to love and care for it. For the same reason, Epicurus says that a wise person shouldn't get involved in politics, because he understands what is required of someone who engages in politics. Of course, if you are going to live among people as if you were just another fly among flies, then what is stopping you? But even though Epicurus knows this, he still dares to say, "Let's not raise children." Yet, a sheep doesn't abandon its own lamb, nor does a wolf abandon its cub; so, should a human abandon their child? What do you want us to do? Should we be as foolish as sheep? But even they do not desert their offspring. Should we be as fierce as wolves? But even they do not desert their offspring. Come on, who would follow your advice when they see their child fallen on the ground and crying?

In my opinion, if your mother and father had known that you were going to say such things, they would not have abandoned you!

Chapter 24
How We Should Deal with Life's Challenges

It's in tough situations that people show who they really are. So, when a difficulty comes your way, remember that God, like a coach, has paired you with a strong opponent. Why? someone might ask. So that you can become a champion, like an Olympic victor; but that can't happen without some hard work and sweat. In my opinion, no one has a better challenge than the one you have, if only you're willing to use it the way an athlete uses a sparring partner to get better.

And now we're sending you to Rome as a scout, to check things out. But no one sends a coward as a scout, someone who, at the first noise or shadow, comes running back in fear, saying, "The enemy is already upon us." So now, if you come back and tell us, "The situation in Rome is terrifying; death is terrible, exile is terrible, insults are terrible, poverty is terrible; run away, everyone, the enemy is here!" we'll say to you, "Go away and keep your warnings to yourself! Our mistake was sending someone like you as a scout."

Diogenes, who was sent as a scout before you, brought back a different report. He says, "Death is not a bad thing, since it's not dishonorable"; he says, "Bad reputation is just noise made by madmen." And what a report he gave us about hard work, pleasure, and poverty! He says, "Being naked is better than wearing a fancy red robe; and sleeping on the bare ground," he says, "is the softest bed." And he proves these points with his own courage, his calmness, his freedom, and even his body, which is healthy and strong. "There's no enemy nearby," he says; "everything is peaceful." How do you know, Diogenes? "Look!" he says, "I haven't been hit by any missile, have I? I haven't been wounded, have I? I haven't run away from anyone, have I?"

This is what it means to be a true scout, but you come back and report one fear after another. Won't you go back out and observe more carefully, without this cowardice?

What should I do, then?—What do you do when you get off a ship? You don't pick up the rudder or the oars, do you? What do you pick up, then? Your own luggage, your oil flask, your bag. So now, if you remember what belongs to you, you'll never claim what belongs to someone else. He says to you, "Give up your fancy red robe." Here, take the plain one. "Give that up too." Here's the simple toga. "Give up your toga." Here, I'm naked. "But you make me jealous." Fine, then, take my whole body. Am I still afraid of the man to whom I can throw my body? But he won't leave me as his heir. So what? Did I forget that none of these things belong to me? How, then, do we call them "mine"? Just like we call the bed in the inn "mine." If the innkeeper dies and leaves you the beds, you'll have them; but if he leaves them to someone else, they'll have them, and you'll look for another bed.

If you don't find one, you'll have to sleep on the ground; just do so with courage, snoring and remembering that tragedies happen among the rich and powerful, but no poor man plays a tragic role except as part of the chorus. Now the kings start off in a state of prosperity:

"Hang the palace with garlands";
then, about the third or fourth act, comes—
"Alas, Cithaeron, why did you receive me?"

Slave, where are your crowns, where's your diadem? Do your guards help you at all? So, when you approach one of these powerful people, remember that you're approaching a tragic character, not the actor, but Oedipus himself. "But so-and-so is blessed; he has many companions to walk with." So do I; I fall in line with the crowd and have many companions to walk with.

But, to sum it all up: remember that the door has been left open. Don't be more of a coward than children, who say, "I won't play anymore," when the game doesn't please them. So, when things seem unbearable to you, just say, "I won't play anymore," and leave; but if you stay, stop complaining.

Chapter 25
On The Same Theme

If all this is true, and we're not just being foolish or pretending when we say, "What's good or bad for a person lies in their moral choices, and everything else doesn't really matter to us," then why are we still worried and afraid? No one has control over the things we truly care about, and the things other people do have control over don't concern us. So, what else is there to talk about?—"But give me some instructions."—What instructions can I give you? Hasn't Zeus already given you directions? Hasn't he given you something that is truly yours, something that can't be hindered or restrained, while everything else that isn't yours can be controlled by others? What instructions did you bring with you when you came into this world from him? What orders? Protect what's truly yours by all means, but don't go after what belongs to someone else. Your faithfulness is yours, your self-respect is yours; so who can take these things from you? Who but you can stop you from using them? But how do you act? When you chase after things that aren't yours, you lose what is truly yours.

Since you have these directions from Zeus, what more do you want from me? Am I greater than Zeus or more trustworthy? But if you follow his commands, do you need any others? Hasn't he already given you these instructions? Bring out your preconceptions, bring out the proofs of the philosophers, bring out what you've often heard, bring out what you've said yourself, bring out what you've practiced.

So, how long should we follow these teachings and not give up? As long as the game is enjoyable. During the Saturnalia festival, a king is chosen by lot because it's part of the game. The king gives orders: "You drink, you mix wine, you sing, you go, you come." I obey, so as not to spoil the game. "Come, suppose you're in a bad situation." I don't suppose that; and who can force me to think that? Again, we've agreed to play the story of Agamemnon and Achilles. The one who plays Agamemnon says to me, "Go to Achilles and take away Briseis." I go. He says, "Come," and I come. Just as we behave in these hypothetical scenarios, we should behave the same way in real life. "Let it be night." So be it. "What then? Is it day?" No, because I've agreed that it's night. "Let's suppose you think it's night." So be it. "But go on and think it's night." That doesn't fit the situation.

In the same way, let's suppose you're unhappy. So be it. "Are you, then, unfortunate?" Yes. "What then? Are you troubled by bad luck?" Yes. "But go on and assume you're in a terrible state." That doesn't fit the situation; plus, there's another force that stops me from thinking that.

So, how long should we follow such commands? As long as it's useful, and that means as long as I keep my dignity and stay consistent.

Furthermore, some people are too grumpy and sharp-tongued and say, "I can't stand dining at this person's house where I have to listen to him every day talk about how he fought in Moesia: 'I told you, brother, how I climbed to the top of the hill; well, now I'm under siege again.'" But another person might say, "I'd rather dine there and let him babble all he wants." It's up to you to weigh these options, but don't do anything feeling burdened, troubled, or thinking you're in a terrible situation; no one is forcing you into this. Has someone made smoke in the house? If it's a little smoke, I'll stay; if it's too much, I'll go outside. You should remember this: the door is always open. But someone says, "Don't live in Nicopolis." I agree not to live there. "Nor in Athens." I agree not to live in Athens, either. "Nor in Rome." I agree not to live in Rome, either.

"Live in Gyara." I agree to live there. But living in Gyara seems like there's too much smoke in the house. I'll leave for a place where no one will stop me from living; that place is open to everyone. And as for the last inner garment, that is, my own body, beyond that, no one has any control over me. That's why Demetrius said to Nero, "You threaten me with death, but nature threatens you." If I care too much about my body, I've made myself a slave; if I care too much about my possessions, I've made myself a slave; because at that moment, I show what I can be caught with, and it will hurt me. Just like when a snake pulls its head back, and someone says, "Strike that part of him that he's protecting," you can be sure that your master will attack you at the point you especially want to protect.

If you remember all this, who will you flatter or fear anymore?

But I want to sit where the senators do.—Do you realize that you're making things cramped for yourself, that you're crowding yourself?—How else can I get a good view in the amphitheater?—Don't become a spectator, and you won't be crowded. Why are you making trouble for yourself? Or wait a little while, and when the show is over, sit down in the senators' seats and relax. In general, remember this: we crowd ourselves, we make things cramped for ourselves, and by that, I mean that the decisions of our will crowd us and make things cramped.

Why, what is the matter of being insulted? Stand by a stone and insult it; what will happen? If a person listens like a stone, what good does it do to insult them? But if the person insulting has found a weak spot, then they accomplish something. "Strip him." Why do you say "him"? Take his cloak and strip that off. "I've offended you." Good for you! This is what Socrates practiced, and that's why he always had the same expression on his face. But we prefer to practice and rehearse anything rather than how to be free and untroubled. "The philosophers talk in riddles," you say. But aren't there riddles in other arts? And what's more puzzling than to cut a man's eye so that he can see? If someone said this to a person who didn't understand surgery, wouldn't they laugh? What's surprising, then, if in philosophy, too, many things that are true seem puzzling to those who don't understand?

Chapter 26
Understanding the Law of Life

As someone was reading the hypothetical arguments, Epictetus said, "There is a rule in dealing with hypotheses: we must accept whatever the hypothesis or premise demands. But much more important is the rule for life: we must do what nature demands. If we want to act according to nature in every situation, it's clear that we should aim to neither avoid what nature requires nor accept what goes against it. That's why philosophers first train us in theory, where things are easier, and then move on to more difficult matters. In theory, nothing stops us from following what we're taught, but in real life, many things pull us away. So, it's ridiculous for someone to say they want to start with the harder things because it's not easy to begin with what's most difficult.

And this is the defense we should use with parents who get angry because their children study philosophy. 'Okay, Father, I'm making mistakes because I don't know what my duties are or what I'm supposed to do. Now, if this is something that can't be taught or learned, why do you blame me? But if it can be taught, then teach me;

and if you can't, let me learn from those who claim they know. What do you think? That I choose to do wrong on purpose and avoid what's good? Of course not! So, what's causing my mistakes? It's my ignorance. Don't you want me to get rid of that? Has anger ever taught anyone how to steer a ship or play music? Do you think your anger will help me learn how to live?'

Only someone who truly dedicates themselves to philosophy can talk like this. But if someone just reads these subjects and goes to philosophers only to show off at a dinner party with their knowledge of hypothetical arguments, what are they really doing? Just trying to impress some senator sitting next to them? In Rome, the opportunities to show off are great, and the wealth in Nicopolis looks like child's play compared to Rome. That's why it's hard for someone to control their desires in Rome because there are so many distractions. I knew a man who clung to the knees of Epaphroditus, crying, because he was miserable—he had nothing left but a million and a half sesterces. What did Epaphroditus do? Did he laugh at him like you're laughing now? No, he just said in amazement, 'Poor man, how did you manage to keep silent? How did you endure it?'

Once, when Epictetus had confused a student who was reading the hypothetical arguments, and the person who had set the passage for him to read laughed at him, Epictetus said to the latter, 'You are laughing at yourself. You didn't give the young man any preparation or check if he could follow these arguments, but you treat him like a reader. Why then,' he added, 'do we trust someone who can't even follow a judgment on a complex argument to give praise or blame, or to judge what is done well or poorly? If this person speaks badly of someone, does that person pay attention to him? If he praises someone, does that person feel proud? When the person giving praise or blame can't even figure out basic logic?'

This is where philosophy starts—with an understanding of the state of one's own mind. Once a person realizes their mind is weak, they won't want to use it on big matters. But as it is now, some people who can't even handle small tasks buy a whole treatise and try to understand everything at once. So they get overwhelmed, suffer from indigestion, and then deal with colics, fluxes, and fevers. They should have first considered whether they were capable of handling it. However, in theory, it's easy to prove someone wrong, but in real life, people don't accept it when they're proven wrong, and we end up hating the person who corrected us. But Socrates used to tell us not to live an unexamined life."

Chapter 27
The Different Types of Appearances and How to Handle Them

External impressions come to us in four different ways: sometimes things really are what they seem to be; sometimes they aren't, and they don't seem to be; sometimes they are, but don't seem to be; and sometimes they aren't, but they seem to be. So, in all these situations, it's the job of an educated person to get things right. Whatever is bothering us, we should bring in the right tools to deal with it. If what's bothering us are tricky arguments from philosophers like Pyrrho and the Academics, we should bring in the right tools to deal with those. If it's the convincing appearances of things that make us think something is good when it isn't, we should bring in tools to handle that. If it's a habit that's troubling us, we should find tools that help us develop a better habit. So, what tools can we find to deal with bad habits? The answer is: build the opposite habit.

You might hear people saying, "That poor person! They died; their father died, and their mother too. They died too young and far from home." When you hear that, think about the arguments on the other side. Pull yourself away from those expressions of pity and build a habit of seeing things differently. To deal with tricky arguments, we need to practice logic and get used to thinking clearly. To deal with convincing appearances, we need to have our preconceptions ready, polished like weapons, and always on hand.

When death seems like a bad thing, we need to be ready with the argument that it's our duty to avoid evil, but death is something that can't be avoided. What can I do? Where can I go to escape it? Imagine I'm Sarpedon, the son of Zeus, so I can nobly say, as he did: "Since I've left home for war, I want to either win the prize for bravery myself or let someone else win it if I can't. If I can't achieve something great, I won't be jealous if someone else does." Even if acting like Sarpedon is too much for us, isn't the other option within our reach? Where can I go to escape death? Show me the place, show me the people who don't die; show me a magic spell against it. If I don't have one, what do you want me to do? I can't avoid death.

Instead of avoiding the fear of it, should I die crying and shaking? The root of sorrow is wanting something that doesn't happen. So, if I can change things to be the way I want, I change them; but if I can't, I might get so frustrated that I want to hurt the person standing in my way. It's human nature not to tolerate losing something good or falling into something bad. Finally, when I can't change things, and I can't harm the person in my way, I sit down and complain, blaming Zeus and the other gods—because if they don't care about me, what good are they to me? "But," you might say, "that's impious." What could be worse than what I'm going through now? In short, we need to remember this: unless piety and self-interest are combined, no one can stay pious. Don't these ideas seem important?

Let the follower of Pyrrho or the Academics come and argue against us. I, for one, don't have time for such debates, nor can I defend commonly accepted opinions. If I had a minor legal case about a piece of land, I would call in someone else to be my lawyer. So, what evidence do I trust? The evidence that fits the situation. When it comes to the question of how perception works—whether it happens through the whole body or just one part—maybe I don't know the answer, and both ideas confuse me. But I'm absolutely sure that you and I aren't the same person. How do I know this? When I want to eat something, I don't bring the food to your mouth but to mine; when I want bread, I don't grab dirt, but I go for the bread as if it's my target. And you, who doubt the evidence of the senses, do you do anything different? When you want to take a bath, do you go to a mill instead?

So, should we do our best to stick to common sense and be on guard against arguments that try to overturn it? Who disagrees with that? But only the person who has the ability and time should focus on these studies, while the person who is trembling, confused, and heartbroken should spend their time on something else.

Chapter 28
Why We Shouldn't Be Angry with Others: And What Is Truly Important and Unimportant in Life

Why do we agree with something? It's because it seems true to us. It's impossible to agree with something that doesn't seem true. Why? Because our mind naturally agrees with what's true, disagrees with what's false, and holds back when it's unsure. How do we know this? Try to feel that it's night right now—it's impossible. Try to stop feeling that it's daytime—you can't do it. Try to believe that the stars are an even number—that's also impossible. So, when someone agrees with something false, remember that they didn't do it because they wanted to. As Plato said, "Every soul is unwillingly deprived of the truth." It only seemed to them that the false thing was true.

Now, when it comes to actions, we have things that are similar to true and false perceptions: what's right and wrong, what's useful and harmful, what's appropriate for me and what's not. "Can someone think something is good for them but still not choose it?" No, they can't. Take the person who says:

"Now, now, I see the terrible things I'm about to do, But my passion is stronger than my better judgment."

This happens because she thinks that following her passion and getting revenge on her husband is better than protecting her children. "But she's mistaken." If you show her clearly that she's wrong, she won't do it. But until you do, what else can she follow besides what seems true to her? Nothing. So why are you angry with her for making such a huge mistake and becoming more like a snake than a person? Why not feel sorry for her instead? Just like we feel sorry for people who are blind or crippled, why don't we feel sorry for those who have become blind or crippled in their ability to reason?

Anyone who remembers that a person's actions are based on what seems true to them—whether it's right or wrong—will understand that if they're right, they're blameless, and if they're wrong, they suffer for it themselves. It's impossible for someone else to suffer the consequences of my mistakes. Whoever keeps this in mind won't get mad at anyone, won't be angry with anyone, won't insult or blame or hate anyone.

So, you think such big and terrible things come from something so small—a wrong impression? Yes, and nothing else. The entire story of the Iliad is just about a sense impression and how a poet used it. Alexander had the impression that he should take Menelaus' wife, and Helen had the impression that she should go with him. Now, if Menelaus had thought it was a good thing to lose such a wife, what would have happened? We wouldn't have the Iliad or the Odyssey.

But do such important things really depend on something so small? What do you mean by "important things"? Wars, conflicts, deaths of many people, and the destruction of cities? What's so important about all that? What, nothing important in that? Why, what's so important about the deaths of many cows and sheep, or the burning of many nests of swallows or storks? How can you compare this to that? It's very similar. People's bodies died in one case, and cows' and sheep's bodies died in the other. People's small houses were burned, and so were the nests of storks. What's so important or scary about that? Or show me how a person's house and a stork's nest are different as places to live.

Does a person really not differ from a stork?—Of course, he does; but not in these things.—In what ways, then, does he differ? Look and you'll find that the difference is in something else. See if it's not in his ability to understand what he's doing, in his ability to live socially, in his faithfulness, self-respect, and intelligence. So where is the great good or evil in people? It's exactly where the difference lies. If that part of us is kept safe and strong, and our self-respect, faithfulness, and intelligence aren't destroyed, then we're safe. But if any of these qualities are destroyed or taken away, then we're destroyed too. And that's where the important things are.

Did Alexander's downfall come when the Greeks attacked Troy with their ships, when they were destroying the land, and when his brothers were dying? Not at all. No one falls because of someone else's actions; what happened then was just like destroying storks' nests. No, Alexander fell when he lost his self-respect, his faithfulness, his respect for the laws of hospitality, and his decency. When did Achilles fall? When Patroclus died? Not at all. Achilles fell when he got angry, when he cried over a captured girl, when he forgot that he was there to fight a war, not to win over a sweetheart.

These are the downfalls that happen to people; this is the siege of their city, the destruction of it—when their correct judgments are torn down, when these are destroyed. So when women are taken into captivity, and children are enslaved, and men are killed, aren't all these things evils? Why do you think that? Let me know where you got that idea. No, instead, let me show you why they aren't evils. Let's look at the evidence, bring out your preconceptions.

This is why I can't understand what people do. When we want to judge weights, we don't just guess; when we want to judge what's straight and what's crooked, we don't just guess; in short, whenever it matters to us to know the truth, we don't just do things at random. Yet when it comes to the most important things—the only causes of doing right or wrong, of success or failure—this is the only time we act randomly and without thought. We don't have anything like a scale or a standard to go by, but some impression comes along, and we immediately act on it. What, am I any better than Agamemnon or Achilles—are they to do and suffer such terrible things because they followed their impressions, while I should be satisfied with mine? And what tragedy comes from anything other than this? What is the Atreus of Euripides? His impression. The Oedipus of Sophocles? His impression. The Phoenix? His impression. The Hippolytus? His impression. What kind of person do you think ignores this? What do we call people who follow every impression they have?—Madmen.— So, are we acting any differently?

Chapter 29
On Steadiness and Determination

The core of what is good comes from a certain kind of decision-making, and the same goes for what is bad. So, what about things outside of us, like events or objects? These are just tools we can use, and how we use them determines whether our decisions are good or bad. How do we make good decisions? By not being overly impressed by these outside things. If our judgments about these things are correct, then our decisions will be good; but if our judgments are wrong, then our decisions will be bad. This is the rule that God has given us, and He says, "If you want something good, get it from yourself." But you might say, "No, I want it from someone else." Don't do that—get it from yourself.

So, when a tyrant threatens me and orders me to come, I ask, "Who are you threatening?" If he says, "I will put you in chains," I reply, "You are threatening my hands and feet." If he says, "I will cut off your head," I reply, "You are threatening my neck." If he says, "I will throw you into prison," I say, "You are threatening my whole body." And if he threatens to send me into exile, I give the same answer. Does this mean he's not threatening me at all? If I believe that none of these things really matter to me, then no, he's not threatening me at all. But if I'm scared of any of these things, then yes, he is threatening me. So, who should I fear? The person who controls things that are under my control? But no one controls those. The person who controls things that aren't under my control? Then why should I care about them?

Do you philosophers teach us to look down on our rulers? Not at all. Who among us tells you to challenge what they have control over? Take my body, take my property, take my reputation, take the people around me. If I encourage anyone to try to control these things, let them accuse me. "Yes, but I want to control your thoughts too." And who gave you that power? How can you control someone else's thoughts? "By scaring them," he says, "I can control them." You don't understand that the thoughts control themselves—they aren't controlled by anything else. Nothing can overpower our decisions, except our decisions themselves. That's why God's rule is fair and just: "Let the better always win over the worse." "Ten are stronger than one," you might say. Stronger for what? For putting someone in chains, for killing them, for dragging them away, for taking their property. Yes, ten can overpower one in that way. But in what way are they worse? If the one has better judgments, and the ten do not. So, can they overpower the one in that way? How could they? But if we weigh them, won't the heavier side go down?

So, could someone like Socrates go through what he did with the Athenians? Don't call it "Socrates' suffering." Let's describe it as it is: The body of Socrates was taken and dragged to prison by stronger people, someone gave poison to Socrates' body, and the body grew cold and died. Does this seem amazing to you? Does it seem unfair? Do you blame God for this? Did Socrates get nothing in return for this? What was truly good for him? Should we listen to you or to Socrates himself? What does Socrates say? "Anytus and Meletus can kill me, but they can't hurt me." And again, "If this is what God wants, then so be it." But can you prove that someone with worse judgments can win over someone with better ones? You can't. You won't even come close. This is a law of nature and of God: "Let the better always win over the worse." Win in what? In what they are better at. One body can be stronger than another; several people can be stronger than one; the thief can be better at staying awake than I am. That's why I lost my lamp—because the thief was better at staying awake. But he paid a high price for the lamp; for a lamp, he became a thief, for a lamp, he became untrustworthy, for a lamp, he became like an animal. This seemed profitable to him!

But now someone grabs me by my cloak and pulls me into the marketplace, and others shout, "Philosopher, what good are your judgments if you're being dragged off to prison or about to be executed?" What kind of philosophy lesson could I have taken that would prevent me from being dragged off if a stronger person grabs my cloak? Or would stop me from being thrown into prison if ten people push me in? Have I learned nothing else? I've learned that everything that happens outside my control doesn't really matter to me. So, have you gained nothing from this understanding? Why are you looking for your benefit in something other than what you've learned is important?

As I sit in prison, I think to myself, "This person who's shouting at me doesn't understand what's really happening, doesn't follow what's being said, and hasn't taken the time to learn what philosophers teach. Don't let it bother you." "But get out of prison." If you don't need me in prison anymore, I'll leave; if you need me here again, I'll come back. For how long? As long as reason decides I should stay with this body; but when reason says it's time to go, then take the body and go. Just make sure I don't give up my life irrationally, out of cowardice, or for a trivial reason. Because God doesn't want that either—He needs this universe, and He needs people who live in it. But if He signals that it's time to retreat, like He did with Socrates, I must obey Him, just like a soldier obeys his general.

What then? Should I tell everyone this? Why? Isn't it enough for me to believe it myself? For example, when children come to us and clap their hands and say, "Today is the festival of Saturnalia," do we tell them, "This is not really a good thing"? No, we clap our hands with them. So, when you can't change someone's mind, remember that they're like a child, and clap your hands with them. But if you don't want to do that, just stay silent.

A person should remember all this and, when faced with a challenge, realize that this is the time to show whether we've learned anything. A young person leaving school and facing a challenge is like someone who has practiced solving puzzles, and if they're given an easy one, they say, "No, give me a harder one so I can really test myself." Athletes don't want to face opponents who are too easy: "He

can't lift me," one might say. "That person over there is stronger."
But when the real test comes, do they cry and say, "I wanted to keep
practicing"? Practice what? If you don't learn to apply these lessons
in real life, what's the point of learning them? I imagine someone
sitting here thinking, "I wish I had a challenge like the one this person
is facing! I'm tired of sitting around—I want to be like an Olympic
champion! When will someone bring me a real test?" That's how you
should all be thinking. Even the gladiators in Caesar's arena complain
if they don't get a chance to fight, and they beg their trainers to let
them fight one-on-one. Will none of you have the same spirit? I
wanted to go to Rome just to see what my athlete is doing, how he's
practicing for his challenge. "I don't want this kind of challenge," he
says. Is it up to you to choose your challenge? You've been given a
body, parents, siblings, a country, and a role in it. And now you come
to me and say, "Change my challenge"? Don't you have the ability to
use what you've been given? You should say, "It's your job to set the
challenge, and mine to face it well." No, instead you say, "Don't give
me this kind of puzzle, give me another one; don't challenge me in
this way, challenge me another way." Soon, the actors in tragedies will
start thinking their costumes and masks are who they really are.
Everything we have is just a tool for the task. Show me what you've
got, so we can see if you're a true actor or just playing a role. If
someone took away your costume and mask, and put you on stage
without them, would you still be an actor? If you have a voice, you
are.

And so it is in life. "Take on a leadership role." I take it, and I
show how an educated person behaves. "Give up your status and
wear simple clothes." What then? Haven't I learned to use my voice
well? "What role are you playing now?" I'm a witness summoned by
God. God says, "Go and testify for Me; you are worthy of being My
witness. Is there anything outside of your control that is truly good

or bad? Do I harm anyone? Have I put anyone's well-being under the control of anyone but themselves?" What kind of witness will you be for God? "I'm struggling, Lord, and suffering; no one cares about me, no one helps me, everyone blames and criticizes me." Is this the testimony you're going to give? Is this how you'll disgrace the honor God gave you, deeming you worthy to be brought forward as a witness for such an important matter?

But the person in power over you declares, "I judge you to be impious and wicked." What has happened to you? "I've been judged impious and wicked." Nothing else? "Nothing." But if he had judged a logical argument and declared, "I judge that the statement, 'If it is day, there is light,' is false," what would happen to the logical argument? Who is being judged here, who has been condemned? The logical argument, or the person who made a mistake in judgment? Who is this person who has the authority to judge you? Does he know what piety or wickedness is? Has he studied it? Has he learned it? Where? Under whom? Yet a musician doesn't care if someone says that a low note is high, nor does a mathematician care if someone says that the lines from the center to the edge of a circle are not equal; but should an educated person care when an ignorant person judges what is holy and unholy, or what is just and unjust?

How unfair it is for educated people to act like this! Is this what you've learned here? Will you leave the petty arguments to those who can't think deeply, so they can sit in a corner and collect their small fees, or complain because no one gives them anything? Won't you instead step forward and use what you've learned? What's missing now is not arguments; the books of the Stoics are full of them. What's missing now? A person who will use them, who will bear witness to these teachings through their actions. This is the role I want you to take, so that we no longer need to use old examples in school but can have an example from our own time. Whose job is it to think about

75

these things? The person who is dedicated to learning; because humans are naturally curious. But it's shameful to think about these things like runaway slaves; instead, sit free from distractions and listen, now to a tragic actor and now to a musician, not like runaway slaves do. For at the very moment when one of them is listening and praising the actor, he glances around, and if someone mentions the word "master," they all panic. It's shameful for philosophers to contemplate the works of nature in this way. What is a "master"? One person is not the master of another person, but life and death, pleasure and pain are their masters. Bring Caesar to me without these things, and you'll see how steadfast I am. But when he comes with them, thundering and lightning, and I'm afraid, what have I done but recognized my master, like the runaway slave? But as long as I have, in a way, a break from these threats, I'm acting like a runaway slave watching a play; I bathe, I drink, I sing, but I do it all in fear and misery. But if I free myself from these masters, those things that make masters terrifying, what trouble do I have left, what master do I still have?

What then? Should I announce this to everyone? No, but I should treat those who are not philosophers with consideration and say, "This person advises me as he thinks best for himself; so I excuse him." Socrates excused the jailer who cried for him when he was about to drink the poison, and said, "How kindly he cried for us!" Did he then say to the jailer, "This is why we sent the women away"? No, he said that to his close friends, those who were ready to hear it; but he treated the jailer with kindness, like a child.

Chapter 30
What We Should Keep in Mind During Tough Times

When you come into the presence of some important person, remember that Another, by Zeus, watches from above what is happening, and you must strive to please Him rather than this person. The One above might ask you, "In your teachings, what did you call exile, imprisonment, chains, death, and dishonor?" You would reply, "I called them 'things that don't really matter.'" "What, then, do you call them now? Have they changed in any way?" "No, they haven't changed." "Have you, then, changed?" "No, I haven't changed." "Tell me then, what are 'things that don't really matter'?" "Those that are independent of our moral choices." "Tell me also what follows." "Things independent of our moral choices are nothing to me." "Tell me also what you thought were 'the good things'?" "A proper moral purpose and a correct use of external impressions." "And what was your goal?" "To follow You."

"Do you say all that even now?" "I say the same things even now." Then enter in, full of confidence and mindful of all this, and you will see what it means to be a young man who has studied what he ought, even when he is in the presence of men who have not studied. As for me, by Zeus, I imagine that you will feel somewhat like this: "Why did we make such great and elaborate preparations for something that amounts to nothing? Was this what authority really is? Was this what all the grand entrances, the chamberlains, the armed guards amounted to? Did I really spend so much time listening to those long discourses for something so insignificant? All this never amounted to anything, but I was preparing for it as though it were something of great importance."

Book II

Chapter 1
That There Is No Conflict Between Confidence and Caution

Some people might find what the philosophers say to be strange, but let's do our best to understand if it's true that "we should do everything with both caution and confidence at the same time." Caution might seem like it's the opposite of confidence, and opposites don't usually go together. But what seems confusing to most people is actually about something different: If we said a person should be both cautious and confident about the same thing, then it would make sense to say that we're mixing things that don't go together. But that's not what's happening here.

Think about it this way: If we've often heard and learned that "the nature of what's good or bad depends on how we use our thoughts and feelings, and that things outside our control are neither good nor bad," then there's nothing strange about what the philosophers say. If they say, "When it comes to things outside our control, we should be confident, but when it comes to things within our control, we should be cautious," it makes sense. If the bad things come from using our moral choices poorly, then we should be cautious about these things. But if things outside our control aren't really good or bad, then we can be confident about them.

So, we can be cautious and confident at the same time, and by Zeus, we can be confident because we're cautious. Because we're careful about the things that are truly bad, we can be confident about the things that aren't.

But sometimes we act like deer that run away from feathers and into a net. They mix up what they should be afraid of and what they should be confident about, and this gets them into trouble. We do the same thing; we're afraid of things that are outside our control, but we're confident about things that actually matter. To be fooled, or to act rashly, or to do something shameful, or to desire something wrong doesn't matter to us as long as we get what we want in things that lie outside our control. But when we face death, exile, hardship, or dishonor, that's when we panic and run away.

As a result, we mix up what's really important and what isn't. We turn our natural confidence into boldness, desperation, recklessness, and shamelessness, while we turn our natural caution and self-respect into fear, cowardice, and anxiety. If a person directed their caution toward moral choices and actions, then they would also gain control over their will to avoid bad things. But if they use their caution on things outside their control, which depend on other people, they'll end up full of fear, instability, and anxiety. It's not death or hardship that's really scary, but the fear of death or hardship. That's why we praise the person who said, "Not death is dreadful, but a shameful death."

So, our confidence should be about death, and our caution should be about the fear of death. But we do the opposite—we run away from death, but we don't care much about how we judge death. Socrates was right when he called these things "bugbears." Just like how masks seem scary to children because they don't understand them, we're also afraid of events because we don't understand them. And it's for the same reason that children are scared of "boogeymen." What is a child? Someone who doesn't know much. What is a child? Someone who needs to learn. When a child knows something, they're no worse than we are. What is death? It's a bugbear. Look at it closely, and you'll see it doesn't bite. The body will be separated from the spirit, either now or later, just as it was separate before. Why are you upset if this happens now? If it doesn't happen now, it will happen later. Why? Because the universe needs it to keep moving forward. It needs things that are happening now, things that will happen, and things that have already happened.

What is hardship? It's a bugbear. Look at it closely, and you'll see what it really is. The body is treated roughly, and then it's treated kindly again. If you can't handle it, the door is open; if you can, then endure it. The door should always be open, and then we won't have any trouble.

So, what's the result of learning these ideas? It's the best and most fitting thing for someone who's truly educated—peace of mind, fearlessness, and freedom. We shouldn't listen to the crowd, who say, "Only the free can be educated," but instead listen to the philosophers, who say, "Only the educated are free." What does that mean? It means that at this time, freedom is nothing but the right to live as we want. "Nothing else." Tell me, then, do you want to live in error? "We do not." Well, no one who lives in error is free. Do you want to live in fear, sorrow, or turmoil? "Of course not." Then, no one who lives in fear, sorrow, or turmoil is free. But whoever gets rid of these things is also free from slavery.

So, how can we still trust those lawmakers who say that only the free should be educated? The philosophers say, "We don't let anyone but the educated be free"; that is, God doesn't allow it. So, when a man turns his slave around before the praetor, has he really done anything? He has done something—he turned his slave around. What else? He has to pay a tax of five percent of the slave's value. But does this make the slave free? Not really. Just like a person who has power over others might not be free if they're still a slave to money, a lover, a child, a tyrant, or even a friend of a tyrant. If they're afraid of any of these things, then they're still a slave.

That's why I keep saying, "Practice these things and be ready—know what you should face with confidence and what you should face with caution." Face with confidence what's outside your control, and with caution what's within your control.

"But haven't I read to you, and don't you know what I'm doing?" What have you been working on? Fancy words! Keep your fancy words! Show me instead how you handle desire and aversion—

whether you don't fail to get what you want, or don't fall into what you don't want. As for your fancy phrases, if you're wise, you'll take them somewhere else and erase them. "But didn't Socrates write?" Yes, and who wrote more than he did? But how did he write? He couldn't always have someone around to test his ideas, so he tested himself and practiced what he preached. That's what a philosopher writes about, not fancy phrases and "said he, said I."

When the time comes, are you going to show off your fancy writing and boast, "Look how I write dialogues"? Don't do that. Instead, boast like this: "Look how I handle my desires and aversions. Bring on death, bring on hardship, bring on imprisonment, bring on dishonor, bring on condemnation, and see how I face them." That's the right way for a young person to show what they've learned. Leave the other things to others—don't talk about them, and if someone praises you for them, don't accept it. Let yourself be known as someone who knows how to handle their desires and aversions. Let others practice lawsuits, problems, and logic puzzles. You practice how to die, how to be chained, how to be tortured, how to be exiled. Do all these things with confidence, trusting in the One who called you to face them and deemed you worthy of this position. When you do, you'll show what a rational mind can do when it faces challenges beyond its control.

And so, the paradox we talked about won't seem impossible or strange anymore—because you'll see that you can be both cautious and confident at the same time: confident in what's outside your control, and cautious in what's within your control.

Chapter 2
On Peace of Mind

Think about what you want to achieve when you go to court and what you want to protect. If you want to maintain your freedom to make moral choices and keep your inner peace, then you have nothing to worry about. If you focus on controlling what is within your power and are satisfied with that, then what else matters? Who can take that away from you? If you want to be self-respecting and honorable, who can stop you? If you don't want to be forced to do something, who can make you desire what you don't want or avoid what you think is right?

But what if the judge does something that seems terrifying? Even then, how can he make you fear what you are facing? If your desires and fears are under your own control, what more do you need? This is your defense, your proof, and your victory.

This is why Socrates, when told to prepare for his trial, said, "Haven't I been preparing for this all my life?" When asked how, he replied, "By focusing on what is within my control." "How did you do that?" he was asked. "I have never done anything wrong, whether in private or public life," Socrates answered.

But if you want to protect external things like your body, money, or reputation, then start preparing right now. Study your judge and opponent carefully. If you need to beg, beg. If you need to cry, cry. If you need to groan, groan. Once you hand over control of your own things to external forces, you become their slave. Don't let yourself be pulled in different directions—decide now whether you want to be free or a slave, educated or uneducated, brave or cowardly. Either endure to the end or give up right away. But don't take many blows only to give up in the end. If that seems shameful, then start thinking right now about where true good and evil lie. Where truth is, that's where caution and confidence should be.

Do you think that if Socrates had cared about protecting external things, he would have said, "Anytus and Meletus can kill me, but they cannot harm me"? Was he so foolish that he didn't see this approach wouldn't lead to that goal, but to something else? Why wouldn't he add something provocative, like my friend Heracleitus, who had a small lawsuit over a piece of land in Rhodes? After he made his case, he added, "But I'm not going to beg you, and I don't care what your decision is. It's you who are on trial, not me." And he ruined his case because of that. What was the point of saying that? Just don't beg, but don't add, "I'm not going to beg," unless it's the right time, like when Socrates deliberately provoked his judges. If you plan to say something like that, why even bother showing up? Why answer the summons at all? If you want to be crucified, just wait—the cross will come. But if reason tells you to answer the summons and do your best to persuade, then do that, but always keep true to your character.

Looking at it this way, it's silly to say, "Give me advice." What advice can I give you? Instead, you should say, "Help my mind to adapt to whatever happens." Asking for advice is like an uneducated person saying, "Tell me what to write when someone tells me what to write." If I say, "Write Dio," and then the teacher says, "No, write Theo," what will he write? But if you've practiced writing, you'll be able to write whatever is dictated to you. If you haven't practiced, what advice can I give you now? If circumstances change, what will you say or do?

So remember this general rule, and you won't be at a loss for advice. But if you're obsessed with external things, you'll be tossed around by the will of your master. And who is your master? The person who has power over anything you care about or wish to avoid.

Chapter 3
For Those Who Refer Others to Philosophers

Diogenes gave an excellent answer to a man who asked him for a letter of recommendation. He said, "That you are a man, he will know at a glance. But whether you are a good man or a bad one, he will only discover if he has the skill to tell the difference between good and bad. And if he doesn't have that skill, he won't discover the truth, even if I write him a thousand letters."

It's like if a silver coin asked to be recommended to someone to be tested. If the person is an expert at testing silver, the coin will prove itself. We should have something similar in our daily lives so that I can say, just like the silver tester does, "Bring me any coin, and I will tell you if it's real."

Now, when it comes to logical arguments, I say, "Bring me any argument, and I will tell you whether it can be analyzed correctly or not." How so? Because I know how to analyze arguments myself. I have the skill needed to evaluate whether someone is handling arguments properly.

But what do I do in everyday life? Sometimes I call something good, and sometimes I call it bad. What is the reason? The opposite of what happens with arguments—in this case, it's because of ignorance and inexperience.

Chapter 4
To the Man Who Committed Adultery

Epictetus was talking about how humans are naturally meant to be loyal and trustworthy. He said that if someone destroys this trust, they are destroying what makes them truly human. At that moment, a man walked in who was known as a scholar, but who had also once been caught committing adultery in the city. Epictetus continued, saying that if we give up on being loyal, which is something we're naturally meant to be, and start making plans to be with someone else's wife, what are we really doing? We are ruining and destroying not just ourselves, but the very idea of trust, self-respect, and respect for the gods. Is that all? No, we are also destroying friendships, our communities, and the state itself.

So, what kind of person does this make us? How am I supposed to treat you now? As a neighbor, a friend? What kind of friend? As a fellow citizen? How can I trust you? If you were a broken pot that couldn't be used for anything, we would throw you out on the trash heap, and even there, no one would pick you up. But if, as a person, you can't act like a decent human being, what are we supposed to do with you? If you can't even be a friend, can you at least be a good servant? And who is going to trust you to do that? Should we just throw you out on the trash heap like a useless piece of garbage? And yet, you still say, "But I'm a scholar!" No, you are a bad person, and you are useless. It's like if wasps complained that no one cares about them, when everyone actually runs away from them and, if they can, they swat them down. You sting everyone you touch, causing trouble and pain. What do you want us to do with you? There is no place for you.

You might say, "But aren't women naturally meant to be shared?" I agree. And a little pig at a feast is also meant to be shared by the guests. But after the portions have been handed out, if you really want to, go ahead and grab someone else's portion, steal it secretly, or slip your hand in and take some for yourself. If you can't tear off a piece of the meat, at least get your fingers greasy and lick them. You would be a great companion at a feast, right? A dinner guest worthy of Socrates! Come on now, isn't the theater also shared by all the citizens? So, if people are sitting there, go ahead and throw one of them out of their seat if you want.

In the same way, women are also shared by nature. But when the law, like a host at a banquet, has given them out, aren't you willing to look for your own share instead of stealing from someone else? "But I'm a scholar and I understand what Archedemus said." Fine, then, understand what Archedemus said and go ahead and be an adulterer, a liar, a wolf, or a monkey instead of a decent person. What is stopping you?

Chapter 5
How Living Carefully Aligns with Having a Noble Spirit

Things themselves are neutral, but how we use them is not neutral. So how can someone stay strong and peaceful while also being careful and neither reckless nor negligent? It's like playing a game with dice. The dice themselves are neutral, and we can't control how they land. But using what happens wisely and carefully, that's our job. In the same way, the main job in life is this: to look at situations and compare them, and say to yourself, "What happens outside of me isn't under my control; my choices are under my control. So where do I look for good and bad? Inside myself, in what is truly mine." But when it comes to what belongs to someone else, never call it "good" or "bad" or "a benefit" or "a harm."

Does that mean we should be careless with things outside our control? Not at all. Because being careless with them would harm our moral character, which is unnatural. We should use these things carefully because how we use them is important, but we should do so with steadiness and peace of mind, knowing that the things themselves are neutral. In what really matters—our choices—no one can stop or force us. The things that can be stopped or forced are not truly good or bad, but how we use them can be good or bad, and that is under our control. It is hard to balance carefulness with material things and calmness in the face of them, but it's not impossible. Otherwise, happiness would be impossible.

We should act like we are on a voyage. What can I control? I can choose the captain, the crew, the day, and the moment to sail. Then, a storm comes. What can I do then? My job is done. Now it's the captain's job. But what if the ship sinks? Then what do I do? What I can do—I drown without fear, without screaming or blaming the gods, but knowing that everything born must die. I'm not eternal; I'm a human, just a part of the whole, like an hour in a day. I must come like the hour and pass like the hour. So what difference does it make if I pass by drowning or by illness? I must pass away somehow.

This is like how skilled ball players play. They don't care whether the ball is good or bad; they care about how they throw and catch it. Skill and grace are what matter, not the ball itself. But if we catch or throw the ball with fear or panic, where's the fun? How can we stay calm or see what's coming next in the game? But one player might say, "Throw!" Another might say, "Don't throw!" And another, "Don't throw it up!" That would be a fight, not a game.

Socrates knew how to play ball in life. How? He knew how to handle himself in court. He said, "Tell me, Anytus, what do you mean when you say I don't believe in God? Who do you think the daemons are? Aren't they either the offspring of gods or a mix of gods and humans?" When Anytus agreed, Socrates said, "Who would believe in mules but not believe in horses?" In speaking like this, he was playing the game well. At that moment, his "ball" was imprisonment, exile, drinking poison, leaving his wife and making his children orphans. These were the things he was dealing with, but he played the game well.

We should also act like this, focusing on playing the game well, but being indifferent to the actual "ball" because it's just a ball. We should try to do well with whatever material we're given, but not let it define us. Like a weaver works with whatever wool he's given, another might give you food, money, and even your body, and can take them away too. You should take what you're given and do your best with it. Then, if you come through it without harm, others might congratulate you, but the one who truly understands will praise you for how you handled yourself, not just that you got out unharmed.

But if you escaped by doing something dishonorable, they will feel the opposite.

So, how can we say that some external things are natural and others are not? It's like thinking that the foot is separate from the body. If you think of the foot alone, it's natural for it to stay clean. But if you think of it as part of the body, it's natural for it to step in mud, get scratched, and even sometimes be cut off to save the whole body. Otherwise, it's not really a foot.

We should think the same about ourselves. What are you? A person. If you think of yourself as separate, it's natural to want to live a long life, be rich, and stay healthy. But if you think of yourself as part of a whole, it's natural to sometimes be sick, take risks, be in need, and even die before your time. Why are you upset? Don't you know that if the foot were separate, it wouldn't be a foot anymore? And if you are separate, you're not really a person anymore. What is a person? A part of society; first, of the society of gods and people, and then of the smaller societies that are like copies of the whole universe.

"Do I have to go on trial now?" Well, would you have someone else get sick now, or someone else take a risk, or someone else die, or someone else be judged? In a world like ours, with these bodies and these fellow humans, these things are bound to happen, some to one person, some to another. It's your job to step up and do your part, to handle things as they should be handled. Then if the judge says, "You're guilty," you can say, "I hope things go well for you. I've done my part; now you should see if you've done yours." Remember, the judge takes a risk too.

Chapter 6
Understanding What 'Indifferent' Things Are

A hypothetical statement is neutral: the judgment you make about it is not neutral; it is either knowledge, an opinion, or a mistake. In the same way, life itself is neutral, but how you live it is not. So when someone tells you that certain things in life are neutral, don't become careless. And when someone urges you to be cautious, don't become obsessed with material things. It's important to know your own abilities and limits so that in areas where you're not prepared, you can stay calm and not get upset if others do better than you. For example, in logical arguments, you might be better than others, and if they feel bad about it, you can remind them, "I've learned this, and you haven't." Similarly, in areas where practice is needed, don't seek things that require experience you don't have; let those with practice take the lead, and stay strong-minded.

When you go to greet someone, how should you do it? Not in a lowly way. If you're shut out because you didn't know how to push your way in through a window, and you find the door closed, you'll either leave or climb through the window. But still, speak to him. How? Not in a lowly way. But what if you don't get what you want? Was that your responsibility or his? Why do you claim something that belongs to someone else? Always remember what belongs to you and what belongs to others, and you won't be disturbed. Chrysippus wisely said, "As long as the future is uncertain, I always stick to what is most likely to preserve what is natural." For God has given me the ability to make choices. But if I knew it was my fate to get sick, I would move toward it; for if a foot had a mind, it would willingly step into the mud. Why are ears of corn grown? Is it not so they can dry out? And don't they dry out so they can be harvested? They are not separate from the cycle of nature. If they had awareness, should they wish never to be harvested? But it would be a curse for ears of corn to never be harvested. So we should understand that it is also a curse for people to never die, just like it would be to never ripen or be harvested. But since we must be harvested, and we know we will be, we get upset about it. This happens because we don't know what we are or haven't studied what it means to be human, the way horse experts know what it means to be a horse. But Chrysantas, when he was about to strike an enemy, stopped when he heard the trumpet signal to retreat. He thought it was better to follow the general's orders than his own desires. But we don't choose to obey when necessity calls, and instead, we cry and complain about our situation, calling them "circumstances." What kind of circumstances? If you call everything around you circumstances, then all things are circumstances. But if you only call hardships by this name, what hardship is there in the natural process of dying? What kills you might be a sword, a wheel, the sea, a tile, or a tyrant. Why do you care how you go to the underworld? All ways are equal. But if you want the truth, the way the tyrant sends you is quicker. A tyrant never took six months to kill a man, but a fever often takes a year. These things are just sounds and the noise of meaningless words.

"I'm in danger of losing my life because of Caesar." And am I not in danger living in Nicopolis, where there are so many earthquakes? And when you cross the Adriatic Sea, aren't you risking your life? "But I'm also in danger of my reputation." Your own? How? Who can force you to hold an opinion you don't want? But are you worried about someone else's opinion? And what danger do you face if others have false opinions? "But I'm in danger of being exiled." What does it mean to be exiled? To be somewhere other than Rome? "Yes, but what if I'm sent to Gyara?" If you like it, you'll go; if not, you can go somewhere else, just like the one who sent you there will also go, whether he wants to or not. Why then do you make such a big deal out of going to Rome? It's not worth all this trouble for a young person to say, "It wasn't worth it to have listened so much, written so much, and spent so much time with an old man who isn't worth much." Just remember to distinguish between what belongs to you and what doesn't, and never claim what belongs to others. A court and a prison are both places, one high and the other low, but you can keep your will steady if you choose to, no matter where you are. We will be like Socrates when we can write hymns in prison. But as we are now, could we endure someone in prison asking, "Would you like me to read hymns to you?" "Why are you bothering me? Don't you know the suffering I'm going through? How can I listen to hymns in such a situation?" What situation? "I'm going to die." And will other people live forever?

Chapter 7
How We Should Approach and Use Divination

Because of an unreasonable belief in divination, many of us neglect our duties. What more can a fortune teller predict than death, danger, or illness, or things like that? If I must face danger for a friend or if it is my duty to die for him, why do I need a fortune teller? Don't I already have within me a sense that tells me what is good and what is bad, and what the signs of both are? So why do I need to look at animal guts or the flight of birds? And why do I listen when someone says, "This is for your own good"? Does he know what is good for me? Does he know what is truly good? And just because he knows how to read animal organs, does that mean he understands the difference between good and evil? If he knows that, then he must also know what is beautiful and ugly, what is just and unjust. Tell me, what exactly is this sign you're seeing for me? Is it life or death, poverty or wealth? But whether these things are good for me or not, I won't ask you. Why don't you give advice on grammar instead? Why do you give advice on matters we all argue about and don't fully understand? The woman who planned to send a month's worth of supplies to Gratilla while she was in exile gave a good answer when someone said that Domitian would take what she sent. She replied, "I'd rather have Domitian take everything than not send it at all."

So what makes us keep going to fortune tellers? It's fear, the fear of what will happen. This is why we flatter them. "Will I inherit my father's property?" "Let's see; let's sacrifice to find out." Yes, whatever the gods decide. When the fortune teller says, "You will inherit it," we thank him as if he gave it to us. This is why they take advantage of us.

So what should we do? We should approach divination without desire or fear, just like a traveler asks a local which of two roads leads to his destination. He doesn't prefer one road over the other; he just wants the road that will get him where he needs to go. In the same way, we should look to God as our guide, like we use our eyes—not asking them to show us what we want to see, but accepting whatever they show us. But now, we nervously grab the hand of the fortune teller, ask God for help, and beg the fortune teller, saying, "Please, master, let me get through this safely." Fool, would you want anything other than what's best? Is there anything better than what God wants? Why are you trying to corrupt your own judge and mislead your advisor?

Chapter 8
Understanding the Nature of Goodness

God is good. But good is also beneficial. It makes sense then that where God's nature is, there also is the nature of good. So what is the nature of God? Is it flesh? No. Is it land or wealth? No. Fame? No. Is it intelligence, knowledge, and reason? Yes. So that is where the nature of good is—right here in reason. You wouldn't look for it in a plant, would you? No. Would you look for it in an animal? No. If you're looking for it in a rational being, then why are you still looking anywhere other than in what makes rational beings better than irrational ones? Plants don't even have the ability to understand what they see, and that's why you wouldn't call them good. So the good must involve understanding what we see. But is that all it takes? If you say that's enough, then you would have to say that animals can be good or bad too. But you don't, and you're right not to. Even if animals can understand what they see, they don't know how to use that understanding. And this makes sense because they exist to serve others and have no authority over anything. The donkey doesn't exist to be better than others. No, but we needed an animal strong enough to carry loads, so it needed to be able to walk. For that, it needed to understand what it saw. But that's where it stopped. If the donkey could also understand how to use what it saw, then it wouldn't be serving us anymore. It would be equal to us.

So won't you look for the nature of good in rational beings? Because if it's not there, you won't find it anywhere else, not in a plant or an animal. "But aren't plants and animals also made by God?" Yes, they are, but they aren't greater things or parts of the gods. But you are a greater thing; you are a piece of God himself. Why don't you know your noble origin? Why don't you remember where you came from? When you eat, do you not remember who you are and what you are feeding? When you are with a woman, do you not remember who you are? When you are talking, exercising, or just being social, do you not realize that you are nourishing a god within you? Fool, you carry a god with you, and you don't even know it. Do you think I'm talking about a god made of silver or gold, something outside of you? No, you carry him within you. But you pollute him with your dirty thoughts and actions. If you had a statue of God, you would never dare to do the things you do. But when God himself is present within you, watching and listening to everything you do, you're not ashamed of your actions or thoughts. You don't even know your own nature, and you provoke God's anger.

So why do we worry when we send a young man out into the world, afraid that he will act improperly, eat improperly, or behave badly with women? Are we worried that his ragged clothes will humiliate him, or that fancy clothes will make him proud? If he acts this way, he doesn't know his own god. He doesn't know with whom he is going out into the world. Can we stand it when he says, "I wish I had God with me"? Don't you already have God with you? Why are you looking for another when he's already with you? Or do you think God would tell you anything different? If you were a statue made by a famous artist, like Athena or Zeus, you would think about both yourself and the artist. And if you had any sense, you would try to do nothing that would shame the artist or yourself, and you'd try to appear in a way that honors the artist's work. But now, since Zeus made you, do you not care how you appear? Is the artist who made a statue the same as the one who made you? Is the statue's craftsmanship like your own? A statue is just marble, bronze, gold, or ivory, and once it's made, it stays the same forever. But God's works, like you, can move, breathe, and think. You can use your senses and understand what you see. Being made by such a creator, how could you dishonor him?

Not only did God make you, but he also trusted you to take care of yourself. He said, "There is no one else more suitable to watch over you than you." So he entrusted you to yourself, to keep yourself modest, faithful, brave, and free from fear or distress. And yet, you fail to do this. Some may ask, "Where did this person get such arrogance and pride?" I am not yet as serious as a philosopher should be because I'm still not fully confident in what I've learned. I'm still afraid of my own weaknesses. But once I gain confidence, you will see in me the face and the posture of a true philosopher. Then I will show you the perfected and polished statue. What do you expect? A proud and arrogant face? Does the Zeus in Olympia lift his eyebrows in pride? No, his expression is calm, like one ready to say, "My word is final and will not change." This is how I will show myself to you—faithful, modest, noble, and calm. What, do you expect me to be immortal too, never to grow old or get sick? No, but I will face death and illness in a way that befits a god. This is the power I have. This I can do. The rest I do not possess, nor can I do. But I will show you the strength of a philosopher. What strength is that? It is having desires that are never frustrated, avoiding things that are within your control, having the right goals, working hard, and being wise in what you agree to. These are what you will see.

Chapter 9
When We Fail to Live as We Should, We Turn to Philosophy

It is not an easy thing to do just one thing: to live up to what it means to be a man. So, what is a man? A man is a rational being who is also mortal. What separates us from wild animals? It's our ability to reason. And what separates us from other creatures, like sheep? It's the same thing. So, make sure you don't act like a wild animal, because if you do, you lose what it means to be a man. Make sure you don't act like a sheep, because if you do, you also lose what it means to be a man. What do we do when we act like sheep? When we eat too much, act lewdly, or do things without thinking, we lower ourselves to the level of sheep. What do we lose? Our ability to reason. When we act violently, argue all the time, or behave with anger, we lower ourselves to the level of wild animals. So, some of us become like big wild animals, and others like small, bad-tempered ones. This is why some people say, "I'd rather be eaten by a lion." But in all these ways, we destroy what it means to act like a man. When is a complex statement correct? When it fulfills the promise of its nature. The same goes for a flute, a lyre, a horse, or a dog—they are preserved when they do what they are meant to do. So, is it any wonder that a person is also preserved or lost in the same way? Each person is improved and preserved by doing what they are meant to do: a carpenter by doing carpentry, a grammarian by doing grammar. But if a man gets used to writing badly, his skill will naturally be corrupted and destroyed. In the same way, modest actions keep a person modest, and immodest actions destroy that modesty. Honest actions keep a person honest, and dishonest actions destroy honesty. On the other hand, bad actions strengthen bad habits: shamelessness makes a person more shameless, dishonesty makes a person more dishonest, abusive words make a person more abusive, and greed makes a person more greedy.

This is why philosophers tell us not to be satisfied with just learning but also to add practice and study. We've spent a long time doing the wrong things, and we've practiced opinions that are contrary to the truth. If we don't also practice the right opinions, we will be nothing more than people who repeat the ideas of others. Who among us can't talk about good and bad things according to the rules of philosophy? We can say that some things are good, some are bad, and some are neutral. Good things are virtues and the things that come from virtues. Bad things are the opposite, and neutral things are wealth, health, and reputation. But what happens if, in the middle of this discussion, there's a loud noise or someone laughs at us? We get disturbed. Philosopher, where are those ideas you were just talking about? Where did they come from? Only from your lips. Why do you misuse the wisdom others have provided? Why do you treat serious matters like a game of dice? It's one thing to store up bread and wine in a pantry, and another thing to eat them. What you eat gets digested, turns into muscle, flesh, bones, blood, healthy skin, and healthy breath. Whatever is stored up can be taken out and shown whenever you want, but it doesn't benefit you unless it's used. What's the difference between explaining these doctrines and explaining the ideas of others with different views? Sit down and explain Epicurus's ideas according to the rules of philosophy, and maybe you'll explain them better than Epicurus himself. Why then do you call yourself a Stoic? Why do you deceive people? Why do you act like a Jew when you're a Greek? Don't you see why someone is called a Jew, a Syrian, or an Egyptian? And when we see a person who tries to act in two different ways, we say, "This person isn't a Jew, but he's acting like one." But when someone fully embraces Jewish teachings and lives by them, then he is both in name and in fact a Jew. In the same way, we too, when we are not true to ourselves, are Jews in name but not in fact. Our actions don't match our words; we're far from practicing what we say and what we claim to know. So, when we can't even live up to what it means to be a man, we add the burden of claiming to be a philosopher. This is like a man who can't lift ten pounds trying to lift the stone that Ajax lifted.

Chapter 10
How to Discover a Man's Duties Based on the Titles He Holds

First, think about who you are. You are a human being, and as a human, nothing is more important than your ability to make choices. Everything else is under your control, and your ability to choose is free and not controlled by anyone else. Now, think about how your ability to reason separates you from other beings. It separates you from wild animals and from domesticated animals like sheep. Additionally, you are a citizen of the world, a part of it—not a servant, but one of the leading parts because you have the ability to understand how the world works and see the connections between things. So, what does it mean to be a good citizen? It means that you don't just think about what is good for you personally, but you consider the whole community, acting as a hand or foot would if they had the ability to reason. They would never move or desire anything without thinking about how it affects the whole body. Philosophers say that if a good person knew what the future held, they would even accept their own sickness, death, or injury because they understand that these things happen according to the larger plan of the universe, and that the whole is more important than the part, and the community is more important than the individual. But since we don't know the future, our duty is to stick to the things that are naturally better choices, because we were made for this purpose.

Next, remember that you are a son. What does it mean to be a son? It means understanding that everything a son has belongs to the father. It means obeying him in all things, never blaming him to others, never saying or doing anything that would harm him, and always yielding to him and helping him as much as you can. After this, know that you are also a brother, and as a brother, you should make concessions, be easily persuaded, speak well of your brother, never argue over things that are outside of your control, and readily give them up so you can gain more of the things that are within your control. Think about how much better it is to gain a good attitude rather than a piece of lettuce or a seat. How much greater is that advantage!

Then, if you are a senator, remember that you are a senator. If you are a young person, remember that you are young. If you are old, remember that you are old. Each of these roles comes with specific duties. But if you go and blame your brother, I would say to you: You have forgotten who you are and what your role is. If you were a blacksmith and misused a hammer, you would have forgotten what it means to be a blacksmith. And if you forget what it means to be a brother and instead become an enemy, would that not mean you've

98

changed into something else? And if instead of being a human, who is a social and tame animal, you become a harmful wild animal, treacherous and biting, have you not lost something important? But do you think the only loss that matters is losing money? Do you think no other loss harms a person? If you lost the ability to read or play music, would you consider that a loss? And if you lose modesty, self-control, and gentleness, do you think that's nothing? The first losses I mentioned are caused by things outside of your control, but the second set of losses happen because of our own choices. And while it's not shameful to lose the first set, it is shameful and unfortunate to lose the second set.

What does someone lose if they become immoral? They lose their humanity. What does someone lose if they cause someone else to become immoral? They lose many other things, and they also lose their humanity. What does someone lose if they commit adultery? They lose their modesty, self-control, decency, and their sense of being a good citizen and neighbor. What does someone lose if they become angry? They lose something else. What does a coward lose? Something different. No one becomes bad without suffering some loss or damage. If you only look for damage in the loss of money, then you would say that none of these people have been harmed. In fact, they might even gain something if they acquire some money by their actions. But if you think this way, then even someone who loses their nose wouldn't be harmed in your eyes. "But," you say, "they are physically mutilated." Well, what about someone who only loses their sense of smell? Don't they lose anything? Is there no part of the soul that benefits the one who has it and harms the one who loses it? "Tell me what you mean by that." Don't we have a natural sense of modesty? "Yes, we do." So, if someone loses this, don't they suffer damage? Don't they lose something that belongs to them? Don't we also have a natural sense of loyalty, affection, and a desire to help others? The person who allows themselves to be harmed in these ways, can they really be free from harm and injury?

"What then? Should I not hurt the person who has hurt me?" First, think about what harm really is, and remember what you've learned from philosophers. If good comes from your choices and actions, and evil also comes from your choices and actions, then think about what you're really saying: "Since this person has hurt themselves by doing something unjust to me, should I hurt myself by doing something unjust to them?" Why don't we think this way? But when there is some harm to our body or possessions, we consider it harm; and when the same thing happens to our ability to choose and act, we think it's no big deal. Someone who has been deceived or who has done something unjust doesn't suffer in their head, their eye, or their hip, and they don't lose their property, so we think it doesn't matter. But whether we have a will that is modest and loyal or shameless and disloyal, we don't care much about it, except when we're in school and talking about philosophy. That's why our progress is limited to just a few words, and beyond that, it doesn't exist at all.

Chapter 11
What The Beginning of Philosophy Is

The beginning of philosophy, for someone who starts it the right way, is realizing how weak and unprepared we are in understanding important things. When we are born, we don't naturally know what a right-angled triangle is, or what a quarter tone or a half tone in music is. We learn these things through teaching and practice. Because of this, people who don't know these things are aware that they don't know them. But when it comes to concepts like good and bad, beautiful and ugly, right and wrong, happiness and misfortune, proper and improper behavior, and what we should or shouldn't do, who ever came into the world without some idea of them? That's why we all use these words and try to match them to different situations, saying things like: "He did well," "He didn't do well," "He did what he should," "He didn't do what he should," "He was lucky," "He was unlucky," "He is just," "He is unjust." Who doesn't use these terms? Who among us waits to learn them like we wait to learn about shapes or sounds? The reason for this is that we come into the world already knowing some things naturally, and we add our own confidence to them. A person might say, "Why shouldn't I know what is beautiful and what is ugly? Don't I already have a sense of it?" Yes, you do. "Don't I apply it to specific things?" Yes, you do. "Don't I apply it correctly?" That's the big question, and that's where confidence comes in. People start with what everyone agrees on, but then they move to what is debated by applying their ideas incorrectly. If they had the power to apply these ideas correctly, what would stop them from being perfect? But now, since you think you're applying these ideas correctly, tell me why you think that. "Because I believe it's right." But another person doesn't see it the same way, and they believe they're right too. Or don't they? "They do believe so." Is it possible for both of you to be right when you have opposite views? "No, it's not possible." So, can you show us anything better than just thinking you're right? Does a madman do anything other than what seems right to him? Is his feeling that something is right enough for him? "No, it's not enough." Then, look for something beyond just what seems right. "What is that?"

This is the beginning of philosophy: realizing that people disagree with each other, wondering why they disagree, rejecting and doubting what only seems to be true, investigating whether what seems true really is true, and finding some standard, like how we use a scale to weigh things or a ruler to check if something is straight. This is the beginning of philosophy. Should we say that everything that seems right to everyone really is right? How can that be when people's opinions contradict each other? So, not everything that seems right is right, but only what seems right to us? Why should our views be better than those of the Syrians or the Egyptians, or better than mine or any other person's? They aren't better. So, what seems right to everyone isn't enough to decide what really is right. In the case of weights or measurements, we don't trust just what we see; we use a standard. In this case, is there no standard higher than what seems right? How could it be that the most important things in life have no clear sign or standard to guide us? There must be a standard. So why don't we look for that standard, find it, and then use it consistently, not even moving a finger without it? I believe this is what cures the madness of those who rely only on what seems right and misuse it. When we find that standard, we can then use it to judge things accurately based on principles that are clear and well-understood.

What are we trying to understand? For example, pleasure. Subject it to the standard, weigh it on the scale. Should the good be something we can trust and rely on? Yes. Should it be something secure? Yes, it should. Is pleasure something secure? No. Then take it off the scale and throw it far away from the category of good things. But if you can't see this clearly, and one scale isn't enough for you, use another. Is it right to be proud of what is good? Yes. Is it right to be proud of present pleasure? Be careful not to say it is. But if you do, then I won't even consider you worthy of using the scale. This is how things are tested and weighed when we have the right standards. And to philosophize is to examine and confirm these standards. Then, using them once we know them is the mark of a wise and good person.

Chapter 12
On the Art of Discussion

What a person needs to learn in order to be able to engage in the art of disputation has been clearly explained by our philosophers (the Stoics); but when it comes to actually using these skills, we lack practice. If you give any one of us an uneducated person to discuss with, we often don't know how to handle the situation. When the uneducated person starts to say things that don't make sense, we don't know how to guide the conversation. Instead, we either insult or make fun of the person, saying, "He's uneducated; it's impossible to do anything with him." But a good guide, when he finds someone lost, helps him find the right path. He doesn't mock or scold him and then leave him behind. You should also try to show the uneducated person the truth, and you will see that he follows it. But if you can't show him the truth, don't mock him—recognize your own shortcomings instead.

How did Socrates handle this? He would make his opponent in a debate agree with him and didn't need any other witnesses. That's why he could say, "I don't care for other witnesses; I'm always satisfied with the evidence from my opponent, and I don't need the opinions of others—just the opinion of the person I'm debating with." Socrates made the conclusions from natural ideas so clear that everyone could see the contradiction if there was one, and they would back away from it. For example, he would ask, "Does an envious person feel joy?" "No, he feels pain," they would answer. Then he would ask, "Is envy pain over bad things?" The person would respond, "What envy is there of bad things?" So, Socrates made the person admit that envy is pain over good things. Then, he would ask, "Would anyone envy people who mean nothing to them?" "No, they wouldn't." Once the person clearly understood what envy was, Socrates would move on without asking for a definition of envy. If the person had defined envy, Socrates wouldn't have said, "You've defined it badly," or, "The words of your definition don't match what envy is." These are technical terms that are hard for uneducated people to understand, and philosophers can't just abandon these terms. But we should be able to make an uneducated person, who follows their natural instincts, either agree with or reject something without needing to use these difficult terms. Knowing our own limitations, we often avoid these kinds of discussions; at least those of us who are careful do. But most people, especially the rash ones, jump into these debates, confusing themselves and others. In the end, they walk away after insulting their opponents and getting insulted themselves.

Socrates, however, had a special ability: he never got angry in a debate, never said anything insulting, and never used abusive language. Instead, he would patiently deal with abusive people and find a way to end the argument. If you want to understand the great power he had in this way, read Xenophon's Symposium, and you'll see how many arguments he was able to resolve. This is why poets often praise this ability:

"Quickly with skill he settles great disputes." – Hesiod

However, in our current time, especially in Rome, it's not safe to do this. If you try, you can't do it secretly; you'll have to approach someone of high rank or wealth and ask him questions like, "Can you tell me to whom you've entrusted your horses?" "Of course, I can." "Have you entrusted them to just anyone, or to someone who knows about horses?" "Certainly not to just anyone." "What about your gold or silver, or your clothes?" "I'm careful about those too." "And what about your body? Have you entrusted its care to anyone?" "Yes, I have." "To someone with experience, like a doctor or a trainer?" "Without a doubt." "Are these the best things you own, or do you have something even more valuable?" "What do you mean?" "I mean the thing that uses these other things and judges each of them." "You mean the soul?" "Yes, that's exactly what I mean." "I agree; the soul is much more valuable than anything else I have." "Then can you show us how you've taken care of your soul? It's not likely that someone as wise and respected as you would allow the most valuable thing you possess to be neglected or ruined." "Certainly not." "But have you taken care of your soul yourself, or have you learned from someone else how to do it, or have you figured it out on your own?"

This is where it gets risky, because the person might say, "What business is this of yours? Who are you?" And if you keep pressing, he might even raise his hands and hit you. I used to admire this way of teaching until I found myself in similar dangerous situations.

☐

Chapter 13
On Anxiety (Solicitude)

When I see someone anxious, I ask: What does this person want? If he didn't want something that's not in his control, how could he be anxious? For example, when a musician is playing alone, he doesn't feel anxious. But when he performs in front of an audience, he becomes anxious, even if he has a good voice and plays the instrument well. Why? Because he doesn't just want to play well; he also wants to get applause, which is something not in his control. So, where he has skill, he is confident. If you bring in someone who knows nothing about music, the musician doesn't worry about him. But in situations where a person lacks knowledge or practice, that's where anxiety appears. What kind of situation is this? It's when someone doesn't understand what a crowd is or what it means to receive their praise. The musician may know how to play the highest and lowest notes, but he doesn't know what public praise means or what power it has in life. Because of this, he's bound to tremble and turn pale. So, when I see someone afraid, I don't say he's not a musician, but I do say other things, and not just one thing, but many. First of all, I say he's a stranger who doesn't know where he is. Even though he's been here a long time, he doesn't know the laws of the place, the customs, or what is allowed and what isn't. He hasn't even hired a lawyer to explain the rules to him.

A person wouldn't write a will without knowing how it should be written, or without hiring someone who knows. Nor would he carelessly sign a contract or write a security note. But he uses his desires without getting advice, and he acts, moves, and makes decisions without any guidance. "What do you mean without advice?" He doesn't realize that he's wanting things he's not allowed to have, and he doesn't want what he's forced to have. He doesn't know what's truly his and what belongs to someone else. But if he did know, he would never be stopped or hindered, and he wouldn't be anxious. "How is that possible?" Is anyone afraid of things that aren't bad? No. Is anyone afraid of bad things that are still within his control so that they might not happen? No, certainly not. If the things that are beyond our control are neither good nor bad, and all the things that are within our control are up to us, and no one can take them from us or give them to us unless we allow it, then where is the room for anxiety?

But we are anxious about our bodies, our little bit of property, and what Caesar might decide, but we're not anxious about our internal thoughts. Are we worried about not forming false opinions? No, because that's in our control. Are we worried about not acting against nature? No, not even that. So, when you see someone turn pale, just like a doctor would say by looking at the complexion, "This person's spleen is not right, or this person's liver is off," you should say, "This person's desires and fears are not in order. He's not on the right path; he's feverish." Nothing else makes a person change color, tremble, chatter his teeth, or make his knees weak and shift from foot to foot.

That's why when Zeno was going to meet Antigonus, he wasn't anxious. Antigonus had no power over the things that Zeno cared about, and Zeno didn't care about the things that were in Antigonus's power. But Antigonus was anxious when he was going to meet Zeno because he wanted to please Zeno. But this was something outside his control. Zeno didn't want to please Antigonus, because no one who is skilled in any art cares about pleasing someone who has no skill in that area.

Should I try to please you? Why? Do you know the standard by which one person judges another? Have you made an effort to understand what makes a person good or bad, and how a person becomes one or the other? Then why aren't you good yourself? "How," he asks, "am I not good?" Because no good person laments, groans, or cries. No good person turns pale and trembles or worries about how someone will receive him or listen to him. Slave, it will be however it pleases the other person. Why do you worry about what belongs to others? Is it the other person's fault if he receives what you say poorly? "Certainly." And can one person's fault be in someone else? "No." Then why are you anxious about something that belongs to someone else? "Your question makes sense, but I'm worried about how I'll talk to him." Can't you talk to him however you choose? "But I'm afraid I might get flustered." If you were going to write the name "Dion," would you be afraid of getting flustered? "Of course not." Why? Is it because you've practiced writing the name? "Yes, that's why." Well, if you were going to read the name, wouldn't you feel the same way? Why? Because every skill brings with it a certain level of confidence in what belongs to that skill.

Have you not practiced speaking? What else did you learn in school? Syllogisms and tricky arguments? For what purpose? Wasn't it to learn how to speak well? And isn't speaking well the same as speaking at the right time, carefully, intelligently, without making mistakes, and with confidence? "Yes." So, when you're riding a horse and go out into an open field, do you worry about being matched against someone on foot? Do you worry about something you've practiced and the other person hasn't? "Yes, but that person I'm going to talk to has the power to kill me." Then tell the truth, unfortunate man, and don't brag or claim to be a philosopher. Don't refuse to acknowledge those who have power over you. As long as you are focused on your body, follow anyone who is stronger than you. Socrates practiced speaking, and he spoke the way he did to tyrants, to judges, and even in prison. Diogenes practiced speaking, and he spoke the way he did to Alexander, to pirates, and to the person who bought him. These men were confident in the things they practiced. But you should go back to your own affairs and stay out of things. Go sit in a corner, work on your arguments, and propose them to someone else. You don't have what it takes to lead a state.

Chapter 14
On Naso

When a certain Roman entered with his son and listened to someone reading, Epictetus said: "This is the method of instruction," and then he stopped. When the Roman asked him to continue, Epictetus said: "Every art, when it is being taught, causes effort for those who are not familiar with it and who are unskilled. The things that come from the arts immediately show their use for the purpose they were made, and most of them contain something attractive and pleasing. For example, watching a shoemaker learn is not a pleasant thing, but the shoes he makes are useful and also nice to look at. The process of a blacksmith learning is very unpleasant to someone who doesn't understand the art, but the work shows the use of the skill. You see this even more in music; if you watch someone learning, the process seems very unpleasant, yet the results of music are pleasing and enjoyable even to those who know nothing about it."

In the same way, we think the work of a philosopher is something similar: he must align his desires with what is happening so that nothing that happens goes against what he wants, and nothing that doesn't happen is something he wishes for. From this alignment comes the ability to pass through life without failing in desires, without encountering things we would avoid, and without uneasiness, fear, or distress. The philosopher lives in harmony with himself and with others, maintaining both natural and acquired relationships, like being a son, a father, a brother, a citizen, a husband, a neighbor, a fellow traveler, a ruler, or one who is ruled. This is how we see the work of a philosopher. The next question is how this should be done.

We see that when a carpenter learns certain things, he becomes a carpenter. When a pilot learns certain things, he becomes a pilot. Isn't it the same with philosophy? Is it enough to just want to be wise and good, or is there also a need to learn certain things? We then ask what these things are. Philosophers say that first, we must learn that there is a God and that he provides for everything. Also, that it is impossible to hide our actions, intentions, or thoughts from him. The next thing to learn is the nature of the gods, because once we know what they are like, anyone who wants to please and obey them must try to be like them. If God is faithful, then man must also be faithful. If God is free, man must also be free. If God is kind, man must also be kind. If God is great, man must also be great. By being an imitator of God, man must do and say everything in a way that is consistent with this fact.

Where should we begin? If you want to enter into this discussion, I'll tell you that the first thing you must understand is the meaning of words. "So, you're saying that I don't understand words now?" You don't understand them. "Then how do I use them?" You use them just like an illiterate person uses written language, or like cattle use their senses: using is one thing, understanding is another. But if you think you understand them, pick any word you like, and let's see if we both understand it the same way. "But it's unpleasant to be corrected, especially when I'm old and have maybe served in the military three times." I know that too: you come to me as if you're not lacking anything, and what could you even imagine you're missing? You're rich, you have children and a wife, and probably many slaves. Caesar knows you, and in Rome, you have many friends. You fulfill your obligations to everyone; you know how to repay someone who does you a favor and how to return the same kind of treatment to someone who wrongs you. So, what do you lack? If I show you that you lack the most necessary and important things for happiness, and that until now you've focused on everything except what you should, and to top it off, that you don't know what God is, what man is, what is good, or what is bad, and if I say that you know nothing about yourself, how could you stand me and stay here? It's impossible; you'd leave in anger. But what harm have I done to you? Is it like a mirror offending an ugly man because it shows him his true reflection? Is it like a doctor insulting a sick man when he says, "You're not well. You have a fever; don't eat today and just drink water"? No one says, "What an insult!" But if you tell a man, "Your desires are out of control, your fears are too low, your intentions are inconsistent, your actions don't align with nature, your opinions are rash and false," he immediately leaves, saying, "I've been insulted."

Our way of dealing with life is like being at a crowded market. Beasts are brought to be sold, along with oxen, and most people come to buy and sell. But there are a few who come just to watch the market, to see how it's run, why it's happening, who set it up, and for what purpose. The same is true in life: some people, like cattle, are only concerned with things like possessions, lands, slaves, and government positions. These are just like fodder to them. But there are a few who attend life's market to observe, to think about what the world is, who governs it, and whether it has a purpose or if it all happens by chance. If it has an administrator, what kind of administrator is he, and how does he govern? Who are we, who were created by him, and for what purpose? Do we have some connection or relationship with him, or not? This is how these few people think, and then they focus on understanding this one thing, and then they leave. What happens then? They are ridiculed by the majority, just like spectators at a fair are mocked by traders. And if the animals had any understanding, they would mock those who admired anything other than fodder.

Chapter 15
On Those Who Stubbornly Hold on to Their Beliefs

When some people hear that a person should be firm in their decisions, and that our will is naturally free and cannot be forced, while everything else can be hindered and is under the control of others, they think they should stick to everything they've decided without changing. But first of all, what they have decided must be reasonable. I want strength in the body, but the kind of strength that exists in a healthy, well-trained body. If I see that you have the strength of someone who is frantic and boast about it, I would tell you to see a doctor because that is not true strength, but a lack of proper strength. In a similar way, those who hear these teachings the wrong way may experience the same problem. This happened to one of my companions who, for no good reason, decided to starve himself to death. I heard about it on the third day of his fasting and went to see what was going on. He said, "I have decided." But tell me, what made you decide this? If you have decided wisely, we will sit with you and help you on your way. But if your decision was unreasonable, then change your mind. "We must stick to our decisions," he said. What are you saying? We should stick to our decisions only if they are right. If you are now convinced that it's night when it's actually day, do not change your mind if you wish, but stay firm and say, "We must stick to our decisions." Shouldn't you first check whether your decision is sound and reasonable, and only then build firmness and security on it? But if you lay a rotten and weak foundation, won't your little building fall even faster, the more and stronger the materials you put on it? Would you leave us and life behind without any good reason, even though you are a friend, a companion, and a fellow citizen of both the large and small community? And while you are committing this act of destroying a person who has done no wrong, do you say that you must stick to your decision? And if one day you decide to kill me, should you stick to that decision too?

This man was eventually persuaded to change his mind, but it's impossible to convince some people nowadays. So now I understand what I didn't before: the saying that you can't persuade or break a fool. May I never have the misfortune of having a foolish wise man as my friend—nothing is more stubborn. "I'm determined," the man says. Madmen are also determined, but the more firmly they hold to things that don't exist, the more medicine they need. Shouldn't you act like a sick person and call for a doctor? "I'm sick, master, help me; tell me what I should do. It's my duty to obey you." The same applies here: "I don't know what I should do, but I've come to learn." "No, talk to me about something else. I've already made up my mind about this." What else should we talk about that's more important and useful than convincing you that it's not enough to just make a decision and never change it? That's the attitude of madness, not of health. "I'll die if you force me to change this." Why? What's happened? "I've decided." I'm lucky that you haven't decided to kill me. "I don't take money." Why not? "I've decided." Be careful, because the same determination that makes you refuse money now might later make you take it for no reason and say, "I've decided." Just like in a sick body where fluids move from one part to another, a troubled soul doesn't know which way to go. But if stubbornness is added to that confusion, then the problem becomes impossible to cure.

Where is the good? In the will. Where is the bad? In the will. Where is neither good nor bad? In things that are beyond our control. But do any of us really think about these lessons outside of the classroom? Does anyone practice answering these questions on their own? Is it day? Yes. Is it night? No. Is the number of stars even? I can't say. When someone offers you money, have you practiced saying that money is not a good thing? Have you trained yourself in these answers, or only in arguing about tricky questions? Why then are you surprised that in the areas you've studied, you improve, but in the areas you haven't, you remain the same? When a public speaker knows that he's written a good speech, memorized it, and has a good voice, why is he still anxious? Because he's not satisfied with just practicing. What does he want? He wants praise from the audience. He's trained in giving speeches, but not in handling praise and criticism. When did he learn what praise is, what blame is, what their nature is, what kind of praise to seek, or what kind of blame to avoid? And when did he practice the discipline that comes with these things? So why are you still surprised that in the things a person has learned, they excel, but in those they haven't, they're just like everyone else?

The musician knows how to play, sings well, and has a fine appearance, but he trembles when he steps on stage. He understands music, but he doesn't understand what a crowd is, what applause is, or what ridicule is. He doesn't know what anxiety is, whether it's something we control or something outside of us, whether it can be stopped or not. That's why, if he's praised, he leaves the stage feeling proud, but if he's ridiculed, his pride is punctured, and he deflates.

This is how we are too. What do we admire? External things. What are we focused on? External things. So, is it any wonder that we fear and feel anxious? What happens when we think the things happening to us are bad? It's not in our power not to be afraid or anxious. Then we say, "Oh God, how can I not be anxious?" Fool, don't you have hands? Didn't God give them to you? Sit down and pray that your nose won't run. Wipe it instead and don't blame him. What has God given you in this situation? Hasn't he given you endurance? Hasn't he given you strength of mind? Hasn't he given you courage? When you have these things, do you still need someone else to wipe your nose? But we neither study these things nor care about them. Show me someone who cares about how they do something, not just about getting the thing done. Who, when they're walking, cares about how they're walking, not just about getting somewhere? Who, when they're planning something, cares about how they're planning, not just about achieving their goal? If he succeeds, he's elated and says, "Didn't I tell you that when we plan something, it's bound to happen?" But if things turn out differently, the poor man is crushed and doesn't even know what to say. Who among us has consulted an oracle about how to act, not just about the outcome? Who among us hasn't gone through life asleep, indifferent? Who? Show me someone, and I'll finally see the person I've been searching for, someone who is truly noble and sincere, whether young or old.

So why are we still surprised when we're well-practiced in thinking about things, but in our actions, we're low, indecent, worthless, cowardly, and impatient? We don't care about these things, nor do we study them. But if we had feared not death or exile, but fear itself, we would have studied to avoid what we consider to be evils. Now, in the classroom, we're argumentative and full of talk, but drag us into real-life practice, and we fall apart miserably. Let some challenging situation arise, and you'll see what we've really been studying. Because we lack discipline, we exaggerate situations and make them worse than they are. For example, when I'm on a ship and look at the deep sea, or when I see no land, I lose my mind and imagine that I'll have to drink all this water if I'm shipwrecked, even though only a small amount would be enough. What really disturbs me? The sea? No, it's my opinion. When an earthquake happens, I imagine the whole city will collapse on me, but isn't just one small stone enough to crush my skull?

So what really weighs on us and disturbs us? What else but our opinions? What else but our opinions burdens someone who leaves behind friends, family, familiar places, and routines? Children, for example, cry when the nurse leaves them for a short time, but they forget their sorrow if they get a small treat. Do you want us to compare you to little children? No, by Zeus, because I don't want to be comforted by a small treat, but by right opinions. And what are these? They're the things a person should study all day, so they're not affected by anything that's not theirs, whether it's a person, a place, a gymnasium, or even their own body. They should always remember the law and keep it in mind. And what is the divine law? It's to keep what is truly ours and not to desire what belongs to others. It's to use what is given to us, and when it's taken away, to give it up readily and with gratitude for the time we had it, without crying for our "nurse and mother." Because what difference does it make what we're attached to? What makes you better than someone who cries for a lost love if you grieve over a gymnasium, a portico, young men, or places of entertainment? Someone else might lament that they can no longer drink the water from a certain stream. Is the water from another source worse? But I was used to the first water. And you'll get used to the other one too. Then, if you become attached to that as well, you'll cry for that too and write a sad poem about it.

When then shall I see Athens again and the Acropolis? Wretch, are you not content with what you see daily? Is there anything better or greater to see than the sun, the moon, the stars, the whole earth, and the sea? But if you understand the one who governs the Whole and carry him within yourself, do you still desire small stones and a beautiful rock? When you're about to leave behind even the sun and moon, will you sit and cry like children? What have you been doing in the school? What did you hear, what did you learn? Why did you write yourself down as a philosopher, when you could have written the truth: "I attended some introductory lectures, and I read some Chrysippus, but I didn't even approach the door of a philosopher." How could I possess anything like what Socrates had, who died the way he did, who lived the way he did, or anything like what Diogenes had? Do you think any of those men wept or grieved because they wouldn't see a certain person, or be in Athens or Corinth, or because they would be in Susa or Ecbatana instead? If a person can leave a banquet when they choose, and no longer be entertained, do they stay and complain? Do they not stay only as long as they enjoy it? Such a person, I suppose, would endure perpetual exile or even be condemned to death. Will you not grow up now, like children, and take on more solid responsibilities, and stop crying for "mothers and nurses," which are the lamentations of old women? "But if I leave, I'll make them sad." Will you make them sad? No, it's not you causing them sorrow, but the same thing that causes you sorrow: their opinion. What should you do then? Change your own opinion, and if these women are wise, they will change theirs too. If they don't, they will mourn by their own fault.

My friend, as the saying goes, make a desperate effort for peace of mind, freedom, and greatness of soul. Lift up your head at last as if released from slavery. Dare to look up to God and say, "Deal with me however you will; I am of the same mind as you; I am yours. I refuse nothing that pleases you: lead me where you will: clothe me in whatever way you choose. Do you want me to hold office, to be a private citizen, to stay here or be exiled, to be poor or rich? I will defend your decisions to others, showing them what each situation truly is." But you won't do this; instead, you'll sit in a corner and wait for your "mother" to feed you. Who would Hercules have been if he had stayed at home? He would have been Eurystheus, not Hercules. Well, and in his travels, how many close friends did he have? But nothing was dearer to him than God. That's why it was believed he was the son of God, and he was. In obedience to God, he went about purging the world of injustice and lawlessness. But you're not Hercules, and you can't cleanse the wickedness of others; nor are you Theseus, able to purge Attica of its evils. Clear away your own. From yourself, from your thoughts, cast out sadness, fear, desire, envy, malice, greed, weakness, and excess. But you can't get rid of these things unless you focus only on God, fix your thoughts on him, and dedicate yourself to his commands. If you choose anything else, you'll be forced to follow what's stronger than you, always seeking peace and never finding it because you're looking for it where it isn't, and ignoring it where it is.

Chapter 16
How to Apply General Ideas to Specific Situations

Where does good come from? It comes from our choices. Where does evil come from? It also comes from our choices. Where can we find neither good nor evil? In things that are beyond our control. But do any of us really think about these lessons outside of school? Do we practice by ourselves to give the right answers to questions, like we do in class? Is it day? Yes. Is it night? No. Is the number of stars even? I can't say. When money is offered to you, have you practiced responding correctly, saying that money isn't really good? Have you trained yourself in giving these answers, or just against tricky arguments? Why are you surprised, then, if you've improved in things you've studied but stayed the same in things you haven't?

When a speaker knows they've written well, memorized their speech, and has a pleasant voice, why are they still anxious? Because they aren't satisfied with just studying. What else do they want? They want to be praised by the audience. So, they've practiced speaking well, but they haven't practiced how to handle praise and criticism. When did they learn what praise is, what blame is, or what kind of praise to seek and what kind of blame to avoid? When did they practice the discipline that comes with understanding these things? So why are you still surprised that a person excels in what they've learned but is just like everyone else in areas they haven't studied?

A musician knows how to play the lute, sings well, and wears fine clothes, but they still tremble when they step on stage. They understand the music, but they don't understand what a crowd is, what the shouts of a crowd mean, or what ridicule is. They don't know what anxiety is, whether it comes from us or from others, or whether it can be stopped. That's why if they're praised, they leave the stage feeling puffed up, but if they're ridiculed, their confidence deflates like a punctured balloon.

The same goes for us. What do we admire? External things. What do we focus on? External things. So is it any wonder that we fear and worry? What happens when we think something bad is coming our way? It's not in our power not to be afraid; it's not in our power not to worry. Then we ask, "Oh God, how can I stop worrying?" Fool, don't you have hands? Didn't God give them to you? Sit down and pray that your nose doesn't run. Or instead, just wipe it and don't blame God. What, has God given you nothing to deal with your problems? Hasn't he given you endurance? Hasn't he given you courage? Hasn't he given you strength? When you have these tools, do you still look for someone else to wipe your nose? But we don't study these things or care about them.

Show me a person who cares about how they do something, not just about getting something. Who cares about their own effort, not just the result? When someone is making a decision, do they care about the decision itself, or just about getting what they want? And if they succeed, they're proud and say, "Didn't I tell you it would work out?" But if it doesn't, they're crushed, not even knowing what to say about what happened. Who among us has ever consulted a seer about our actions? Who hasn't just drifted through life without paying attention?

So why are we still surprised that we're good at thinking about things, but in our actions, we're weak, indecent, lazy, and cowardly? We don't care about these things or study them. But if we feared fear itself, not death or exile, we would have studied how not to fall into what we see as evil. Now, in the classroom, we're quick to argue and full of words. But when it comes to real-life practice, we're a mess. Let something troubling happen, and you'll see what we've really been studying and practicing. Without discipline, we always make things seem worse than they are.

For example, when I'm on a ship and look out at the deep sea, or see that there's no land in sight, I panic and imagine that if we're shipwrecked, I'll have to drink all that water. I forget that only a few pints would be enough to drown me. What really disturbs me? The sea? No, it's my opinion. Again, when there's an earthquake, I imagine the whole city is going to collapse on me, but isn't one small stone enough to kill me?

So what really weighs us down and disturbs us? What else but our opinions? What else but opinions makes someone sad when they leave their friends, home, and routines? Little children cry when their nurse leaves, but they forget their sadness if they get a small treat. Do you want us to compare you to little children? No, because I don't want to be comforted by a small treat, but by the right opinions.

And what are these right opinions? They're the ones we should study all day, so we're not affected by anything that isn't ours—not by a friend, a place, a gym, not even by our own body. Instead, we should remember the law and keep it in mind. And what is the divine law? To keep what's ours, not to claim what belongs to others, but to use what's given and not desire what isn't. And when something is taken away, to give it up willingly and be thankful for the time we had it. If you do that, you won't cry for your nurse or your mom. What does it matter what controls a person, whether it's something big or small? How are you any better than someone who cries for a girl, if you're upset over a gym or a group of young people or places of amusement? Another person might complain that they'll no longer drink from the Dirce spring. Is the water from the Marcian aqueduct any worse than the water from Dirce? But I was used to the water from Dirce. And you'll get used to the other water too. Then if you get attached to that, you'll cry over it too, just like Euripides wrote about the hot baths of Nero and the Marcian water. That's how tragedy is made when ordinary things happen to silly people.

When will I see Athens again and the Acropolis? You fool, aren't you content with what you see every day? Is there anything better or greater to see than the sun, the moon, the stars, the whole earth, and the sea? But if you understand the one who controls everything, and carry that understanding within you, do you still desire small stones and a pretty rock? What will you do when you have to leave even the sun and the moon? Will you sit and cry like a child? What have you been doing in school? What did you hear and learn? Why did you call yourself a philosopher when you should have just said, "I learned a few things, read Chrysippus, but I never really became a philosopher"?

How could I possess anything like what Socrates had, who lived and died as he did, or anything like what Diogenes had? Do you think any of these men wept or grieved because they wouldn't see a certain person, or a certain place, or be in Athens or Corinth, but instead in Susa or Ecbatana if that's what happened?

If a person can leave a party whenever they want, and stop having fun, do they still stay and complain? Or do they only stay as long as they're enjoying themselves? I suppose such a person would handle exile or a death sentence just fine. Will you not grow up now, like children, and eat more solid food instead of crying for your mom and nurse? "But if I leave, I'll make them sad." You make them sad? No, what makes them sad is the same thing that makes you sad: opinions. What should you do, then? Change your opinion, and if these women are wise, they'll change theirs too. If not, they'll keep crying because of their own foolishness.

My friend, as the saying goes, make a desperate effort for peace of mind, freedom, and greatness of spirit. Lift your head as if you're finally free. Dare to look up to God and say, "From now on, deal with me as you will. I'm on your side. I'm yours. I refuse nothing that pleases you. Lead me where you want. Dress me how you want. Is it your will that I should hold a public office, or live as a private person, stay here, or be exiled, be poor, or be rich? I'll defend all these choices to others. I'll show them the true nature of each situation." But you won't do this. Instead, you'll sit in comfort and wait for your mom to feed you.

Who would Hercules have been if he'd stayed home? He would have been Eurystheus, not Hercules. And how many close friends did he have on his journeys? But nothing was dearer to him than God. That's why people believed he was the son of God, and he was. In obedience to God, he went about ridding the world of injustice and lawlessness. But you're not Hercules, and you can't rid the world of other people's wickedness, just as you're not Theseus, able to clean up Attica. Clean up your own life instead. Get rid of sadness, fear, desire, envy, hatred, greed, laziness, and lack of self-control. But you can't get rid of these things unless you focus only on God, love him above all, and follow his commands. If you choose anything else, you'll always be sighing and groaning, forced to follow what's stronger than you. You'll keep searching for peace of mind but never find it, because you're looking for it where it doesn't exist, and ignoring where it really is.

Chapter 17
How We Should Struggle Against Appearances

What is the first thing someone who wants to be a philosopher should do? They need to let go of pride, which means thinking they already know everything. It's impossible for a person to start learning something if they believe they already know it. When it comes to deciding what should be done or not done, what is good or bad, beautiful or ugly, we all talk about these things randomly and then go to philosophers. We praise, criticize, accuse, blame, judge, and decide on matters of what is honorable and dishonorable. But why do we go to philosophers? Because we want to learn what we don't think we know. And what is it that we want to learn? Theorems, which are ideas or principles. We want to learn what philosophers say because we find their ideas elegant and sharp, and some of us want to learn because we hope to benefit from it.

It's ridiculous to think that a person wants to learn one thing but will end up learning something else, or that someone will make progress in something they don't learn. But many people are deceived by this idea, just like the rhetorician Theopompus was when he criticized Plato for wanting to define everything. Theopompus said, "Did none of us use the words Good or Just before you, or were we just saying these words without understanding what they really mean?" But who told you, Theopompus, that we didn't have natural ideas of these things, like preconceptions? We can't apply preconceptions to real situations if we haven't broken them down and figured out what specific thing should be connected to each preconception.

You could make the same argument against doctors. Before Hippocrates, who didn't use the words healthy and unhealthy, or were we just saying these words without meaning? We also have a basic idea of what health is, but we struggle to apply it correctly. That's why one doctor might say, "Don't eat," another says, "Eat more," another says, "Let out blood," and another says, "Use cupping." What's the reason for this? Isn't it because people can't properly apply the idea of health to specific situations?

The same thing happens in life. Who among us doesn't talk about what is good and bad, or what is useful and not useful? We all have some idea of these things, but is our understanding clear and complete? Prove it. How do you prove it? By correctly applying the idea to specific situations. For example, Plato applies definitions to the idea of what is useful, but you apply them to the idea of what is useless. Can both of you be right? How is that possible? Doesn't one person apply the idea of good to wealth, while another applies it to pleasure or health? If we all know what these words mean, why do we argue, fight, and blame each other?

And why am I bringing this up? If you know how to properly apply your ideas, why are you unhappy, why are you frustrated? Let's not even talk about the second topic, which is about how we pursue things and our duties related to them. Let's also skip the third topic, which is about how we agree to things. I'll give up on those two topics for now. Let's focus on the first topic, which clearly shows that we don't properly apply our preconceptions. Do you now desire what is possible and what is within your power? Then why are you frustrated?

Why are you unhappy? Do you try to avoid things that are unavoidable? Then why do you encounter what you want to avoid? Why are you unlucky? Why, when you want something, does it not happen, and when you don't want something, it does happen? This is the greatest proof of unhappiness and misery: I wish for something, and it doesn't happen. And what could be more miserable than that?

Medea couldn't stand this, and that's why she ended up killing her children. It was an act of a strong spirit, at least in this way: she knew how painful it is when something you wish for doesn't happen. She thought, "This is how I'll get back at him (her husband) for wronging and insulting me. But what will I gain if I punish him this way? How should I do it? I'll kill my children, but I'll also punish myself. But what do I care?" This is what happens when a person's soul is filled with strong but misguided energy. She didn't know where the power to make things happen lies. It's not something you can get from the outside, or by changing and adapting things. Don't desire the man (Jason, Medea's husband), and nothing you desire will fail to happen. Don't stubbornly wish that he will live with you, don't desire to stay in Corinth, and in general, don't desire anything other than what God wills. And who can stop you? Who can force you? No one can force you any more than they can force Zeus.

When you have such a guide and your wishes and desires match his, why do you still fear disappointment? Give up your desire for wealth and your fear of poverty, and you won't be disappointed. Give up your desire for health, and you won't be unlucky. Give up your desire for political positions, honors, your country, friends, children—basically, for anything that's not in your control—and you won't be unlucky. But give your desires to Zeus and the other gods; surrender them to the gods. Let the gods lead, let your desire and aversion align with the gods, and how can you be unhappy anymore? But if you, lazy person, still envy, complain, are jealous, and afraid, and you never stop complaining about yourself and the gods, why do you still talk about being educated? What kind of education do you mean? Do you think you've been learning sophistical arguments? Wouldn't it be better if you could unlearn all these things and start from the beginning, realizing that you haven't even touched the heart of the matter yet? Then, starting from this foundation, you should build everything else so that nothing happens that you don't want, and nothing you want fails to happen.

Show me one young person who has come to a philosophy school with this intention, who has become a champion for this cause and says, "I'll give up everything else, and it's enough for me if I can live my life free from obstacles and troubles, to hold my head high like a free person, and to look up to heaven as a friend of God, fearing nothing that might happen." Point out such a person to me so I can say, "Come, young person, and take possession of what is rightfully yours, for it is your destiny to excel in philosophy: these books are yours, these teachings are yours." Then, after they've worked hard and practiced in this area, let them come back to me and say, "I want to be free from passions and worries; I want to know, as a pious person and philosopher, what my duties are to the gods, to my parents, to my brothers, to my country, and to strangers." I would say, "Come to the second area of study; this too is yours."

"But I've now studied the second area enough, and I would love to be steady and unshaken, not only when I'm awake, but also when I'm asleep, when I'm drunk, and when I'm feeling down." You are aiming high, like a god, with these ambitions.

No, instead, "I want to understand what Chrysippus says in his treatise on the Pseudomenos (the Liar)." Won't you hang yourself, wretched person, with such a goal? And what good will it do you? You'll read the whole thing with sadness, and you'll speak about it to others with trembling. That's what you do. "Brother, do you want me to read to you, and you read to me?" You write excellently, my friend, just like Xenophon, and you, just like Plato, and you, just like Antisthenes. Then, after sharing your dreams with each other, you go back to the same things: your desires are the same, your aversions are the same, your pursuits are the same, your goals are the same, you wish for the same things, and work for the same things.

Then, you don't even seek out someone to give you advice, but you get upset when you hear things like what I'm saying now. You say, "That old man was so mean: when I was leaving, he didn't cry or say, 'You're going into danger. If you come back safely, my child, I'll light candles.'" This is what a kind person would do, right? It would be a great thing if you did come back safely, and maybe it would be worth lighting candles for such a person because you should be immortal and free from illness.

As I said, we need to throw away this conceit of thinking we know something useful. We need to approach philosophy like we approach geometry or music. If we don't, we won't make any progress, even if we read all the works of Chrysippus, Antipater, and Archedemus.

Chapter 18
How We Must Struggle Against Impressions

Every habit and skill grows stronger and increases by practicing the related actions: the habit of walking grows by walking, and the habit of running grows by running. If you want to be a good reader, then read; if you want to be a writer, then write. But if you haven't read for thirty days straight and have done something else instead, you will notice the effect. Similarly, if you have been lying down for ten days, try to get up and take a long walk, and you will see how weak your legs have become. In general, if you want to develop any habit, practice it regularly; if you don't want to develop a habit, avoid doing it and do something else instead.

The same is true for the emotions and feelings in your mind: when you get angry, you need to understand that not only has this negative thing happened to you, but you have also strengthened the habit of anger, like adding fuel to a fire. When you have given in to sexual desire with someone, don't just think of this one defeat; realize that you have also increased your lack of self-control. It is impossible for habits and skills to not be created when they didn't exist before, and for them not to be increased and strengthened by repeated actions.

This is also how, as philosophers say, diseases of the mind develop. For example, when you first desire money, if you apply reason to see the harm in this desire, you can stop it, and your mind's ability to control itself is restored. But if you don't take steps to cure this, your mind will no longer return to its original state, and the desire will become stronger the next time it appears. When this happens repeatedly, your mind becomes hardened, and the obsession with money becomes a mental illness. Just like someone who has had a fever and hasn't fully recovered, the same thing happens with diseases of the mind. Certain traces and marks are left behind, and unless you completely get rid of them, when the problem arises again, it will cause even more damage. If you don't want to be someone with a bad temper, don't feed the habit: don't do anything that will make it stronger. At first, stay calm, and count the days you haven't been angry. Maybe you used to get mad every day; then it was every other day; then every third day, then every fourth. But if you manage to go thirty days without getting angry, make a sacrifice to God. The habit first starts to weaken, and then it is completely destroyed. "I haven't gotten upset today, or yesterday, or any day for two or three months. But I was careful when something frustrating happened." If you can say that, you're on the right track.

Today, when I saw an attractive person, I didn't think, "I wish I could be with her," and I didn't feel jealous of her husband. For anyone who thinks that way is also wishing to be an adulterer. I didn't let myself imagine anything more. I patted myself on the back and thought, "Well done, Epictetus, you've solved a tricky problem, even better than those famous puzzles." And if the person showed interest in me, sent signals, or even came close, and I still resisted and won over my desire, that would be a victory greater than solving any riddle. Such a victory is something to be proud of, not just solving logical puzzles.

How can this be done? Be willing to approve of yourself, be willing to appear beautiful to God, and desire to be pure in your mind and in your relationship with God. Then, when any temptation comes to you, as Plato says, seek purification, go to the temples of the gods who protect people from harm. Or just surround yourself with good and just people, whether they're alive or dead. Go to Socrates and think of him lying next to Alcibiades, ignoring his beauty: consider what a victory he gained over himself, like an Olympic champion, even greater than Hercules. One might rightly greet him, "Hail, wondrous man, who has conquered more than just boxers or wrestlers." By keeping these examples in mind, you'll be able to resist temptation. But first, don't let yourself be swept away by the first impression. Pause and say, "Wait a moment, let me see what you really are." Don't let the first impression paint a vivid picture that draws you in; instead, bring up a better, noble thought to push away the bad one. If you practice this regularly, you'll see how strong you become.

This is the true athlete, the person who trains against temptations. Stop, don't get carried away. The struggle is great; it's for kingship, freedom, happiness, and peace of mind. Remember God: call on Him for help and protection, just as sailors call on the gods during a storm. For what is a greater storm than the one caused by overwhelming desires that take away reason? The storm itself is just an appearance.

If you remove the fear of death, no matter how much thunder and lightning there is, you'll see calmness and peace in your mind. But if you lose the battle and think you'll win next time, and then say the same thing again, you'll eventually be in such a bad state that you won't even know you're doing wrong. You'll even start making excuses for your actions, proving the old saying true: "The one who delays suffers more."

Chapter 19
To Those Who Embrace Philosophical Ideas Only for Debate

There's a famous argument called "the ruling argument," which comes from a contradiction between three ideas. The ideas are: that everything in the past must be true; that an impossible thing cannot come from a possible thing; and that something is possible even if it's not true and never will be. Diodorus noticed this contradiction and used the first two ideas to prove that nothing is possible unless it's true or will be true. Another person might believe that something can be possible even if it's not true and never will be, and that an impossible thing cannot follow a possible thing. But this person won't agree that everything in the past must be true, as some followers of Cleanthes believed, and which Antipater strongly defended. Others believe that something can be possible even if it's not true and never will be, and that everything in the past is necessarily true. However, they would say that an impossible thing can follow a possible thing. But it's impossible to believe all three ideas at the same time because they contradict each other.

So, if someone were to ask me, "Which of these ideas do you believe?" I would say that I don't know, but I've heard the story. Diodorus believed one thing, the followers of Panthoides and Cleanthes believed another, and Chrysippus believed a third. "What's your opinion, then?" I wasn't made to examine these ideas, compare what others have said, and form my own opinion on the matter. So, I'm not much different from a person who just memorizes facts. Who was Hector's father? Priam. Who were his brothers? Alexander and Deiphobus. Who was their mother? Hecuba. I've heard this story. From whom? From Homer. And Hellanicus also wrote about the same things, and maybe others like him too. And what do I know about the ruling argument? Nothing. But, if I want to show off, especially at a party, I might impress the guests by listing those who have written on these topics. Chrysippus wrote brilliantly about possibilities, Cleanthes wrote specifically on the subject, and Archedemus also wrote about it. Antipater not only wrote about possibilities but also separately about the ruling argument. "Haven't you read their works?" I haven't read them. "Read them." And what will you gain from reading them? You'll just become more foolish and annoying than you are now; because what else have you gained from reading them? What's your opinion on the matter? None; but you'll talk about Helen and Priam, and the island of Calypso, which never was and never will be. And in this case, it's not so important if you only remember the story and don't form your own opinion. But in matters of ethics and morality, this happens to us much more than in the things we're discussing now.

"Tell me about good and evil." Listen:

The wind from Ilium to Ciconian shores brought me. —Odyssey

Some things are good, some are bad, and others are indifferent. The good things are virtues and things that relate to virtues; the bad things are vices and things that relate to vices; and the indifferent things are those that lie between virtues and vices, like wealth, health, life, death, pleasure, and pain. "How do you know this?" Hellanicus says it in his Egyptian history; what difference does it make if he says it, or if Diogenes says it in his ethics, or if Chrysippus or Cleanthes says it? Have you examined any of these things and formed your own opinion? Show me how you behave during a storm at sea. Do you remember this distinction between things when the sail is flapping and someone who knows nothing about navigation stands by you while you're panicking and says, "Tell me, by the Gods, what you were just saying: Is it a vice to suffer shipwreck? Does it have anything to do with vice?" Won't you pick up a stick and hit him on the head? "What does that matter now? We're drowning, and you come to mock us?" But if Caesar calls you to court, do you remember the distinction then? If you're walking in pale and trembling, and someone comes up to you and says, "Why are you trembling, man? What are you so worried about? Does Caesar, who's inside, have the power to give virtue and vice to those who come before him?" You would reply, "Why do you mock me and add to my troubles?" "Still, tell me, philosopher, why are you trembling? Are you afraid of death, prison, physical pain, banishment, or disgrace? What else is there? Is there any vice or anything that partakes of vice? What did you use to say about these things?" "What business do you have with me, man? My own troubles are enough for me." And you're right. Your own troubles are enough, your lack of courage, your boasting when you sat in the lecture hall. Why did you show off with ideas that weren't yours? Why did you call yourself a Stoic?

Observe your actions, and you'll see which philosophy you truly follow. You'll find that most of you are Epicureans, a few are Peripatetics, and they're weak ones at that. How will you show that you truly value virtue above all else or even consider it superior? But show me a real Stoic, if you can. Where or how? But you can show me plenty of people who can repeat the arguments of the Stoics. Do these same people recite the Epicurean ideas any worse? And the Peripatetic ideas, don't they handle them just as well? So who is a Stoic? Just as we call a statue a work of Phidias if it's made according to his art, show me a person who lives according to the teachings they speak about. Show me a person who is sick and happy, in danger and happy, dying and happy, in exile and happy, in disgrace and happy. Show me such a person: I truly want to see a Stoic. You can't show me someone who's fully formed, but at least show me someone who's on the path, who's making progress toward becoming a Stoic. Do me this favor: let an old man see something he's never seen before. Do you think you need to show me the Zeus of Phidias or the Athena, a statue made of ivory and gold? No, show me a human soul ready to think as God does, ready not to blame either God or man, ready not to be disappointed by anything, not to feel harmed by anything, not to be angry, not to be envious, not to be jealous; and why not say it directly? A person who is aiming to go from being a human to being like God, and who, while still in this mortal body, thinks of themselves as united with Zeus. Show me such a person. But you can't. So why do you deceive yourselves and others? Why do you put on a disguise that doesn't belong to you and walk around as thieves, stealing names and ideas that aren't yours?

Now, I am your teacher, and you are my students. My goal is to make you free from restraint, compulsion, and hindrance; to make you free, prosperous, happy, and to look to God in all things, big and small. You are here to learn and practice these things. So why don't you finish the work if you have the purpose you ought to have, and if I have the qualities I ought to have? What's missing? When I see a craftsman with the materials he needs, I expect to see the finished work. Here is the craftsman, here are the materials; what is lacking? Isn't this something that can be taught? It is. Isn't it within our power? Yes, it's the only thing that's fully within our power. Neither wealth, nor health, nor reputation, nor anything else is in our power except the right use of our thoughts and perceptions. This right use is naturally free from restraint and impediment. So why don't you finish the work? Tell me why. Is it because of me, or because of you, or because of the nature of the thing itself? The thing itself is possible and is the only thing fully within our power. So it must be either my fault or your fault, or, more likely, both of ours. So, are you willing that we finally begin to work toward this goal in this school, and to forget about the past? Let's make a start. Trust me, and you will see.

Chapter 20
Against Followers of Epicurus and of the Academy

Ideas that are true and clear are so important that even those who argue against them end up using them. You might think that the best proof something is true is when even the person who denies it still needs to rely on it. For example, if someone says that nothing is universally true, they still must agree that the statement "nothing is universally true" is true in every case. What else could this be but admitting that everything universally affirmed is false? Similarly, if someone says, "You can't know anything for sure," or "You shouldn't believe anything," or "It's not possible to learn anything," they are contradicting themselves because they are trying to teach you that nothing can be taught.

How is this different from those who say, "No one agrees with anyone," but still want you to agree with them? Epicurus, for example, tried to destroy the idea that people are naturally connected, but he had to use the very thing he was trying to deny. He would say, "Don't be fooled, people; there's no natural connection between rational beings; believe me. Those who say otherwise are deceiving you." But if he didn't believe in natural connections, why did he care if we were deceived? Why did he put so much effort into convincing us? If what he said was true, he should have just lived quietly, eating, drinking, and enjoying himself without worrying about what others believed.

Why should he lose sleep, write so many books, and argue so much if it didn't matter? It's like he's saying to his fellow Epicureans, "Let's tell everyone that natural connections don't exist, but let's keep the benefits of them for ourselves." So, what woke Epicurus from his peaceful life and made him write all those things? It was nature itself, which is stronger than any human reasoning. Nature pulled him to do what she wanted, even though he resisted. Just as a vine grows like a vine and an olive tree grows like an olive tree, a human cannot completely lose the qualities of being human. Even someone who tries to deny natural desires cannot fully remove them.

Epicurus tried to deny all the responsibilities of being a person, a family member, a citizen, or a friend, but he couldn't get rid of basic human desires because that's impossible. What a shame it is when a person, who has been given the ability to understand truth by nature, doesn't try to improve and build on that understanding but instead tries to destroy the very tools that allow us to know the truth. What do you say, philosopher? Do you think piety and holiness are good things? "Yes, I can prove they are good." Then prove it so that people can learn to respect the divine and not be careless about the most important things. "Do you have the proof?" Yes, I do, and I'm glad.

"Then listen to the opposite view: There are no gods, and if there are, they don't care about us. There's no connection between us and them, and this talk about piety and holiness is just lies made up by boastful people or lawmakers trying to scare wrongdoers." Congratulations, philosopher, you've managed to convince young people to dismiss divine things. "Doesn't that make you happy?" Not at all. You've also taught that justice doesn't exist, modesty is foolish, and that relationships like father and son don't matter. Congratulations again, philosopher, keep persuading young people so that more will share your views.

These ideas are definitely not what helped build strong cities or the values that held Spartan society together. Do you think the Spartans died at Thermopylae because they believed that everything was meaningless? Then these same people get married, have children, and take part in public life, even becoming priests and interpreters of the gods they claim don't exist. What hypocrisy and deception! What are you doing, man? Are you contradicting yourself every day and still not giving up these cold arguments? When you eat, where do you put your hand? To your mouth or your eye? When you wash, do you call a pot a dish or a ladle a spit?

If I were a slave to one of these people, even if I had to suffer daily, I would trick them. If they asked for olive oil, I'd bring them vinegar and pour it on their heads. "What is this?" they would ask. "It looked like oil to me," I'd say. Or if they asked for a barley drink, I'd bring them a bowl of something sour. "Didn't I ask for barley drink?" they would say. "Yes, master," I'd reply. "This is it; smell and taste it. How do you know if your senses are deceiving you?" If I had a few like-minded friends, we could drive them mad or make them change their ways. But instead, they mock us while using all the things that nature provides and then try to deny their reality.

How ungrateful and shameless can people be when they eat bread every day and still claim they don't know if there is a Demeter, Persephone, or Pluto? They enjoy the night, day, seasons, stars, sea, and land, along with the cooperation of humanity, and yet they don't consider any of these things. They just want to spout their little arguments, and after filling their bellies, they head off to the bath without a care about what they've said or who they've influenced. They don't care if a young person who hears them loses their moral values, or if an adulterer uses their words to justify their actions, or if someone neglecting their parents finds excuses in these teachings. What is good or bad to you? This or that?

Why should anyone bother responding to such people or trying to convince them? It's more likely to change the mind of a stubborn person than to make these people see their own mistakes.

Chapter 21
On the Inconsistency of the Mind

Some things people easily admit, while others they don't. No one will admit that they are foolish or lack understanding; instead, you'll hear everyone say, "I wish my luck matched my intelligence." But people do admit they are timid, saying, "I'm a bit timid, I admit, but in other ways, you won't find me foolish." A person won't easily admit to being reckless, and they definitely won't admit to being unjust. They will never confess to being envious or a busybody. However, most people will admit to being compassionate. Why is this? The main reason is inconsistency and confusion about what is good and bad. But different people have different reasons. Generally, they won't admit to things they believe are disgraceful. They think timidity is a sign of a good nature and that compassion is also good, while foolishness is seen as the mark of a slave. They won't admit to things that are harmful to society. But in the case of most mistakes, they confess them because they believe there is something involuntary about them, like with timidity and compassion. If someone admits they are reckless, they usually blame love or passion as an excuse for their lack of control. But people don't think injustice is involuntary at all. They also believe jealousy has something involuntary about it, which is why they admit to being jealous too.

Living among people who are so confused, so unaware of what they say, of the problems they have or don't have, why they have them, or how they can be fixed, it's worth asking yourself constantly, "Am I like them? What do I think of myself? How do I behave? Do I act wisely? Do I act with self-control? Do I ever say, 'I've been taught to be ready for anything that might happen'?" Do I have the humility to admit when I don't know something? Do I go to my teacher like someone seeking answers from an oracle, ready to obey? Or do I, like a whining child, go to school just to learn facts and understand books that I didn't understand before, so I can explain them to others? Man, you've had an argument with a poor servant at home, you've turned your household upside down, you've scared the neighbors, and now you come to me pretending to be a wise man, judging how I explain a word, and how I babble whatever comes to mind. You come full of envy and feeling low because you bring nothing valuable from home, and you sit through the discussion thinking of nothing but how your father and brother feel about you. "What are they saying about me? Do they think I'm improving? Are they saying, 'He'll return with all knowledge'? I wish I could learn everything before I return, but it takes so much effort, and no one sends me anything. The baths at Nicopolis are dirty, everything is bad at home, and everything is bad here."

Then they say, no one benefits from going to school. Why? Who goes to school to improve themselves? Who goes to have their opinions purified? Who goes to learn what they need? Why are you surprised if you leave school with the same things you brought in? You didn't come to change your beliefs or correct them or to receive new ones. Not at all. You're more interested in whether you already have what you came for. You want to talk about theories? What then? Don't you just become a bigger fool? Don't your little theories give you a chance to show off? You solve tricky logical problems. Don't you examine the tricky question called the "Liar"? Don't you look into hypothetical problems? Why, then, are you upset if you get exactly what you came for in school? "Yes, but if my child dies or my brother, or if I have to face death or torture, what good will these things do me?" Well, did you come here for that? Did you sit by my side for that? Did you ever stay up late or get up early with this in mind? Or when you went out for a walk, did you ever bring up a real-life situation instead of a theoretical problem, and discuss it with your friends? Where and when did you do this? Then you say, "Theories are useless." To whom? To those who misuse them. Eye drops aren't useless to those who use them correctly. Bandages aren't useless. Weights aren't useless; they're useful to some and useless to others. If you ask me now if logical problems are useful, I'll tell you they are, and if you want, I'll prove it. "How, then, will they be useful to me?" Did you ask if they're useful to you, or if they're useful in general? Let someone with a serious illness ask me if vinegar is useful; I'll say it is. "Will it be useful to me?" I'll say no. First, get your illness under control and heal your sores. And you, O people, first heal your mind and stop your distractions; bring it calm and clear to school, and you'll see what power reason has.

Chapter 22
On Friendship

When someone works hard at something, they naturally begin to love it. Do people work hard on things that are bad? Not at all. Do they put effort into things that don't matter to them? No, they don't. So, they must be focusing on things that are good, and if they focus on them, they love them too. This means that anyone who understands what is good also knows how to love. But if someone can't tell the difference between what's good and what's bad, or between things that are neither good nor bad, how can they truly love? Only those who are wise have the power to really love.

But someone might say, "I'm not wise, but I still love my child." I'm surprised you admit that you're not wise. What are you missing? Can't you see and hear? Don't you notice things around you? Don't you eat food that's good for you and wear clothes that fit you? So

138

why do you say you're not wise? It's because you often get confused and tricked by what you see. Sometimes you think something is good, then later think it's bad, or sometimes you think it's neither good nor bad. You get upset, scared, jealous, and you change your mind a lot. That's why you say you're not wise. And aren't you also inconsistent in your love? Do you sometimes think wealth and pleasure are good and other times bad? Do you sometimes think certain people are good, then later think they're bad? Do you sometimes like them and other times dislike them? Do you sometimes praise them and other times criticize them? "Yes, I do that too." So, do you think someone who has been tricked by another person is really their friend? "No, I don't." And if someone chooses a friend but keeps changing their mind, do they really care about that person? "They don't." And if someone criticizes a person one moment and admires them the next, do they have true affection for them? "No, they don't."

Think about little dogs playing together, and you might say there's nothing more friendly than that. But to see what friendship really is, throw a piece of meat between them, and you'll see what happens. Now imagine putting a small piece of property between you and your child; you'll quickly find out how much your child might want you gone, and how much you might want your child gone. Then you'll say, "What kind of child did I raise? They've been wanting to get rid of me for a long time." Or imagine an old man and a young man both liking the same woman; they'll both want her, and you'll see how quickly their feelings change. The same goes for fame or danger—it will be just like that. You'll end up like Admetus's father, saying:

"Life gives you pleasure: and why not your father?"

Do you think Admetus didn't love his own child when the child was little? That he wasn't deeply worried when the child was sick? That he didn't often wish he could take the child's place when the child had a fever? But when a real test came, look at what he said.

139

Weren't Eteocles and Polynices from the same mother and father? Didn't they grow up together, live together, eat together, sleep together, and even kiss each other often? If anyone had seen them, they would have laughed at philosophers who say friendship is tricky. But when they fought over the throne, like dogs fighting over a piece of meat, look at what they said:

Polynices: "Where will you stand in front of the towers?" Eteocles: "Why do you ask me?" Polynices: "I'll stand across from you and try to kill you." Eteocles: "I want to do the same."

These were their true feelings.

Don't be fooled: every living thing cares about its own interests more than anything else. So, when something gets in the way of those interests, whether it's a brother, father, child, or someone they love, they'll hate, reject, and curse it. They love their own interests more than anything else. That's their true family, their country, and even their god. So, when they think the gods are getting in the way, they curse them, tear down their statues, and burn their temples, just like Alexander burned the temples of Aesculapius when his dear friend died.

Because of this, if a person puts their interests, their sense of what's right, their goodness, and their love for their country and family all in the same place, they'll be secure in all those things. But if they separate their interests from these other things, putting them in different places, their interests will always win. Wherever someone's "self" and "mine" are, that's where they'll lean. If their self is in their body, they'll be controlled by their physical desires. If it's in their will, they'll be controlled by their choices. If it's in external things, they'll be controlled by those things. If I place myself where my will is, then I can be a good friend, a good son, and a good father because my interest will be in being trustworthy, modest, patient, self-controlled, helpful, and respectful. But if I put myself in one place and honesty in another, then I'll follow Epicurus's idea that honesty is either meaningless or just what people think it is.

This kind of ignorance is why the Athenians fought with the Spartans, why the Thebans fought with both, why the great king fought with the Greeks, why the Macedonians fought with everyone, and why the Romans fought with the Getae. And even before that, the Trojan War happened for these reasons. Alexander was a guest of Menelaus, and if anyone had seen their friendly relationship, they wouldn't have believed anyone who said they weren't friends. But then a beautiful woman came between them, and they went to war over her. So, when you see brothers who seem like close friends, don't assume their friendship is real, not even if they swear it and say they'll never be apart. The ruling principle of a bad person can't be trusted. It's unstable, has no solid direction, and gets overwhelmed by different thoughts at different times. Don't just look at whether they were born to the same parents, grew up together, or had the same teacher. Look at where they place their interests—are they in external things or in their will? If they're in external things, don't call them friends, just like you wouldn't call them trustworthy, brave, or free. Don't even call them human, if you have any sense. For it's not human nature to bite, abuse, and take over empty places or public spaces like wild animals, or to act like robbers in court, or to be indulgent, adulterous, or corrupt. These behaviors come from placing oneself and one's interests in things outside of one's control. But if you hear that someone truly thinks the good lies in their will and in how they see things, don't worry whether they're father and son, brothers, or longtime companions. Once you've figured that out, you can confidently say they're friends, just as you can say they're faithful and just. For where else can friendship exist but where there is faithfulness, modesty, and a shared sense of what's right?

But you might say, "This person treated me well for so long; didn't they love me?" How do you know they didn't see you the same way they see a sponge to clean their shoes or as they care for their pet? How do you know that when you're no longer useful, they won't discard you like a broken dish? "But this woman is my wife, and we've been together for so long." And how long did Eriphyle live with Amphiaraus and have children with him? But then a necklace came between them. And what was the necklace? It was the idea that these things matter. That was what broke the friendship between husband and wife and stopped the woman from being a wife or mother. So, anyone who really wants to be a true friend or have a true friend should remove these ideas, hate them, and drive them out of their soul. Then, first of all, they won't blame themselves, won't be at odds with themselves, won't change their mind, and won't torment themselves. Next, they'll be a true friend to someone who is like them, completely and totally. They'll be patient with someone who is different, kind to them, gentle, and ready to forgive them because they know the person is mistaken about what really matters. They won't be harsh to anyone because they'll understand, as Plato said, that every mind loses the truth against its will. If you can't do this, you can still do what friends do—drink together, live together, travel together, and be born to the same parents—like snakes do. But neither they nor you will be friends as long as you hold onto these wild and cursed beliefs.

Chapter 23
On the Power of Speaking

Everyone finds it easier and more enjoyable to read a book when the words are clear and well-written. Similarly, people are more likely to listen and understand when words are used in a proper and fitting way. Therefore, we cannot say that the ability to express ourselves doesn't matter because that would be both disrespectful to the gifts given by God and a sign of fear. It would be disrespectful because it would mean we are undervaluing the talents given by God, just as if we ignored the gift of sight or hearing. Did God give us eyes for no reason? Did He give them the amazing ability to see far and to understand the things we see for nothing? What is faster or more accurate than sight? Did He create the air, which allows us to see, or the light, without which nothing would be visible, for no reason?

We should not be ungrateful for these gifts, nor should we forget the things that are even more important. We should thank God for our ability to see and hear, for life itself, and for the things that keep us alive, like food, wine, and oil. But we must also remember that God has given us something even better: the ability to use these gifts, to understand them, and to judge their value. What tells us the value of each of these abilities? Is it the ability itself? Have you ever heard your eyesight say anything about itself? Or your hearing? Or any other . object? No, they are here to serve the ability that can make use of what we perceive. When you ask what the value of something is, who answers? How can any ability be stronger than the one that uses the others and judges them? Which of these abilities knows what it is and what it's worth? Which one knows when it should be used and when it shouldn't? What ability opens and closes your eyes, decides what you should look at, and what you should avoid? Is it your eyesight? No, it's your will. What ability opens and closes your ears, making you curious or uninterested in what you hear? Is it your hearing? No, it's your will.

So, if the will is the one that controls all these other abilities that are blind and silent, only able to do what they're meant to do, and if the will alone can see clearly and understand the value of everything else, will it ever say that something else is more important than itself? What does your eye do when it's open other than see? But who tells you whether you should look at a certain person's wife and how to do so? The will. And who tells you whether you should believe something you hear or not, and whether you should be affected by it? Isn't it the will? The ability to speak and make words sound good, if it exists as a separate ability, only arranges words like a hairdresser styles hair. But who tells us whether it's better to speak or stay silent, whether to speak in one way or another, and what is appropriate or not? Isn't it the will? Should the will then come forward and say that something else is more important than itself?

What does this mean? Can the thing that serves be greater than the thing it serves? Can a horse be greater than its rider, a dog greater than its hunter, a tool greater than the one who uses it, or a servant greater than the king? What controls everything else? The will. What takes care of everything? The will. What can destroy a person by making them starve, hang themselves, or jump off a cliff? The will. Is there anything stronger in a person than this? And how can things that are controlled by other forces be stronger than the thing that controls itself? What things naturally get in the way of your ability to see? Both your will and things outside of your control. It's the same with hearing and speaking. But what can naturally hinder the will? Nothing outside of the will; only the will itself, when it's twisted. Therefore, the will is either the source of all good or the source of all evil.

Being such a powerful ability, the will should tell us that the most important thing of all is the flesh. But even if the flesh itself claimed to be the best, no one would accept that. But what is it, Epicurus, that tells us what the purpose of life is, what the nature of things is, what the rule of truth is, that leads you to grow a beard, that writes when you're dying that you're spending your last day happily? Is it the flesh or the will? So, do you admit that you possess something greater than the will? Aren't you mad? Are you really so blind and deaf?

Does anyone despise the other abilities? I hope not. Does anyone say that the ability to speak is useless? I hope not. That would be foolish, disrespectful, and ungrateful to God. But a person should give each thing its proper value. For example, even a donkey has some use, but not as much as an ox. A dog has some use, but not as much as a slave. A slave has some use, but not as much as a citizen. A citizen has some use, but not as much as a leader. Just because some things are better than others doesn't mean we should undervalue the usefulness of other things. The ability to speak has value, but it's not as great as the will. When I say this, don't think I'm asking you to neglect the ability to speak, just like I wouldn't ask you to neglect your eyes, ears, hands, feet, clothes, or shoes. But if you ask me what the most important thing is, what should I say? I can't say the ability to speak, but the will, when it's right. Because the will uses the ability to speak, along with all the other small and great abilities. When the will is correct, a bad person becomes good; when it fails, a person becomes bad. It's through the will that we are happy or unhappy, that we blame or praise each other. In short, it's the will that, if we neglect it, causes unhappiness, and if we take care of it, brings happiness.

To deny the importance of the ability to speak and to say that it doesn't exist is not only ungrateful to those who gave it but also cowardly. Such a person seems to fear that if this ability exists, we won't be able to ignore it. This is similar to those who say there's no difference between beauty and ugliness. But if that were true, it would mean that a person would react the same way to seeing an ugly person as they would to seeing a beautiful one, or to seeing something beautiful as they would to seeing something plain. But these are foolish ideas from people who don't understand the nature of things and are afraid that if someone sees the difference, they will be overwhelmed by it. The important thing is to recognize the value of each ability, to understand what is truly the most important, and to always pursue that, considering everything else of lesser value but still taking care of those other things as much as we can. We must take care of our eyes, not because they are the most important thing, but because they help us take care of the most important thing. Our will won't be in its best condition if it doesn't use the other abilities correctly and prioritize some things over others.

What usually happens? People often act like a traveler on their way home who stops at a nice inn and decides to stay there. They forget their purpose: they weren't traveling to the inn, they were just passing through. "But this inn is nice," they might say. And how many other inns are nice? And how many meadows are beautiful? But they're all just places to pass through. Your real purpose is to return home, to relieve your family's worries, to fulfill your duties as a citizen, to marry, to have children, and to take on the responsibilities of a leader. You weren't born to choose the most pleasant places to live, but to live in the place where you were born and where you were made a citizen. This is similar to what we're talking about. Since you must use speech and communication to reach perfection, to purify your will, and to correct how you perceive things, and since teaching often requires a certain way of speaking with variety and sharpness, some people get so captivated by these things that they stay there, one drawn in by the way words are expressed, another by logical puzzles, another by tricky arguments, and still another by something else like these, and they waste away as if they were enchanted by Sirens.

Your purpose was to make yourself able to use your perceptions in a way that's in harmony with nature, to not be frustrated in your desires, to avoid what you should avoid, to never be unlucky or unhappy, to be free, not hindered, not forced, to align yourself with the order of the universe, to obey it, to be content with it, blaming no one, accusing no one, and being able to say with all your heart:

"Lead me, O Zeus, and Destiny."

But if, instead, you get caught up in some clever way of speaking, in some logical puzzle, do you stay there, forgetting your real purpose and saying, "These things are great"? Who says they're not great? But they're only great as a way to reach your real purpose, like inns are along the way. What stops you from being an unhappy person, even if you speak like Demosthenes? And what stops you from being miserable, from feeling sorrow, envy, or disturbance, from being unhappy, even if you solve logical puzzles like Chrysippus? Nothing. You see, these things are just tools, and your real purpose is something else. When I speak like this to some people, they think I'm saying that we should ignore the ability to speak or ignore logical puzzles. But I'm not saying that. I'm saying that we shouldn't get stuck on these things and think they are the most important. If my teaching causes harm to those who listen, then count me among those who do harm. For I cannot see one thing that is truly excellent and supreme and say that something else is, just to please you.

Chapter 24
To Someone Who Was Not Valued by Him

Someone once said to Epictetus, "I've often wanted to hear from you and came to you many times, but you never responded to me. Now, if possible, I beg you to say something to me." Epictetus replied, "Do you think that, just as there is skill in anything else, there is also skill in speaking, and that those who have the skill speak well, while those who don't have it speak poorly?" The person answered, "Yes, I do think so."

Epictetus continued, "So, someone who benefits from speaking and can help others by speaking will do so skillfully. But someone who harms themselves and others by speaking, will they be unskilled in this art of speaking? You may find that some people are harmed and others are helped by what they say. Do you think that everyone who hears something is helped by it, or do you believe that some are helped and some are harmed?" The person replied, "Both types exist."

"In that case," Epictetus said, "those who listen skillfully are helped, and those who listen poorly are harmed. Would you agree that there is a skill in listening just as there is in speaking?" The person agreed. "If you like, consider it this way too. Who practices music? A musician. Who makes statues? A sculptor. Do you think looking at a statue well requires no skill?" The person replied, "It does require skill."

"Then if speaking properly is the work of a skilled person, do you see that listening properly, to gain benefit, is also the work of a skilled person? But let's put aside for now the idea of speaking and listening perfectly, because we are both far from that level. Still, I believe everyone would agree that anyone who wants to listen to philosophers needs some practice in listening. Don't you agree?"

"Tell me, then, what I should talk to you about. What subject can you listen to?" The person said, "About good and evil." Epictetus asked, "Good and evil in what? In a horse?" The person replied, "No." Epictetus continued, "In an ox?" Again, the person said, "No." "Then in what?" asked Epictetus. The person answered, "In a human being."

Epictetus asked, "Do we know what a human being is? Do we understand what the idea of a human being is? Or have we practiced listening to this kind of topic? Do you understand what nature is? Can you even begin to understand me if I say I'm going to explain it to you? Do you understand what explaining something is, how something is explained, or by what methods? Do you know what is true or false? What follows from a certain point, what contradicts it, or what is consistent or inconsistent?"

Epictetus went on, "But should I push you to study philosophy? And how should I do that? Should I show you how people's opinions clash because they don't agree on what is good or bad, or what is useful or harmful, when you don't even know what a contradiction is? Tell me what I will achieve by talking to you. Make me want to do this. Just as grass that is good for a sheep makes the sheep want to eat, but a stone or bread does not, we also have natural desires to speak when the listener seems to be someone worthwhile, when they make us want to speak. But if the listener is like a stone or a blade of grass, how can they make anyone want to speak? Does a vine ask the farmer to take care of it? No, but by showing that it will benefit the farmer if he does, the vine invites him to care for it. When children are lively and cheerful, who doesn't want to play with them, crawl with them, or mimic their baby talk? But who wants to play with a donkey or bray like it? Even if it's a small donkey, it's still a donkey."

"Why do you say nothing to me?" you might ask. I can only say this: A person who doesn't know who they are, why they exist, what this world is, who they live with, what is good or bad, what is beautiful or ugly, who doesn't understand logic or reasoning, who doesn't know what is true or false, and who can't tell the difference between them, will neither desire according to nature nor avoid things correctly. They won't move toward or away from things in the right way, won't make good decisions, won't agree or disagree properly, and won't hold back judgment when needed. In short, they will go around blind and silent, thinking they are someone important when they are really nobody. Is this a new problem? No, ever since people existed, all errors and misfortunes have come from this kind of ignorance. Why did Agamemnon and Achilles fight? Wasn't it because they didn't know what was useful and what wasn't? Didn't one say it was useful to return Chryseis to her father, while the other said it wasn't? Didn't one believe it was right to take someone else's prize, while the other said it wasn't? Didn't they forget who they were and why they had come to Troy?"

"Tell me, why did you come? To win mistresses or to fight?" The answer would be, "To fight." "With whom? The Trojans or the Greeks?" The answer would be, "With the Trojans." "Then why do you leave Hector alone and draw your sword against your own king? And you, my good man, why do you neglect your duties as king, you who are supposed to protect the people and take care of important matters, and instead argue about a girl with your strongest ally, whom you should be protecting and supporting? Are you now worse than a well-behaved priest who treats these fierce warriors with respect? Do you see what ignorance about what is useful can lead to?"

"But I am also rich," someone might say. Are you richer than Agamemnon? "But I am also handsome." Are you more handsome than Achilles? "But I have beautiful hair." Didn't Achilles have more beautiful, golden hair, yet he didn't spend time styling it? "But I am also strong." Can you lift as much as Hector or Ajax? "But I am of noble birth." Are you the child of a goddess? Is your father descended from Zeus? What good are these things to you if you end up sitting and crying over a girl? "But I am a skilled speaker." Wasn't Achilles also skilled? Didn't he handle the best Greek speakers, like Odysseus and Phoenix, and silence them?

This is all I have to say to you, and I say it unwillingly. Why? Because you haven't inspired me. What do I need to be inspired, like a skilled rider is inspired by a spirited horse? Should I look at your body? You don't take care of it. Should I look at your clothes? They are extravagant. Should I look at your behavior or your expression?

They mean nothing. When you come to listen to a philosopher, don't say, "You tell me nothing." Instead, show yourself as someone worth talking to, and you will see how you inspire the speaker.

Chapter 25
How The Art of Reasoning is Necessary

When someone who was present said, "Convince me that logic is necessary," Epictetus replied, "Do you want me to prove this to you?" The person answered, "Yes." Then Epictetus said, "To prove it, I must use a logical form of speech." The person agreed. Epictetus then asked, "How will you know if I am tricking you with my argument?" The person was silent. Epictetus then said, "Do you see that you are admitting logic is necessary, since without it, you wouldn't even know whether logic is necessary or not?"

Chapter 26
Understanding the Nature of Mistakes

Every mistake involves a contradiction, because when someone makes a mistake, they don't want to be wrong—they want to be right. It's clear that they don't do what they wish to do. For example, what does a thief want to do? They want to do what benefits them. But if stealing doesn't actually benefit them, they are not doing what they really want.

Every rational mind naturally dislikes contradictions. As long as someone doesn't understand that they are contradicting themselves, they will continue to do contradictory things. But when they do understand the contradiction, they will avoid it as much as a person avoids something false when they recognize it as false. But as long as something false doesn't appear false to them, they will accept it as true.

The person who is strong in argument and has the ability to encourage and correct others can show each person the contradiction that leads them into error, and can clearly prove how they are not doing what they wish to do, and instead are doing what they don't wish to do. If someone shows this to a person, that person will stop doing what they're doing. But as long as this isn't shown to them, don't be surprised if they keep doing it, because it seems to them that they are doing the right thing.

For this reason, Socrates, trusting in this power, used to say, "I don't need any other witness to what I say; I am always satisfied with the person I am discussing with, and I ask them to give their opinion and to be my witness. Even if they are the only one, they are enough in place of everyone." Socrates knew how the rational mind works, just like a pair of scales that must tip when it sees a contradiction, whether it wants to or not. Show the rational mind a contradiction, and it will move away from it. But if you don't show it, you should blame yourself, not the person who isn't persuaded.

Book III

Chapter 1
On Adornment

A young man, who was studying to be a public speaker, came to see Epictetus. His hair was styled more carefully than usual, and he was dressed in fancy clothes. Epictetus asked him, "Tell me, do you not think that some dogs are beautiful and some horses are beautiful, just like all other animals?" The young man replied, "Yes, I do think so." Epictetus then asked, "Are not some men also beautiful and others ugly?" The young man answered, "Certainly."

Epictetus continued, "Do we call each of these animals beautiful for the same reason, or is each one beautiful for something specific?

Think about it this way: A dog is made for one thing, a horse for another, and a nightingale for yet another. We can generally say that each of these animals is beautiful when it is excellent according to its nature. But since the nature of each is different, they each seem beautiful in a different way. Is it not so?" The young man admitted that it was true. Epictetus then said, "So, what makes a dog beautiful might make a horse ugly, and what makes a horse beautiful might make a dog ugly, if their natures are different." The young man agreed, "It seems to be so."

Epictetus then added, "For example, what makes a Pancratiast beautiful might make a wrestler not good, and what makes a runner beautiful might make him look ridiculous. Someone who is beautiful for the Pentathlon might be very ugly for wrestling." The young man agreed again, saying, "It is so." Epictetus asked, "What then makes a man beautiful? Is it the same thing that makes both a dog and a horse beautiful?" The young man responded, "It is." Epictetus then asked, "What makes a dog beautiful?" The young man answered, "The possession of the excellence of a dog." Epictetus continued, "And what makes a horse beautiful?" The young man replied, "The possession of the excellence of a horse." Then Epictetus asked, "What then makes a man beautiful? Is it not the possession of the excellence of a man?"

Epictetus then advised the young man, "If you want to be beautiful, young man, work on acquiring human excellence. But what is human excellence? Think about whom you yourself praise when you praise many people without partiality. Do you praise the just or the unjust? You praise the just. Do you praise the moderate or the immoderate? You praise the moderate. Do you praise the temperate or the intemperate? You praise the temperate. If you make yourself such a person, you will know that you will make yourself beautiful.

But if you neglect these things, you must be ugly, even though you do all you can to appear beautiful."

Epictetus then reflected, "I do not know what more to say to you. For if I say what I think, I may offend you, and you might leave and never come back. But if I do not say what I think, see how I would be acting. If you come to me to be improved, and I do not improve you at all, if you come to me as to a philosopher, and I say nothing to you as a philosopher, how cruel it would be to leave you uncorrected. If at any time later you gain some sense, you might blame me, and say, 'What did Epictetus see in me that when he saw me in such a bad condition, he neglected me and never said a word? Did he so much despair of me? Was I not young? Was I not able to listen to reason? And how many other young men at my age make similar mistakes? I heard that a certain Polemon, who was a very dissolute youth, went through a great change. Well, even if Epictetus did not think I would become like Polemon, he might have at least told me to fix my hair, take off my decorations, and stop plucking the hair out of my body. But when he saw me dressed like this, he kept silent.' I do not say like what; but you will understand when you come to your senses, and know what it is, and what kind of people wear such clothing."

Epictetus then questioned, "If you bring this charge against me later, what defense will I have? Should I say that you would not have been persuaded by me? Was Laius persuaded by Apollo? Did he not ignore the oracle and get drunk instead? Well then, for this reason, did Apollo refuse to tell him the truth? I do not know whether you will be persuaded by me or not; but Apollo knew for sure that Laius would not be persuaded, and yet he still spoke. But why did he speak? I would say in reply: Why is he Apollo, and why does he deliver oracles? Why has he fixed himself in this place as a prophet and a source of truth for the inhabitants of the world to come to him? And why are the words 'Know yourself' written in front of the temple, though no one pays attention to them?"

Epictetus continued, "Did Socrates persuade all his listeners to take care of themselves? Not even one in a thousand. But still, after he had been placed in this position by the deity, as he himself said, he never left it. And what did he say even to his judges? 'If you acquit me on the condition that I stop doing what I do now, I will not agree, and I will not stop. I will go to young and old alike, and speak plainly to every person I meet. I will ask the questions that I ask now, and most especially to you, my fellow citizens, because you are more closely related to me.' Are you so curious, Socrates, and such a busybody? And how does it concern you how we act? And what is it that you say? Being of the same community and of the same kin, you neglect yourself and show yourself to be a bad citizen to the state, a bad kinsman to your kin, and a bad neighbor to your neighbors. Who then are you? Here it is a great thing to say, 'I am the one whose duty it is to take care of men. For it is not every little heifer that dares to resist a lion; but if the bull comes up and resists him, say to the bull, if you like, "Who are you, and what business do you have here?"' In every kind, there is something produced that excels; in oxen, in dogs, in bees, in horses. So do not say to that which excels, 'Who then are you?' If you do, it will find a way to speak and say, 'I am like the purple in a garment; do not expect me to be like the others, or blame my nature for making me different from the rest of men.'"

Epictetus then questioned himself, "What then? Am I such a man? Certainly not. And are you such a man who can listen to the truth? I wish you were. But since I am in a way condemned to wear a white beard and a cloak, and you come to me as to a philosopher, I will not treat you cruelly, nor act as if I despair of you. But I will say: Young man, whom do you wish to make beautiful? First, know who you are, and then adorn yourself accordingly. You are a human being, and this is a mortal animal that has the power to use appearances rationally. But what does it mean to use appearances rationally? It means acting in conformity with nature and doing so completely. So what do you possess that is unique? Is it the animal part? No. Is it the condition of mortality? No. Is it the power to use appearances? No. You possess the rational faculty as something unique. Adorn and beautify this, but leave your hair to the one who made it as he chose."

Epictetus asked, "Come, what other labels do you have? Are you a man or a woman? A man. Then adorn yourself as a man, not as a woman. A woman is naturally smooth and delicate, and if she has much hair on her body, she is seen as a monster and is exhibited in Rome among other monsters. And in a man, it is monstrous not to have hair. If he has no hair, he is a monster; but if he cuts off his hair and plucks it out, what should we do with him? Where should we exhibit him, and under what name should we show him? I will exhibit to you a man who chooses to be a woman rather than a man. What a terrible sight! There is no man who will not wonder at such a notice. Indeed, I think that the men who pluck out their hair do so without understanding what they are doing."

Epictetus then asked, "Man, what fault do you find with your nature? That it made you a man? Should nature have made all human creatures women? And what advantage would you have had in being adorned? For whom would you have adorned yourself if all human creatures were women? But you are not pleased with this. So set to work on the whole business. Take away—what is its name?—that which causes the hair to grow. Make yourself a woman in all respects, so that we may not be mistaken. Do not make one half man and the other half woman. Whom do you wish to please? The women? Please them as a man. But they like smooth men. Will you not hang yourself? And if women took delight in catamites, would you become one? Is this your purpose? Were you born for this, that dissolute women should delight in you? Should we make someone like you a citizen of Corinth, perhaps a leader of the city, or the head of the youth, or a general or supervisor of the games? Well, when you have taken a wife, do you intend to have your hair plucked out? To please whom and for what purpose? And when you have children, will you raise them with the habit of plucking their hair? A beautiful citizen, a senator, a rhetorician. We ought to pray that such young men are born among us and raised well."

Epictetus then pleaded, "Do not do this, I beg you by the Gods, young man. But when you have heard these words, go away and say to yourself, 'Epictetus did not say this to me; for how could he? But some kind God spoke through him. For it would never have occurred to him to say this, since he is not accustomed to talking like this with anyone. Come, let us obey God, so that we may not be subject to his anger.' You say, 'No.' But I say, if a crow's croaking means something to you, it is not the crow that means something, but God speaking through the crow. And if God signifies something through a human voice, will he not cause the man to say this to you, so that you may know the power of the divine? That he signifies to some in this way and to others in that way? And concerning the greatest things and the chief, he signifies through the noblest messenger."

Epictetus ended with, "What else does the poet say? 'For we ourselves have warned him, and have sent Hermes, the careful watcher, the slayer of Argus, to warn the husband not to kill nor wed the wife.' Was Hermes going to come down from heaven to say this to him? And now the Gods say this to you and send the messenger, the slayer of Argus, to warn you not to distort what is well arranged, nor to meddle with it, but to allow a man to be a man, and a woman to be a woman, a beautiful man to be a beautiful man, and an ugly man to be an ugly man. For you are not just flesh and hair, but you are will (proairesis); and if your will is beautiful, then you will be beautiful. But up to now, I dare not tell you that you are ugly, for I think you are more willing to hear anything than this. But see what Socrates says to the most beautiful and blooming of men, Alcibiades: 'Try then to be beautiful.' What does he say to him? Dress your hair and pluck the hairs from your legs? Nothing of that kind. But adorn your will, take away bad opinions. What about the body? Leave it as it is by nature. Another has looked after these things. Trust them to him. What then, must a man be unclean? Certainly not. But what you are and what you are made by nature, cleanse this. A man should be clean as a man, a woman as a woman, a child as a child. You say no, but let us also pluck out the lion's mane so that he may not be unclean, and the cock's comb because he too ought to be clean. Granted, but as a cock, and the lion as a lion, and the hunting dog as a hunting dog."

With this, Epictetus ended his lesson, leaving the young man to reflect on what truly makes someone beautiful.

Chapter 2
What to Focus on for Real Progress: And How We Often Ignore What's Most Important

There are three main areas where a person should practice if they want to be wise and good. The first area is about our likes and dislikes. This means that a person should work on getting what they really want and avoiding what they don't want. The second area is about our actions, like moving toward something or away from something. It also means doing what's right, according to reason, and not being careless. The third area is about not being fooled or making quick decisions. This means being careful when we agree with something, making sure we are thinking wisely.

Out of these three areas, the most important one is about our feelings. Feelings get stirred up when we don't get what we want or when we end up in situations we want to avoid. This makes us feel upset, unlucky, sad, or jealous. These feelings can make it hard for us to listen to reason. The second area is about what duties we have. This means that while we shouldn't be emotionless like a statue, we should still be a good person, a respectful child, a responsible parent, or a good citizen.

The third area is especially important for those who are making progress. It helps secure the other two areas so that even when we are asleep, drunk, or feeling down, we don't make bad choices. Some people might say this is too hard, but many modern philosophers often ignore the first and second areas (feelings and duties) and focus only on the third. They use tricky arguments, draw conclusions from questions, use ideas that aren't real, and sometimes lie. They say a person must be careful not to be fooled. But who needs to do this? A wise and good person. Is this the only thing left for you to work on? Have you already mastered everything else? Are you free from being fooled by money? If you see a beautiful girl, can you resist being swayed by her looks? If your neighbor inherits land, do you not feel jealous? If you still struggle with these things, do you really think you only need to work on being completely steady?

Poor soul, you hear these things with fear and worry, afraid that someone might look down on you or wonder what others might say about you. If someone tells you that during a conversation about who is the best philosopher, a person said that someone else was the best, your small and anxious heart suddenly swells with pride. But if another person says, "You are mistaken; that person is not worth listening to; they only know the basics and nothing more," you become confused, pale, and immediately want to prove that you are a great philosopher. But it's already clear from how you react to these words. Why do you need to prove it further? Don't you know that Diogenes pointed out one of the sophists by simply sticking out his middle finger? When the man got angry, Diogenes said, "This is the person I was talking about; I have pointed him out to you." A person is not shown by pointing, like a rock or a piece of wood, but by showing what they believe in.

Let's also look at what you believe in. Isn't it clear that you don't value your own choices at all? Instead, you focus on things outside your control, like what others will say about you, whether people will think you are smart, or whether you have read the works of famous philosophers like Chrysippus or Antipater. If you have even read Archedemus, you feel like you have achieved everything. But why are you still uneasy, feeling the need to prove who you are? Do you want me to tell you what kind of person you have shown yourself to be? You have shown yourself to be mean, always complaining, easily angered, fearful, critical of everything, blaming everyone, never at peace, and vain. This is what you have shown us. Now, go away and read Archedemus. But know that if a mouse jumps down and makes a noise, you will be scared to death, just like that man—what was his name?—Crinis, who was also proud because he understood Archedemus.

Poor soul, will you not let go of these things that don't concern you at all? These things are meant for those who can learn them without being upset, for those who can say, "I am not controlled by anger, sadness, or envy. I am not held back or stopped. What is left for me? I have free time, I am calm. Let me now study how to deal with tricky arguments, and how, when a person accepts an idea, they should not be led to something silly." Such things belong to them. For those who are happy, it is appropriate to light a fire, have a meal, and, if they choose, sing and dance. But when the ship is sinking, you come to me and try to raise the sails.

Chapter 3
What a Good Person Should Focus On and Practice Most

The thing that a wise and good person should focus on is their own mind and how they think. Just like a doctor works with the body and a farmer works with the land, a good person's job is to use their mind in a way that matches what is natural and true. It is natural for every mind to agree with what is true, to reject what is false, and to be unsure about what we don't know. It is also natural to want good things and avoid bad things, and to feel neutral about things that are neither good nor bad. Just like a banker can't refuse to accept the emperor's coin, our minds naturally accept what seems good and reject what seems bad.

This is why good is more important than anything else, even our closest relationships. There is no closer connection to me than the good itself. You might think I am hard-hearted for saying this, but that's how I am made; it's like a coin that God has given me. So, if something is good but not beautiful or just, I would still choose the good over my father, my brother, or even my country. Should I give up my own good so that someone else can have it? Why should I? Just because you're my father? But you are not my good. Just because you're my brother? But you are not my good either. But if we believe that good is found in making the right choices, then being a good son, father, or citizen is also good. And if we give up some external things, we can still hold on to what is truly good. If your father takes away your property, he hasn't really harmed you. If your brother gets more of the inheritance, that doesn't take away your sense of right and wrong, your honesty, or your love for your family. No one can take these things from you, not even Zeus, because he has made these things yours alone, free from anyone's control.

So, when you deal with people who value different things, like money or power, they will respond to those things. If a corrupt official comes to your town, he might want silver. If you show him silver, he will give you what you want. If someone loves pleasure, they might want young girls or boys. If someone is a hunter, they might want a good horse or dog. Everyone has their own "coin" that they value, and they will trade what they have for it.

This is why it's important to practice understanding what things really are. When you wake up in the morning, look at everyone you meet or hear about, and ask yourself: What have I seen? Is it something that depends on me or not? If it's not, let it go. Did you see someone who looks good? That's something outside of your control. Did you see someone grieving? Death is outside of your control. Did you meet a powerful official? His position is outside of your control. Let these things go; they are not yours to worry about.

If we practiced this every day, from morning to night, we would really make progress. But instead, we often get caught up in things while we're not fully awake, and only occasionally wake up a little when we are in school. Then, when we see someone grieving, we think, "This person is ruined." When we see someone with power, we think, "This person is happy." When we see someone who has been exiled, we think, "This person is miserable." When we see someone who is poor, we think, "This person is wretched because they have nothing to eat."

We need to get rid of these wrong ideas, and that's where we should focus our efforts. What is crying and grieving? It's an opinion. What is bad luck? It's an opinion. What is political conflict, disagreement, blame, accusation, or disrespect? These are all just opinions, and nothing more. These are opinions about things outside our control, as if they were good or bad. But if we change these opinions to focus on things we can control, I promise that you will become strong and steady, no matter what happens around you. The mind is like a dish of water, and appearances are like light shining on it. When the water is disturbed, the light seems to move, but it really doesn't. When a person feels confused, it's not their knowledge or skills that are shaken, but the part of the mind that holds these things. If the mind is calmed, everything else returns to normal.

With this, Epictetus leaves us to think about what truly matters and what we should focus on in our lives.

Chapter 4
Speaking Out Against Someone Who Acted Inappropriately in a Theatre

The governor of Epirus showed his support for an actor in a way that was not appropriate, and people criticized him for it. Later, the governor told Epictetus that he was upset by the criticism and that he was angry at those who blamed him. Epictetus responded, "What harm did they do? They were just showing support, just like you were." The governor replied, "But does anyone show their support like that?" Epictetus then said, "When people see you, their governor, a friend of Caesar and his representative, showing support in that way, wouldn't you expect them to do the same? If it's not right to show support like that, then don't do it yourself. But if it is right, why are you angry when they follow your example? Who do the people look up to except you, their leader? Whose example should they follow when they go to the theatre, if not yours?

Look at how Caesar's representative acts: he shouts out, so I will shout out too. He jumps up from his seat, so I will jump up too. His servants sit in different parts of the theatre and shout. I don't have servants, but I will shout as loud as I can, just like them. You should realize that when you enter the theatre, you are setting a rule and example for everyone else on how they should watch the play."

Epictetus continued, "So why did they blame you? Because everyone hates being stopped from getting what they want. They wanted one person to win, and you wanted another. They got in your way, and you got in theirs. You were stronger, so they did the only thing they could: they blamed what blocked them. What do you expect? That you can do whatever you want, but they can't even say what they want? Why are you surprised? Don't farmers curse Zeus when their crops are ruined? Don't sailors curse him during storms? Don't people always complain about Caesar? What then? Doesn't Zeus know this? Isn't Caesar told about it? What do they do? They know that if they punished everyone who complained, they wouldn't have anyone left to rule over.

So, when you go to the theatre, don't just say, 'I want Sophron (an actor) to win.' Instead, say this: 'Let me keep my mind in control and act according to nature. No one is more important to me than myself. It would be silly for me to get upset just because an actor wins or loses. Who do I want to win? The actor who actually wins. That way, whoever wins is the one I wanted to win.' But if you really want Sophron to win, then hold your own games at home—Nemean, Pythian, Isthmian, Olympian—and declare him the winner. But in public, don't try to take more than your share or act like you own the place. If you don't agree with this, then be prepared to be criticized. When you act like everyone else, you put yourself on their level."

With this, Epictetus reminds us that our actions set an example for others, and we must be mindful of the influence we have, especially in public settings.

Chapter 5
Speaking Out Against Those Who Want to Go Home Because of Sickness

"I am sick here," one of the students said, "and I want to go back home." Do you think that at home you will be free from sickness? Have you considered whether you're doing anything here that could help you strengthen your willpower, so you can improve yourself? Because if you're not working on that, there was no point in coming here. Go ahead, go home. Take care of your own matters. If you can't keep your mind in a state that follows nature, maybe you can manage your land better, make more money, take care of your father in his old age, spend time in public places, or hold an official position. But if you are a bad person, you will do all these things badly too.

But if you understand yourself and know that you are replacing bad thoughts with better ones, and if you have changed your life from focusing on things outside your control to things within your control, then if you ever say, "Oh no!" it won't be because of your father or your brother but because of yourself. So, do you still blame your sickness? Don't you know that both sickness and death will come while we're doing something? The farmer is busy in the field, the sailor is busy at sea, so what would you be doing when death catches you? It must catch you while you're doing something. If you can be doing something better than this when you're caught, then do it. I want to be caught by sickness or death while I am focused on taking care of my own will, so I can be free from worry, free from obstacles, free from force, and truly free.

I want to be found practicing these things so that I can say to God, "Have I disobeyed any of your commands? Have I misused the powers you gave me? Did I see things the wrong way or have wrong ideas? Have I ever blamed you? Have I ever criticized how you run things? I was sick because that was your will, and so were others, but I accepted being sick. I was poor because that was your will, but I accepted that too. I didn't hold a public office because you didn't want me to, and I never desired it. Have you ever seen me unhappy because of this? Haven't I always approached you with a happy face, ready to follow your commands and do what you signal? Is it now your will that I leave the company of people? I will leave. I thank you for allowing me to be part of this group of people, to see your works, and to understand how you manage everything." May death come while I am thinking about these things, while I am writing and reading like this.

"But my mother won't hold my head when I am sick." Then go to your mother; you are the kind of person who needs someone to hold your head when you're sick. "But at home, I used to lie down on a comfortable bed." Then go to your bed: you are indeed someone who should lie on such a bed, even when you're healthy. So don't miss out on what you can do there at home.

But what does Socrates say? He says that just as one man enjoys improving his land and another enjoys improving his horse, I enjoy seeing myself get better every day. "Better at what? At using fancy words?" Don't say that. "At little bits of knowledge?" What are you talking about? "I don't see what else philosophers spend their time on." Does it seem like nothing to you to have never blamed anyone, neither God nor man? To have never criticized anyone? To always have the same calm face whether you're going out or coming in? This is what Socrates knew, yet he never said he knew anything or taught anything. But if someone wanted fancy words or little bits of knowledge, he would send them to Protagoras or Hippias, and if someone wanted vegetables, he would send them to the gardener. So who among you has this goal in mind? Because if you did, you would be content in sickness, in hunger, and even in death. If any of you have been in love with a charming girl, you know that what I am saying is true.

Chapter 6
Various Sayings

Someone once asked him how it happened that even though people today have developed reason more, the progress made in the past was greater. He replied, "In what way has reason been developed more today, and in what way was the progress greater in the past? Because in whatever way reason has been developed more now, progress will be found in that same area. Today, reason has been developed for solving logical puzzles, and so progress has been made there. But in the past, reason was developed for keeping the mind in a state that follows nature, and that's where progress was made. So don't mix different things together, and don't expect to make progress in one area while working on another. But look and see if any of us who focus on keeping our minds in line with nature and living that way always does not make progress. You won't find such a person."

A good man is unbeatable because he doesn't get into fights where he isn't stronger. If you, his opponent, want to take his land and everything on it, go ahead—take the land, take his slaves, take his job, take his poor body. But you won't make his desires fail or force him into something he wants to avoid. The only fight he enters is about things that are under his control, so how can he not be unbeatable?

Someone else asked him, "What is common sense?" Epictetus replied, "Just like how there's a basic sense of hearing that lets us tell the difference between sounds, and a more trained ear that can distinguish musical notes, there are basic things that people who aren't completely messed up can see with the common understanding that everyone has. This basic understanding is called common sense."

It's not easy to motivate young men who are weak, just like it's not easy to hold soft cheese with a hook. But those who have a good natural character, even if you try to turn them away, will stick to reason even more. That's why Rufus often tried to discourage his students. He used this method to test who had a good natural character and who didn't. He would often say, "Just as a stone, if you throw it up, will fall back to the earth by its own nature, a man whose mind is naturally good will turn even more toward what he is naturally inclined to, no matter how much you push him away."

Chapter 7
Conversation With the Governor of the Free Cities, Who Was an Epicurean

When the administrator, who was an Epicurean, came to visit him, Epictetus said, "It is right for those of us who are not philosophers to ask you who are philosophers, just like people who visit a new city ask the locals, 'What is the best thing in the world?' so that we too can look for what is best and appreciate it, just like visitors do with the sights in a city. Almost everyone agrees that there are three things related to people—soul, body, and external things. Now, it's up to you philosophers to answer what is the best. What should we tell people? Is the flesh the best? Did Maximus sail as far as Cassiope in winter with his son just to satisfy his flesh? When the administrator replied that it was not, and added, 'Far be it from him,' Epictetus asked, 'Isn't it proper, then, to focus on what is truly the best?' The administrator replied, 'It is certainly the most proper thing.'

'What do we have that is better than the flesh?' Epictetus asked. 'The soul,' the administrator replied. 'And are the good things of the soul better, or are the good things of the body better?' 'The good things of the soul,' said the administrator. 'And are the good things of the soul within the power of our will or not?' 'They are within the power of our will,' replied the administrator. 'Is the pleasure of the soul something within our control?' 'It is,' the administrator answered.

'And what does this pleasure depend on?' Epictetus continued. 'Does it depend on itself? That can't be, because first, there must be a certain substance or nature of good, by obtaining which we get pleasure in the soul.' The administrator agreed. 'So, what do we depend on for this pleasure of the soul? Because if it depends on the things of the soul, then the nature of the good is discovered. For the good cannot be one thing, and what gives us rational pleasure something else. Nor can something that is not good lead to something good. If what comes after is good, then what comes before must also be good. But you wouldn't say this if you are thinking clearly, for that would contradict both Epicurus and the rest of your teachings. So it must be that the pleasure of the soul comes from the pleasure of the body, and therefore, bodily things must be the foundation and the essence of the good.'

'For this reason, Maximus acted foolishly if he made that voyage for any reason other than the sake of the flesh, that is, for the sake of what is best. And a person acts foolishly if he refrains from taking what belongs to others when he is a judge and has the power to take it. But if you like, let's consider only how this can be done secretly and safely, so that no one finds out. For even Epicurus doesn't say stealing is bad, but he does say getting caught is bad. And because it's impossible to be completely safe from getting caught, he says, "Don't steal." But I say that if stealing is done cleverly and cautiously, we won't get caught. Besides, we have powerful friends in Rome, both men and women, and the Greeks are weak, and no one would dare go to Rome to complain. Why do you hold back from your own good? This is foolish. And even if you tell me you do hold back, I won't believe you. Just as it is impossible to believe something that appears false or to reject something that appears true, it is also impossible to hold back from what seems good. But wealth is a good thing, and it is certainly effective in producing pleasure. Why don't you go after wealth? And why shouldn't we take our neighbor's wife if we can do it without being caught? And if the husband foolishly complains, why not throw him out of the house? If you want to be a philosopher as you should be, a perfect philosopher consistent with your teachings, you must act this way. If you don't, then you are no different from us who are called Stoics, for we also say one thing and do another. We talk about what is good, but we do what is bad. But you will be contradictory in the opposite way, teaching what is bad and practicing what is good.'

'In the name of God, are you thinking of a city of Epicureans? Someone says, "I won't marry." Another says, "Neither will I, because a man shouldn't marry, and we shouldn't have children or get involved in public matters." What will happen then? Where will the citizens come from? Who will raise them? Who will govern the youth, or oversee their physical training? And what will the teacher instruct them in? Will he teach them what the Spartans learned or what the Athenians learned? Bring up a young man according to your doctrines. The doctrines are bad, destructive to a state, harmful to families, and not suitable for women. Get rid of them, man. You live in a leading city; it is your duty to be a magistrate, to judge fairly, to refrain from taking what belongs to others. No woman should seem beautiful to you except your own wife, and no youth, no silver vessel, no gold vessel, except your own. Seek doctrines that are consistent with what I say, and by following them, you will happily abstain from things that have such persuasive power to lead and overpower us. But if, in addition to the persuasive power of these things, we also create a philosophy that helps push us toward them and strengthens us in this direction, what will be the result? In a piece of art, which is the best part—the silver or the workmanship? The substance of the hand is the flesh, but the work of the hand is the most important part, leading the rest. The duties, then, are also threefold: those directed toward the existence of a thing, those directed toward its existence in a particular kind, and third, the most important things themselves. So, in people, we should not value the material, the poor flesh, but the leading things, the most important aspects. What are these? Engaging in public service, marrying, having children, worshipping God, taking care of parents, and generally, having desires, aversions, and pursuits in the way we ought to and according to our nature. And how are we naturally made? Free, noble, modest. What other animal blushes? What other animal can feel shame? We are made by nature to put pleasure in its place as a servant, to encourage us to act in ways that are in line with nature.'

'But I am rich and want for nothing,' you might say. Why then do you pretend to be a philosopher? Your gold and silver vessels are enough for you. What need do you have for principles? 'But I am also a judge of the Greeks.' Do you know how to judge? Who taught you? 'Caesar wrote me a letter of appointment.' Let him write you an appointment to judge music, and what good will it do you? How did you become a judge? Whose hand did you kiss? The hand of Symphorus or Numenius? In front of whose bedroom did you wait? To whom did you send gifts? Don't you see that being a judge is worth just as much as being Numenius? 'But I can throw anyone I want into prison.' So can you do with a stone. 'But I can beat anyone I want with sticks.' So you can do to a donkey. This is not governing people. Govern us as rational beings: show us what is good for us, and we will follow it; show us what is bad, and we will turn away from it. Make us imitators of you, as Socrates made people imitators of himself. For he was like a governor of people, guiding their desires, aversions, actions, and decisions. He would say, 'Do this; don't do that.' If you don't obey, I will throw you in prison. This is not governing people as rational beings. But I say, 'As Zeus has ordained, so act; if you do not act so, you will feel the consequences, you will be punished.' What will be the punishment? Nothing more than not having done your duty; you will lose the qualities of faithfulness, modesty, and propriety. Don't look for greater penalties than these."

Chapter 8
How We Should Train Ourselves to Deal with Impressions

Just as we practice dealing with tricky questions, we should also practice daily against appearances, because appearances also challenge us with questions. For example, someone's son has died. How should we respond? The event is not within our control, so it's not evil. A father has disinherited his son. What do you think of it? It's something beyond our control, so it's not evil. Caesar has condemned a person. Again, it's beyond our control, so it's not evil. The man is upset by this. Feeling upset is something that depends on our will, so it is evil. But if he has accepted the condemnation bravely, that's within his control, so it's good.

If we train ourselves in this way, we will make progress, because we will never agree to anything unless there's an appearance that we can fully understand. Your son is dead. What has happened? Your son is dead. Anything more? No, that's it. Your ship is lost. What has happened? Your ship is lost. A man has been taken to prison. What has happened? He's been taken to prison. But when people say he has fared badly, they are adding their own opinion.

You might say that Zeus is not doing the right thing in these matters. Why? Because he made you capable of enduring them? Because he made you strong? Because he took away the power of these events to be true evils? Because it's possible for you to be happy even while suffering? Because he has given you an escape when things don't please you? If you don't like what's happening, then leave and don't complain.

If you want to know how the Romans feel about philosophers, listen to this. Italicus, who was the most respected of the philosophers, once got upset with his own friends, and as if he was suffering something unbearable, he said, "I can't stand this; you're killing me! You'll make me just like that man over there," pointing to me.

Chapter 9
To a Rhetorician Who Was Going to Rome for a Trial

When a man came to Epictetus because he was going to Rome for a legal case that concerned his status, Epictetus asked him why he was going to Rome. The man then asked Epictetus what he thought about it. Epictetus replied, "If you ask me what you will do in Rome, whether you will succeed or fail, I can't tell you because I have no rule for this. But if you ask me how you will fare, I can tell you: if you have the right opinions, you will do well; if your opinions are wrong, you will do poorly. For every person acts based on their opinions. Why did you want to be elected governor of the Cnossians? It was your opinion. Why are you now going to Rome? It's your opinion. And you're going in winter, with all its danger and cost. 'I must go,' you say. What tells you this? Your opinion. So, if opinions cause all actions, and a person has bad opinions, the result will match the cause. Do we all have sound opinions, both you and your opponent? How do you differ then? Do you have better opinions than your opponent? Why do you think so? He also believes his opinions are better, just like a madman does. This is not a good way to measure truth. But show me that you have examined your opinions and worked on them.

Just as you are now sailing to Rome to become governor of the Cnossians, and you're not content to stay at home with the honors you already have but desire something greater and more noticeable, when did you ever take a journey to examine your own opinions and get rid of any bad ones? Who have you consulted for this purpose? When have you set aside time for this? At what stage of your life? Look back at the times of your life by yourself if you are ashamed to tell me. When you were a boy, did you examine your own opinions, or did you just do what you did without thinking? When you were a youth and attended the rhetoricians, and practiced rhetoric yourself, did you ever think you were lacking in anything? When you became a young man, involved in public matters, arguing cases, and gaining reputation, who then seemed your equal? And when would you have allowed anyone to examine and show you that your opinions were wrong?

So, what do you want me to say to you now? 'Help me with this matter.' I have no rule for this. And if you came to me for this purpose, you didn't come to me as a philosopher but as you would go to a vegetable seller or a shoemaker. What, then, are philosophers' rules for? They are for this purpose: that whatever may happen, our ruling mind may be and continue to be in line with nature. Does this seem like a small thing to you? 'No; it is the greatest.' What then? Does it require only a short time? Can it be grasped just by passing by? If you can, grasp it.

Then you will say, 'I met with Epictetus just like I would meet with a stone or a statue,' because you saw me and nothing more. But a person truly meets with another as a person when they learn his opinions and, in turn, show their own. Learn my opinions, show me yours, and then say that you have visited me. Let us examine each other: if I have any bad opinions, take them away; if you have any, show them. This is the purpose of meeting with a philosopher. 'Not so,' you might say, 'but this is just a passing visit. While we're hiring the ship, we can also see Epictetus. Let's see what he says.' Then you go away and say, 'Epictetus was nothing; he used bad grammar and spoke in a strange way.' But what else did you come as judges of?

A man might say to me, 'If I pay attention to matters like you do, I will have no land, like you have none; I will have no silver cups, like you have none; nor fine animals, like you have none.' To this, it's enough to say, 'I have no need for such things; but if you possess many things, you have a need for even more. Whether you like it or not, you are poorer than I am.' 'What do I need, then?' 'You need what you do not have: firmness, a mind that is in line with nature, freedom from anxiety. Whether I have a patron or not, what does that matter to me? But it matters to you. I am richer than you: I am not anxious about what Caesar will think of me. That is why I flatter no one. This is what I have instead of silver and gold vessels. You have gold utensils, but your words, your opinions, your decisions, your desires are made of clay. But when I have these things in line with nature, why shouldn't I also focus on reason? I have leisure; my mind is not distracted. What should I do, since I have no distractions? What is more suitable for a person than this? When you have nothing to do, you get bored, you go to the theater, or you wander around without purpose. Why shouldn't the philosopher work to improve his reason? You work on crystal vessels; I work on the problem called 'the liar.' You focus on fancy vessels; I work on the problem called 'the denier.' To you, everything you have seems small; to me, everything I have seems great. Your desire is insatiable; mine is satisfied. This is like when children put their hand into a narrow-necked jar and try to pull out figs and nuts. If they fill their hand, they can't take it out, and then they cry. Let go of a few of them, and you will be able to pull your hand out. In the same way, let go of some of your desires. Don't desire too many things, and you will have what you want."

Chapter 10
How We Should Endure Sickness

When the time comes for each opinion, we should have it ready: at breakfast, the opinions that relate to breakfast; in the bath, those that concern the bath; in bed, those that concern bed.

> "Let sleep not come upon your tired eyes
> Before you have reviewed each day's actions:
> What's been done wrong,
> what's been done right, what's been left undone;
> From start to finish, examine all, and then
> Blame what is wrong, and rejoice in what is right."

We should remember these verses so that we can use them, not just say them out loud, like when people exclaim "Paean Apollo." In the same way, when we have a fever, we should be ready with the opinions that relate to fever; we shouldn't, as soon as the fever starts, lose and forget everything. A man with a fever might say, "If I keep philosophizing, may I be hanged! Wherever I go, I must take care of this poor body so that the fever doesn't come back." But what is philosophizing? Isn't it preparing yourself for things that might happen? Do you realize that you're basically saying, "If I keep preparing myself to handle things patiently, may I be hanged"? That's like someone giving up the Pancratium (a type of athletic competition) after getting hit. In the Pancratium, you can stop and avoid getting hit. But if you give up philosophy, what will you gain?

So, what should a person say when something painful happens? "This is why I trained myself, this is why I disciplined myself." God is asking you to show that you have trained properly, that you've eaten what you should, that you've exercised, that you've followed the coach's instructions. Will you show weakness now that it's time to act? Now is the time for the fever—bear it well. Now is the time for thirst—bear it well. Now is the time for hunger—bear it well. Is it not within your power? Who can stop you? The doctor might stop you from drinking, but he can't stop you from bearing thirst well; he might stop you from eating, but he can't stop you from bearing hunger well.

"But I can't continue my philosophical studies." And what are your studies for? Aren't they so that you may be happy, steady, and in line with nature? What stops you, when you have a fever, from keeping your mind in line with nature? Here is the test of a philosopher. This is part of life, just like walking, sailing, or traveling by land. Fever is part of life too. Do you read while walking? No. Nor do you read when you have a fever. But if you walk well, you have everything that belongs to a person walking. If you bear a fever well, you have everything that belongs to a person with a fever.

What does it mean to bear a fever well? It means not blaming God or people, not being upset about what happens, expecting death calmly and nobly, and doing what must be done. When the doctor comes, don't be afraid of what he says. If he says, "You're doing well," don't be overly happy. What good news has he really given you? And when you were healthy, what good did that bring you? Even if he says, "You're in bad shape," don't lose hope. What does it mean to be sick? Does it mean you're close to the separation of soul and body? What harm is there in that? If you're not close now, won't you be close later? Will the world turn upside down when you die? So why flatter the doctor? Why say, "Please, doctor, I'll be well if you want me to be"? Why give him the chance to act proud? You should treat the doctor like you treat a shoemaker who is measuring your foot or a carpenter who is building your house. The doctor is only dealing with your body, which isn't really yours, but something naturally destined to die.

When you have a fever, you have the chance to act this way. If you do these things, you have done what is within your control. A philosopher doesn't worry about external things, like wine, oil, or even his body, but only about his own ruling mind. So how should he act toward external things? He should not be careless about them. Where, then, is the reason for fear? Where is the reason for anger or fear about things that belong to others or things that have no value? We should have these two principles ready: nothing is good or bad except what depends on the will, and we should not try to control events but follow them.

"My brother shouldn't have treated me this way." No, but he will take care of that. However he behaves, I will act as I should toward him. This is my business; that is someone else's. No one can stop me from doing this, but the other thing can be hindered.

Chapter 11
Miscellaneous Matters

There are certain penalties, almost like laws, for those who disobey the divine order. If someone thinks anything other than what depends on their own will is good, let them feel envy, desire, flattery, and be disturbed. If someone considers anything else to be evil, let them grieve, lament, weep, and be unhappy. And yet, even though we are punished so harshly, we still can't stop.

Remember what the poet says about the stranger:

"Stranger, I must not, even if a worse man comes."

This can even apply to a father: I must not, even if someone worse than you comes, treat my father badly because we are all from Zeus, the father of all. The same applies to a brother, because we are all from Zeus, who watches over families. And in all other relationships in life, we will find that Zeus is watching.

Chapter 12
On Exercise

We should not make our exercises consist of things that are unnatural and meant to impress others. If we do, we, who call ourselves philosophers, won't be any different from jugglers. It's difficult to walk on a tightrope, and not only difficult but also dangerous. Should we practice tightrope walking for this reason? Or should we practice climbing palm trees or hugging statues? Definitely not. Not everything that is difficult and dangerous is good for practice. What is good for practice is what helps us achieve our goals. And what is our goal? To live with desires and aversions that are free from restraint. What does this mean? It means not being disappointed in what you desire and not falling into anything you would avoid. Our practice should be directed toward this goal. Since it's not possible to avoid disappointment and unwanted outcomes without great and constant practice, you must understand that if you let your desires and aversions focus on things outside your control, you will neither achieve what you want nor avoid what you don't want. And since strong habits tend to prevail, and we are used to focusing our desires and aversions on things outside our control, we need to counter this habit with a new one, practicing where we are most likely to slip up.

If I am inclined to seek pleasure, I will purposely incline in the opposite direction for the sake of practice. If I dislike pain, I will train myself against the appearances that try to make me avoid it. Who is truly practicing? The one who practices not using his desires and only applies his aversion to things within his control, and who practices most in the areas that are hardest to conquer. This is why one person must practice more against one thing and another against something else. So what's the point of climbing palm trees or carrying around tents, mortars, and pestles? Instead, practice enduring insults if you're irritable, or not getting upset if you're dishonored. Then you will make so much progress that, even if someone hits you, you will say to yourself, "Imagine that you have hugged a statue." Also, practice using wine properly so you don't drink too much. Some people foolishly practice this too. But first, you should abstain from wine, and from young girls and fancy cakes. Then, if the occasion arises, test yourself at the right time to see if appearances overpower you as they used to. But at first, stay far away from what is stronger than you. The contest is unequal between a charming young girl and a beginner in philosophy. As the saying goes, an earthen pitcher and a rock do not agree.

After desire and aversion, the second topic is about actions and the decisions to act or not. You must be obedient to reason, doing nothing out of place or time or in a way that is improper. The third topic concerns judgments, which relate to things that are persuasive and attractive. As Socrates said, we ought not to live an unexamined life, so we shouldn't accept an appearance without examining it. We should say, "Wait, let me see what you are and where you come from," like the night watchman who says, "Show me your pass." Do you have the signal from nature that says you can be trusted? Finally, whatever exercises are applied to the body, if they help in any way with desires and aversions, they can be good exercises. But if they are just for show, they indicate someone who is focused on external things and is looking for others to say, "What a great person." That's why Apollonius wisely said: When you exercise for your own good and you're thirsty from the heat, take a mouthful of cold water, spit it out, and tell no one.

Chapter 13
What Solitude Is and the Nature of a Solitary Person

Solitude is a condition of someone who feels helpless. Just because a person is alone doesn't mean they are lonely; and just because someone is among a crowd doesn't mean they aren't lonely. When we lose a brother, a son, or a friend we relied on, we say we are left lonely, even if we are in a busy city like Rome, surrounded by crowds, and have many people living nearby, even slaves. A person who is considered lonely is seen as helpless and vulnerable to harm. This is why we often say we feel lonely when we travel and encounter robbers. It's not the presence of other people that removes loneliness, but the presence of someone who is trustworthy, modest, and helpful.

If being alone was enough to make someone lonely, you could say that even Zeus is lonely during the great conflagration (when everything burns) and that he might complain, "Poor me, I have no Hera, no Athena, no Apollo, no brother, no son, no kin." Some people say that this is what he does when he is alone during the conflagration. But they don't understand how a person lives when they are truly alone because they base their ideas on the natural desire for companionship, mutual love, and the joy of conversation. Still, a person should be prepared for solitude, able to be self-sufficient and content with their own company.

Just as Zeus lives with himself, calm and thinking about his own nature and his role in the universe, we too should be able to talk to ourselves, not feel the need for others, and not be without ways to spend our time. We should observe the divine order and how we relate to everything else, consider how we used to feel about the things that happen and how we feel now, think about what still causes us pain, and figure out how to cure and remove those pains. If anything needs improvement, we should work on it with reason.

Caesar seems to provide us with great peace: there are no more enemies, no battles, no large groups of robbers or pirates, and we can travel freely from east to west. But can Caesar protect us from fever, shipwreck, fire, earthquake, or lightning? Can he protect us from love? He cannot. From sorrow? He cannot. From envy? He cannot. In short, he cannot protect us from any of these things. But the teachings of philosophers promise to give us security even from these troubles. And what do they say? "People, if you listen to me, wherever you are, whatever you are doing, you won't feel sorrow, anger, compulsion, or obstacles, but you will live peacefully and free from worry." When a person has this kind of peace—not given by Caesar, for how could he give it, but by God through reason—wouldn't they be content even when alone? When they reflect, "Now nothing bad can happen to me; no robber, no earthquake; everything is full of peace and calm: every road, every city, every neighbor, every companion is harmless." One person provides me with food; another with clothing; another with thoughts and understanding. And if someone doesn't provide what's needed, God gives the signal to leave, opens the door, and says, "Go." Go where? To nothing terrible, but to the place you came from, to your friends and family, to the elements: what was in you of fire returns to fire, what was of earth returns to earth, what was of air returns to air, and what was of water returns to water. There is no Hades, no Acheron, no Cocytus, no Pyriphlegethon, but everything is full of gods and spirits. When a person thinks about these things and sees the sun, the moon, and the stars, and enjoys the earth and sea, they are neither lonely nor helpless.

"Well, what if someone comes upon me when I'm alone and murders me?" Fool, they don't murder you, just your poor body.

What kind of solitude, then, is left? What need is there? Why do we make ourselves worse than children? What do children do when they're left alone? They play with shells and ashes, build something, then knock it down and build something else. They never lack ways to pass the time. Should I, if you sail away, sit down and cry because I've been left alone and lonely? Do I have no shells, no ashes? But children do what they do out of ignorance, and we are unhappy because of our knowledge.

Every great power is dangerous to beginners. You should bear only what you are able, but according to nature. Sometimes practice living like a sick person so that you can someday live like a healthy person. Abstain from food, drink only water, and sometimes abstain entirely from desire, so that someday you can desire according to reason; and if it is according to reason, when you have something good in you, you will desire it well.

But we don't want to wait; we want to live like wise men right away and be useful to others. Useful how? What are you doing? Have you been useful to yourself? But I suppose you want to teach others? Teach them! You want to be useful to them. Show them through your own example what kind of person philosophy makes, and don't waste time. When you are eating, do good to those who eat with you; when you are drinking, do good to those who drink with you; by yielding to others, being patient, and bearing with them, you do them good, and don't spit your bad moods on them.

Chapter 14
Certain Miscellaneous Matters

Just as bad actors in a tragedy can't perform well on their own but need to be part of a group, some people can't walk alone. If you are truly something, then walk alone and talk to yourself. Don't hide in the crowd. Take a moment to look around, examine yourself, and wake up so you can understand who you are.

When a person drinks water or does anything for practice or discipline, they always tell everyone whenever they get the chance: "I drink water." Is that why you drink water, just to say you do it? If drinking water is good for you, then drink it. But if it's not, then you're being foolish. If it's good for you and you do drink it, then say nothing about it to those who don't like water-drinkers. What, do you want to please those very people?

Some things we do have a final purpose, some are done because of the situation, some are done to follow certain rules, and others are done to fit in with others. Some things are done according to a set way of life.

You need to get rid of two things in people: arrogance and distrust. Arrogance is the belief that you don't need anything. Distrust is the belief that you can't be happy when so many things surround you. Arrogance is removed by proving it wrong, and Socrates was the first to practice this. To see that something is not impossible, investigate and search for answers. This search won't hurt you, and in a way, this is what philosophy is: figuring out how to use desire and avoidance without being hindered.

"I am better than you because my father was a consul." Another says, "I was a tribune, but you weren't." If we were horses, would you say, "My father was faster, I have more oats and a fancier bridle"? If you said this to me, I would say, "Fine, then let's race." Isn't there something in a person, like running in a horse, that shows who is better or worse? Isn't there modesty, loyalty, and justice? Show that you are better in these things, and then you can say you are better as a person. If you brag about being able to kick hard, I'll say you are proud of something that is the behavior of a donkey.

Chapter 15
That We Ought to Proceed with Caution in Everything

Before you do anything, consider what comes before and what follows, and then decide. If you don't think about it first, you might start with enthusiasm but later give up when the consequences show up. "I want to win at the Olympic games." [So do I, by the gods, for it's a fine thing]. But think about what comes before and after; and if it's good for you, go ahead. You'll have to follow a strict diet, avoid rich foods, exercise at set times, in heat and cold, drink no cold water, and no wine even when you want it. In short, you must surrender yourself to the trainer like you do to a doctor. Then in the contest, you might get covered in sand, dislocate a hand, sprain an ankle, swallow dust, get whipped; and after all this, you might still lose. After thinking about all these things, if you still want it, go to the training. If you don't think about them, you'll act like children who play as wrestlers, then gladiators, then blow a trumpet, then act in a play, just because they've seen and admired these things. You do the same: one day you're a wrestler, then a gladiator, then a philosopher, then a public speaker; but with your whole soul, you are nothing. Like a monkey, you imitate everything you see; and you always want something new, but once you get used to it, you don't like it anymore. You've never done anything with careful thought or deep examination; you've just jumped into things with shallow desires. Some people hear a philosopher speak like Euphrates and want to be philosophers themselves.

Man, first think about what it is you want to do, and then consider your own nature and what it can handle. If you are a wrestler, look at your shoulders, your legs, your body: different people are naturally made for different things. Do you think that, by living as you do now, you can become a philosopher? Do you think you can eat, drink, and behave as you do now and still be a philosopher? You will need to stay up late, work hard, overcome certain desires, leave your family, be looked down on by your servant, and be laughed at by others. In everything, you will be in a lower position—in honors, in court, in public life. When you've considered all these things, then, if you still want to, pursue philosophy, if you want to trade these things for peace, freedom, and tranquility. If you haven't thought about these things, don't approach philosophy. Don't act like children, being a philosopher one day, a tax collector the next, then a public speaker, then a government official. These things don't go together. You must choose to be either a good person or a bad one: you must either work on your inner self or on external things; you must either be a philosopher or live like the rest of the crowd.

Someone said to Rufus when Galba was murdered, "Is the world still governed by Providence?" But Rufus replied, "Did I ever base my belief in Providence on Galba's life?"

Chapter 16
Why We Must Be Careful in Our Social Relationships

If a person often interacts with others, whether it's through talking, drinking together, or just being social, they will either start to become like those people or try to change them to be more like themselves. It's like putting a piece of cold charcoal next to a piece that is burning: the cold charcoal will either cool down the hot one, or the hot charcoal will make the cold one start burning. Since the risk is so high, we need to be careful about getting too close to ordinary people, and remember that it's impossible to be around someone who is dirty without getting some dirt on yourself. For example, what if someone talks about gladiators, horses, athletes, or even worse, about people in general? They might say someone is bad or good, or comment on what was done well or badly. And if they laugh at or make fun of others, or show a mean attitude? Are any of us like a musician who, when they pick up their instrument, can instantly tell which strings are out of tune and fix them? Do we have the ability that Socrates had, to guide those around him to become better? How can we have this ability? So, if you spend time with ordinary people, you'll end up being influenced by them.

Why are they more powerful than you? Because they speak from their true feelings, but you only speak from your lips. That's why your words lack strength and sound empty, and it's unpleasant to hear your advice and your so-called virtue that everyone talks about. In this way, ordinary people have an advantage over you: their opinions are strong and unshakable. Until you have strong, well-formed opinions and have developed a real sense of security, be careful about associating with ordinary people. If you don't, you'll lose the good things you've learned in your studies, just like wax melts in the sun. Keep away from the sun until you have strong opinions. This is also why philosophers suggest that people leave their home country because old habits distract them and make it hard to start new ones. We can't stand it when people say, "Look, that person is now a philosopher, even though they used to be different." Similarly, doctors send people with long-term illnesses to different places with different climates, and they are right to do so. You should also adopt new habits instead of sticking to old ones. Focus on your opinions and practice them. But you don't do this: you go to a show, a gladiator match, a gym, or a circus, and then return to the same places and people. There's no good habit, no attention to self-improvement, or careful consideration of how to handle different situations. You should ask yourself: "How should I respond to these situations? In a natural way or against nature? Am I responding correctly or incorrectly? Am I ignoring things that are beyond my control?" If you are not in this state yet, you should distance yourself from old habits and ordinary people if you ever want to start becoming better.

Chapter 17
On Providence

When you find yourself complaining about Providence, take a moment to think carefully, and you will see that things have happened for a reason. For example, you might say, "But the unfair person seems to have the advantage." In what way? "In money." Yes, he might have more money because he flatters others, lacks shame, and stays alert. But is that surprising? Look to see if he has the advantage over you in being trustworthy and modest. You will see that he does not. In the areas where you are better, you will find that you actually have the advantage. I once spoke to a man who was upset because Philostorgus was successful. I asked him, "Would you want to be like Sura?" He replied, "I hope that day never comes." So why are you upset if Philostorgus gets something for what he sells? Why do you think he is lucky if he gains things in ways you dislike? Providence is not wrong for giving better things to better people. Isn't it better to be modest than to be rich? He agreed. So why are you upset when you have the better quality? Always remember that it is a natural law that the superior has an advantage in what they are superior at, and you will not be upset.

"But my wife treats me badly." If someone asks you about this, just say, "My wife treats me badly." Is there anything else to it? No, nothing more. "My father gives me nothing." Is that all? Yes, that's all. To call this an evil is something extra and false that we add ourselves. Instead of trying to get rid of poverty, we should get rid of our negative opinions about poverty, and then we will be happy.

Chapter 18
Why We Must Not Let News Upset Us

When you hear any news that might upset you, remember this: the news is about something that is not within your control. Can anyone tell you that you have a bad opinion or a bad desire? No. But they might tell you that someone has died. What does that have to do with you? They might say that someone is talking badly about you. What does that have to do with you? Or that your father is planning something. Who is he planning it against? Against your will? How can he? Is he planning against your body or your possessions? You are safe; it's not against you. But what if a judge says you've done something wrong? Didn't the judges also say the same about Socrates?

Does it matter to you that the judge said this? No. So why are you still upset? Your father has a duty, and if he doesn't do it, he loses the role of being a father and a caring person. Don't wish for him to lose anything else because of this. A person never does wrong in one area and then suffers in another. On the other hand, it is your duty to defend yourself clearly, calmly, and without anger. If you don't, you will also lose the role of being a respectful and generous person. So, is the judge without danger? No; he is in danger too. So why are you still afraid of his decision? What does someone else's wrongdoing have to do with you? Your own problem is giving a poor defense: focus only on this. Whether you are condemned or not is up to someone else and is their problem. If someone threatens you, it's not your problem. If someone blames you, let them handle their own problems. If they are going to condemn you unfairly, that is their fault.

Chapter 19
The Difference Between a Philosopher and an Uneducated Person

The first difference between a regular person and a philosopher is this: a regular person says, "Oh, how miserable I am because of my little child, my brother, my father." A philosopher, if he ever says, "I'm so miserable," stops and says, "But only for myself." Nothing that is outside of your own control can harm or upset your will; only your own will can do that. So, if we start blaming ourselves when things go wrong and remember that our own opinions are the only things that cause us trouble or make us lose our peace, I swear by all the gods that we have made progress. But right now, we are doing the opposite. For example, when we were children, if we stumbled because of carelessness, the nurse would not scold us but would hit the stone we tripped over. But what did the stone do? Should the stone have moved because of your child's mistake? Also, if we came out of the bath and found nothing to eat, the teacher would not check our hunger but would punish the cook. Man, did we make you the teacher of the cook instead of the child? Correct the child; make him better. Even as adults, we act like children. Someone who cannot play music is like a child in music; someone who cannot read is like a child in learning; someone who has not learned life lessons is like a child in life.

Chapter 20
How We Can Benefit From All External Things

When you hear something that could disturb you, remember this principle: that news is about things that are not within your control. Can anyone report to you that you have formed a bad opinion or had a bad desire? Of course not. But maybe they will report that someone has died. What does that have to do with you? They might say that someone is speaking poorly of you. What does that have to do with you? Or that your father is planning something. Planning against whom? Against your will? How can he do that? But is he planning against your body or your possessions? You are safe; it is not against you. But what if a judge says that you have done something wrong? Didn't the judges say the same thing about Socrates? Does it matter that the judge has said this? No. So why worry about it? Your father has a certain duty, and if he doesn't fulfill it, he loses his role as a father and as someone who cares and is gentle. Don't wish for him to lose anything else because of this. Because a person does not do wrong in one area and then suffer in another. On the other hand, it is your duty to defend yourself firmly and politely, without getting angry. But if you do not, you will lose your role as a son and as someone who behaves modestly and generously. Well, is the judge safe from danger? No; he is also in danger. So why are you still afraid of his decision? What does it matter if it is someone else's fault? It is your own fault if you make a bad defense. Be careful of that. But whether you are condemned or not, since it is the action of another person, it is the evil of another person. If someone threatens you, what about it? He is just a person who is blaming you. Let him deal with his own problems. He is going to condemn you unfairly. He is a miserable person.

Chapter 21
To Those Who Take on the Role of Teacher Too Lightly

People who quickly pick up new philosophical ideas often want to share them right away, just like someone with an upset stomach who vomits their food. First, you need to properly understand and digest these ideas. If you don't, they become like poorly prepared food that's not good to eat. After you've digested them, show us how these ideas have changed you, just like athletes show the results of their training in their muscles or artists show their skills through their work. A carpenter doesn't just talk about carpentry; he builds something to prove his skills. You should do something similar: live like a wise person, handle everyday tasks like a responsible adult, and deal with family and neighbors well. Show us that you've truly learned something valuable from philosophy. Instead of just reading philosophical texts out loud, you should be able to handle life's challenges and show real improvement.

Is it really worth leaving your home and family just to listen to someone explain words? Shouldn't you come back with the ability to endure difficulties, interact well with others, and handle life's ups and downs honorably? How can you offer these things if you don't have them yourself? Have you done anything besides solve logic problems and argue? Just because someone else has a school doesn't mean you should have one too. You can't just start a school casually; you need to have the right experience, guidance from the gods, and personal preparation.

No one sets sail without making sacrifices to the gods or sows seeds without asking for Demeter's help. How can you undertake such a big task without divine guidance? What are you really doing? Are you just copying rituals from sacred places without understanding their purpose? You're not following the proper procedures or showing the right respect, and you lack the preparation needed. You only memorize the words and claim they are sacred by themselves.

You need to approach these matters differently: they are important and not meant for everyone. Wisdom alone might not be enough; you also need the right readiness, qualities, and divine guidance, just like Socrates, Diogenes, and other great teachers had. But you're treating this as if it were a simple business. Just because you have some knowledge doesn't mean you know how or when to use it. Don't handle important things carelessly. Leave it to those who are truly qualified. Don't damage the reputation of philosophy through your actions. If you enjoy studying ideas, do so quietly on your own. Never claim to be a philosopher if you haven't changed in your desires, actions, or understanding. If you're not ready to do this properly, then stop pretending and let those who are capable handle it.

Chapter 22
On Cynicism

When one of his students, who seemed inclined towards Cynicism, asked Epictetus what kind of person a Cynic ought to be and what Cynicism really means, Epictetus replied that they would discuss it in more detail later, but he wanted to say this much: anyone who attempts such a serious task without God's guidance is displeasing to

God and is likely to end up behaving improperly in public. Epictetus explained that in a well-managed household, no one steps forward and declares, "I ought to be the head of the household." If someone did that, the master of the house would turn around, see this person giving orders arrogantly, drag him out, and punish him. The same is true in the great city of the world, where there is also a master who governs everything.

The master of the world might say to the sun, "You are the sun; your role is to circle the earth, creating the year and the seasons, making plants grow and flourish, stirring the winds, calming them, and properly warming people's bodies. Go, travel around, and take care of things from the greatest to the smallest." He might say to a calf, "You are a calf; when a lion appears, do what's natural for you— run away! If you don't, you will suffer." Or he might say to a bull, "You are a bull; step forward and fight, for this is what suits you, and you are capable of it. You can lead the army against Troy; be like Agamemnon. You can fight Hector in single combat; be like Achilles." But if Thersites tried to take command, he would either fail to get it, or if he did, he would disgrace himself in front of many witnesses.

So, consider the matter carefully: it's not as easy as it seems to you. If you think, "I'll just wear a cloak like I do now, sleep on the ground like I do now, carry a small bag and a staff, go around begging, and scold people I meet who pluck their hair or dress their hair nicely or wear fine clothes," then Cynicism is not for you. Stay far away from it; don't even think about it. But if you understand what it really is and don't see yourself as unfit for it, then think about the great responsibility you are taking on.

First, when it comes to your own behavior, you must be completely different from what you are now. You must not blame God or other people; you must completely rid yourself of desire, and only avoid things that are within your control. You must not feel anger, resentment, envy, or pity. You must not see a girl as attractive, nor should you care about your reputation, be pleased by a boy, or be enticed by a piece of cake. Remember that other people build walls, live in houses, and hide in darkness when they do such things, and they have many ways to keep things hidden. A man can shut the door, place someone in front of the room, and tell them, "If anyone comes, say I'm not here, that I'm busy." But a Cynic must use modesty as his only protection; if he doesn't, he'll be shamefully exposed in his nakedness under the open sky. Modesty is his house, his door, his guard in front of the bedroom, and his darkness. He should have nothing to hide. If he tries to hide something, he loses the essence of being a Cynic, a person who lives openly under the sky, a free person. He starts to fear something outside of himself, he needs to hide, and he can't find a place to hide even if he wants to. And if by chance this public teacher gets caught, what kind of punishment will he face? When someone fears these things, how can they be bold enough to oversee others? It's impossible.

So first, you must purify your mind and your way of life. You should say to yourself, "My task is to work on my understanding, just as wood is to a carpenter and leather is to a shoemaker; my job is to correctly interpret appearances. The body means nothing to me; its parts mean nothing to me. Death? Let it come whenever it will, whether it's the death of the whole body or just a part of it. Run away, you say? But where? Can anyone throw me out of the world? No, they cannot. But wherever I go, the sun is there, the moon is there, the stars are there, dreams, omens, and communication with the gods are there."

Then, if you are prepared in this way, a true Cynic won't be satisfied just with this. He must also know that he is sent by Zeus as a messenger to people to teach them about what is truly good and bad, to show them that they have gone astray, searching for the essence of good and evil in the wrong places while ignoring where it really is. He is like a spy, just as Diogenes was taken to King Philip after the battle of Chaeronea as a spy. A Cynic is a spy of what is truly good and bad for people, and his duty is to carefully examine things and report back truthfully, without being frightened or confused by appearances.

A Cynic should be able to stand up and speak loudly if needed, like Socrates, who would ask people, "Men, where are you rushing to? What are you doing, you poor souls? You're like blind people wandering aimlessly. You're on the wrong path and have left the right one behind. You're searching for happiness and success where they don't exist, and when someone shows you where they are, you don't believe them. Why are you looking for them outside yourselves?" Socrates might ask, "In the body? It's not there. If you don't believe me, look at Myro and Ophellius. In possessions? It's not there. But if you doubt me, look at Croesus. Look at those who are rich now and see how their lives are filled with misery. In power? It's not there. If it were, then people who were consuls multiple times should be happy, but they aren't. Whom should we believe in these matters? You, who look from the outside and are dazzled by appearances, or the people themselves? What do they say? Listen to them when they groan, when they grieve, when they think they're more miserable and in greater danger because of their consulships and glory. Is it in royal power? No, it isn't. If it were, Nero and Sardanapalus would have been happy. But even Agamemnon wasn't happy, though he was better than Sardanapalus and Nero. While others are sleeping soundly, what is he doing?"

Agamemnon says: "Much from his head he tore his rooted hair: —Iliad, x 15 "I am perplexed," he says, "and Disturb'd I am," and "my heart out of my bosom Is leaping." —Iliad, x 91"

Epictetus explains that Agamemnon wasn't troubled by his possessions or his body. No, he was rich in gold and bronze. So, what was wrong with him? It was the part of him that deals with desires and aversions, the part that moves toward or away from things. That part had been neglected and was corrupt. He didn't understand the nature of the good he was made for or the nature of evil. He didn't know what was truly his and what belonged to others. When something belonging to others went wrong, he would say, "Woe to me, the Greeks are in danger!" His ruling faculty, the part that should guide him, was wretched, neglected, and uncared for. He worried, "The Greeks will be destroyed by the Trojans." But if the Trojans didn't kill them, wouldn't they still die eventually? "Yes, but not all at once," he might say. But what difference does it make? If death is an evil, whether people die all at once or one by one, it's still an evil. Is anything going to happen other than the separation of the soul and body? No, that's all. And if the Greeks die, is the door closed? Can't you still choose to die? Yes, you can. So, why do you lament and say, "Oh, you who are king and hold Zeus's scepter?" There is no such thing as an unhappy king, just as there is no such thing as an unhappy god. So what are you? In truth, you're just a shepherd, because you weep like shepherds do when a wolf takes one of their sheep. The people you govern are like sheep to you. And why did you come here? Was your desire in danger? Was your aversion? Was your ability to act or avoid acting threatened? "No," he says, "but my brother's wife was taken away." Wasn't it a gain to be rid of an adulterous wife? "But we'll be looked down upon by the Trojans!" Are the Trojans wise or foolish? If they're wise, why are you fighting them? If they're foolish, why do you care what they think?

So where is the good, if it's not in these things? Tell us, you who are a lord, a messenger, and a spy. It's not where you think it is or where you're looking for it. If you had chosen to seek it, you would have found it within yourselves, and you wouldn't be wandering off the right path, seeking what belongs to others as if it were your own. Turn your thoughts inward. Reflect on the ideas you already have. What kind of thing do you imagine the good to be? "Something that flows easily, that is happy, that isn't hindered." Isn't it also something great, valuable, and free from harm? In what should you look for something that flows easily, that isn't hindered? In something that serves or in something that's free? "In something that's free." So, is your body free, or is it a slave? "We don't know." Don't you realize that it's a slave to fever, gout, eye infections, dysentery, tyrants, fire, iron, and everything that's stronger than it? "Yes, it's a slave." How, then, can anything that belongs to the body be free from hindrance? And how can something be great or valuable if it's naturally dead, like earth or mud? Well then, do you possess nothing that's free? "Maybe nothing." Who can force you to agree to something that seems false? "No one." Who can force you not to agree to something that seems true? "No one." In this, you can see that there's something in you that's naturally free. But what about desire, aversion, or moving toward or away from something? Can you do any of these things without first receiving the impression that something is useful or necessary? "No one can." In these things, too, you have something that isn't hindered and is free. Miserable people, focus on this, take care of this, seek the good here.

"And how is it possible for a man who has nothing, who is naked, homeless, without a hearth, dirty, without a servant, without a city, to live a life that flows easily?" Look, God has sent you a man to show you that it's possible. Look at me, who has no city, no house, no possessions, no servant; I sleep on the ground; I have no wife, no children, no official post, only the earth and sky, and one poor cloak. And what do I lack? Am I not without sorrow? Am I not without fear? Am I not free? When did any of you see me fail to achieve what

I desire or fall into something I wanted to avoid? Did I ever blame God or man? Did I ever accuse anyone? Did any of you ever see me with a sorrowful face? And how do I deal with those you're afraid of and admire? Don't I treat them like slaves? Who, when he sees me, doesn't think he's seeing his king and master?

This is the language of the Cynics, this is their character, this is their purpose. You might say, "No, but their characteristic is the little wallet, the staff, the big jaws, devouring everything they're given, storing it up, or unreasonably insulting everyone they meet, or showing off their shoulders as if it's something special." Do you see what you're getting into? First, take a mirror, look at your shoulders, observe your loins, and your thighs. You're about to compete in the Olympic Games, not in some small and insignificant contest. In the Olympic Games, you're not just allowed to be defeated and leave; first, you must be disgraced in front of the entire world, not just in front of Athenians, Spartans, or Nicopolitans. Next, you'll be whipped if you've entered the contest rashly, and before being whipped, you'll suffer thirst, heat, and swallow a lot of dust.

Reflect more carefully, know yourself, consult the divine, and don't attempt anything without God. If he advises you to proceed, be assured that he intends for you to become great or to receive many blows. For a Cynic, this amusing quality is part of the package: he must be flogged like a donkey, and when he's flogged, he must love those who flog him, as if he were the father and brother of all. You might say, "No, but if someone flogs you, stand in the public square and shout, 'Caesar, what am I suffering in this state of peace under your protection?' Let's bring the offender before the governor." But what is Caesar to a Cynic, or what is a governor, or anyone else except the one who sent the Cynic down here, whom he serves, namely Zeus? Does he call upon anyone other than Zeus? Isn't he convinced that whatever he suffers, it's Zeus who's training him? Hercules, when he was trained by Eurystheus, didn't think he was miserable; he confidently undertook everything he had to do. And would a Cynic, who's being trained by Zeus, call out and complain, he who's worthy of bearing Diogenes' scepter? Listen to what Diogenes says to passersby when he's sick with a fever, "Miserable people, won't you stop? You're going on such a long journey to Olympia to see athletes fight and destroy each other, but you won't stop to see the fight between a fever and a man?" Would such a man accuse God of treating him unfairly, a man who takes pride in his situation and claims to be an example to those who pass by? What could he accuse God of? For maintaining decent behavior? For making his virtue more evident? Well, and what does he say about poverty, death, and pain? How does he compare his own happiness to that of the great king (the king of Persia)? Or rather, he thought there was no comparison between them. Where there are disturbances, grief, fears, unsatisfied desires, and aversions to things that can't be avoided, how can there be a path to happiness? But where there are corrupt principles, those things must necessarily exist.

When the young man asked if, "When a Cynic falls ill and a friend invites him to stay at his house and be cared for, should the Cynic accept the invitation?" Epictetus replied: "And where will you find a friend of a Cynic? For the person who invites him should be like the Cynic to be worthy of being considered his friend. He should be a partner in the Cynic's scepter and royalty, and a worthy helper, if he wants to be considered worthy of the Cynic's friendship, like Diogenes was a friend to Antisthenes, and Crates was a friend to Diogenes. Do you think that if someone comes to a Cynic, greets him, and offers his house, he's a Cynic's friend, and the Cynic will think him worthy of taking him into his home? So, if you please, reflect on this too: rather look for a convenient place to bear your illness and where you'll be sheltered from the cold. But you seem to want to go to someone's house to be well-fed for a while. Why then do you think of attempting such a great thing as the life of a Cynic?"

"But," the young man asked, "Should marriage and having children, as a chief duty, be undertaken by the Cynic?" If we had a community of wise men, Epictetus replied, perhaps no one would readily apply himself to Cynicism. For whose sake should he undertake this way of life? However, if we suppose that he does, nothing would stop him from marrying and having children because his wife would be like him, his father-in-law would be like him, and his children would be raised like him. But in the present situation, which is like an army in battle formation, is it not appropriate for the Cynic to focus solely on serving God, able to move among people without being tied to common duties or entangled in the ordinary relationships of life, which, if neglected, would cause him to lose his character as an honorable and good man? And if he observes them, he will lose his role as the messenger, spy, and herald of God. Consider that he would have responsibilities toward his father-in-law, other relatives of his wife, and his wife herself (if he has one). Being a Cynic would also prevent him from caring for his family's illnesses and providing for their support. And that's just the beginning; there would be more distractions. Where now is that king, the one who devotes himself to public interests?

The people's guardian and so full of cares. —Iliad, ii 25

It is his duty to look after others, both the married and those with children, to see who treats his wife well and who doesn't, which families are well-managed and which aren't, going around like a doctor checking pulses. He might say to one, "You have a fever," to another, "You have a headache or gout," and to another, "Avoid eating," or, "Eat," or, "Don't bathe," and to another, "You need surgery or cauterization." How can he have time for this if he's tied to the duties of ordinary life? Isn't it his duty to provide clothes for his children and send them to school with writing materials? Shouldn't he also provide them with beds? For they can't be genuine Cynics from birth. If he doesn't do this, it would be better to expose the children as soon as they're born than to kill them in this way. Consider how we're reducing the Cynic's royalty, how we're stripping him of his kingship. "Yes, but Crates took a wife." You're talking about a special case due to love and a woman who was another Crates. But we're discussing ordinary marriages, those that aren't distracting, and we don't find that marriage in this world is especially suited to the Cynic.

How, then, shall a man maintain society? In the name of God, are those who introduce two or three noisy children into the world greater benefactors to society than those who oversee as much of humanity as possible, seeing what they do, how they live, what they pay attention to, and what they neglect contrary to their duty? Did those who left small children to the Thebans do them more good than Epaminondas, who died childless? And did Priam, who fathered fifty worthless sons, or Danaus or Aeolus, contribute more to the community than Homer? So, should the duties of a general or the work of a writer prevent a man from marrying or having children, and should such a man be judged to have chosen a childless life for no reason? And shouldn't the Cynic's kingship be considered an equivalent to having children? Don't we see his greatness, and don't we rightly admire the character of Diogenes? And instead of this, do we look at the present Cynics who are like dogs waiting at tables, imitating the Cynics of old in no way except perhaps in their crude behavior, but in nothing else? Such matters wouldn't have bothered us at all, nor would we have wondered if a Cynic chose not to marry or have children. Man, the Cynic is the father of all men; the men are his sons, the women are his daughters. He visits everyone with care and concern. Do you think he scolds people he meets out of idle meddling? He does it as a father, as a brother, and as the servant of the father of all, the servant of Zeus.

If you please, ask me also if a Cynic should engage in government. Fool, do you seek a greater form of governance than the one he's already engaged in? Do you ask if he should appear before the Athenians and discuss finances and supplies, he who must talk to all men, whether Athenians, Corinthians, or Romans, not about supplies, finances, peace, or war, but about happiness and misery, good fortune and bad fortune, slavery and freedom? When a man has taken on the responsibility of such a state, do you ask if he should engage in the administration of another state? Ask me also if he should hold a government office. Again, I'll say to you: Fool, what greater government could he exercise than the one he already exercises now?

A Cynic also needs to have a certain level of physical fitness because if he looks weak, thin, and pale, his words won't carry the same weight. He must not only prove to ordinary people that it's possible to be a good man without depending on the things they value, but he must also show through his own body that a simple and frugal life in the open air doesn't harm the body. "Look," he says, "I'm living proof of this, and my body is, too." That's what Diogenes did; he went about looking healthy and strong, and his appearance drew people's attention. But if a Cynic seems pitiful, he appears to be nothing more than a beggar. People turn away from him; they're offended by him. He shouldn't look dirty, so he doesn't repel people in that way either; his roughness should be clean and appealing.

A Cynic also needs natural charm and sharpness, and if he doesn't have these qualities, he's just a dull fellow and nothing more. He needs these qualities so that he can handle any situation that comes his way. That's why Diogenes responded to someone who asked, "Are you the Diogenes who doesn't believe in the gods?" by saying, "How could that be when I think that you're hateful to the gods?"

On another occasion, when Alexander the Great stood by him while he was sleeping and quoted Homer's line (Iliad, ii 24),

"A man, a counselor, should not sleep all night,"
Diogenes, still half-asleep, replied,
"The people's guardian and so full of cares."

But above all, a Cynic's ruling faculty must be purer than the sun; otherwise, he will be nothing more than a cunning, deceitful person because while he himself is entangled in some vice, he will criticize others. Consider how things are: Kings and tyrants rely on their guards and weapons to reprimand and punish wrongdoers, even if they themselves are bad. But a Cynic, instead of using weapons and guards, relies on his conscience to give him this power. When he knows that he has watched and worked for the good of humanity, that he has slept with a clear conscience, and that whatever thoughts he had were as a friend of the gods, as a servant, as a participant in Zeus's power, and that he's always ready to say,

"Lead me, O Zeus, and thou, O Destiny;"

and also, "If it so pleases the gods, so let it be," why shouldn't he have the confidence to speak freely to his brothers, his children, to all his kinsmen? That's why he's not a busybody or a meddler when he's in this state of mind; he's not interfering in others' affairs when he's overseeing human matters—he's looking after his own affairs. If that's not the case, you could also say that a general is a meddler when he inspects his soldiers, examines them, watches them, and punishes the disorderly. But if, while you have a stolen cake under your arm, you scold others, I'll say to you, "Why don't you go away into a corner and eat what you've stolen? What business do you have with other people's affairs? Who are you? Are you the bull of the herd or the queen of the bees? Show me the signs of your authority, like the ones they have by nature. But if you're just a drone claiming sovereignty over the bees, don't you think your fellow citizens will put you down, just as the bees do to drones?"

A Cynic must also have such endurance that he seems unfeeling to the average person, like a stone. No one insults him, no one strikes him, no one offends him, but he offers his body to anyone who wants to do what they will with it. He remembers that the weaker must be overpowered by the stronger in what they are weaker in; the body is weaker than many, and the weaker are overpowered by the stronger. So, he never enters into a contest in which he can be overpowered; instead, he immediately withdraws from things that belong to others. He doesn't claim things that are servile. But when it comes to his will and his use of appearances, you'll see how sharp his perception is, so much so that you might say Argus was blind compared to him. Is his assent ever rash? Is his movement toward an object hasty? Does his desire ever miss its mark? Does he ever encounter what he wants to avoid? Is his purpose ever unfulfilled? Does he ever find fault? Is he ever humiliated? Is he ever envious? These are the things he focuses all his attention and energy on; everything else, he treats with indifference. All is peaceful; no thief can take away his will, no tyrant can harm it. But what about his body? I say there is a threat. And his possessions? I say there is a threat. And what about government positions and honors? What does he care for them? When someone tries to frighten him with these things, he says, "Go away, look for children; masks are frightening to them, but I know they're just shells with nothing inside."

This is what you're considering. Therefore, if you please, I urge you in the name of God, delay your decision and first consider if you're prepared for it. Remember what Hector says to Andromache: "Go back inside and weave:

"War is the work of men Of all indeed, but specially 'tis mine."
—Iliad vi 490

Hector knew his own strength and role in war, just as a Cynic must know whether he's truly ready for the challenges of such a life.

Chapter 23
To Those Who Read and Discuss Just to Show Off

First, decide who you want to be, and then do what matches that decision. This is true in almost everything. People who train for sports first decide what they want to be, and then they follow the right steps. If someone wants to run a long-distance race, they follow a specific diet, walking routine, and exercise plan. If someone wants to run a short sprint, their training is different. And if they want to compete in multiple events like the Pentathlon, their training will be even more varied. The same goes for the arts. If you are a carpenter, you will have certain tools and techniques; if you work with metal, you will have different ones. Whatever we do, if we don't have a clear goal, we'll end up doing it without purpose. And if we aim at the wrong goal, we'll miss the mark. There's a general goal that applies to everyone, and then there's a specific goal for each person. First, we must act as a human being. What does that mean? It means we shouldn't be like sheep, even though they're gentle, nor should we be destructive like wild beasts. But the specific goal depends on each person's way of life and will. A musician acts as a musician, a carpenter as a carpenter, a philosopher as a philosopher, and a speaker as a speaker.

So, when you say, "Come and listen to me read," make sure you're not doing it without a purpose. Then, if you find you have a purpose, think about whether it's the right one. Do you want to help others or just be praised? If you want to do good, that's one thing. But if you just want praise, remember what you've heard: "What's the value of praise from the many?" And that's true—praise doesn't make a musician better at music, nor does it help a mathematician. So, if you want to be useful, in what way? Tell us, so we can rush to your reading room. But can anyone be useful to others if they haven't first received something useful themselves? No, they can't. Just like someone can't be a good carpenter if they haven't learned carpentry, or a good shoemaker if they haven't learned how to make shoes.

If you want to know whether you've gained anything useful, show us your thoughts, philosopher. What does desire promise? It promises not to fail in what you want. What does avoiding something promise? It promises not to fall into what you don't want. Well, are you keeping these promises? Tell me the truth; but if you lie, I'll tell you the truth. Recently, when your listeners weren't that enthusiastic and didn't applaud you, you left feeling down. And when you were praised, you went around asking everyone, "What did you think of me?" "Wonderful, master," they might say. "But how did I handle that particular part?" Which part? "The part where I described Pan and the nymphs?" "Excellently." Then you tell me you're acting according to nature in your desires and aversions? Get out of here; try to convince someone else. Didn't you praise someone against your own opinion? Didn't you flatter someone just because they were a senator's son? Would you want your own children to be like that? I hope not. Then why did you praise and flatter him? "He's a smart young man and listens well to speeches." Why? "Because he admires me." Ah, there's your answer. But don't you think these same people secretly despise you? So, when someone who knows they haven't done anything good or even thought about it hears a philosopher say, "You have great natural talent, and you're honest and good-natured," what do you think they're really thinking? Probably something like, "This guy must need something from me." Or tell me, what action has shown that this person has a great mind? Look, he's been around you for a while, listening to your talks and readings; has he become more modest? Has he started reflecting on himself? Has he realized what a bad state he's in? Has he thrown away his arrogance? Is he looking for someone to teach him? Yes, but not someone to teach him how to live—he's looking for someone to teach him how to talk. That's why he admires you too. Listen to what he says: "This man writes beautifully, much better than Dion." That's a whole different thing. Does he say, "This man is modest, trustworthy, and free from disturbances?" Even if he did, I would ask him: "Since this man is trustworthy, tell me what that means." And if he couldn't tell me, I'd say: "First, understand what you're saying, and then speak."

You, who are in a bad state, craving applause and counting your listeners, do you really intend to be useful to others? "Today, a lot more people attended my talk. Yes, many, maybe five hundred." That's nothing; suppose there were a thousand—Dion never had so many listeners—How could he? And they understood what was said beautifully. "What's beautiful can move even a stone." See, these are the words of a philosopher. This is the mindset of someone who will do good for others; here's someone who has listened to talks, who has read about Socrates as Socratic, not just as the writings of Lysias and Isocrates. "I've often wondered by what arguments..." Not so, but "by what argument": this is more precise than that." What, have you read the words any differently than you read little poems? Because if you read them as you should, you wouldn't be focusing on such things; instead, you would be paying attention to these words: "Anytus and Melitus can kill me, but they cannot harm me." "And I am always of such a disposition as to pay regard to nothing of my own except to the reason which, after inquiry, seems to me the best."

So, who ever heard Socrates say, "I know something and I teach?" Instead, he would send different people to different teachers. That's why they would come to him and ask to be introduced to philosophers by him, and he would take them and recommend them. Not so; but as he accompanied them, he would say, "Come listen to me speak today at the house of Quadratus." Why should I listen to you? Do you want to show me that you can put words together cleverly? Go ahead, put them together, and what good will it do you? "But just praise me." What do you mean by praise? "Say to me, 'Admirable, wonderful.'" Fine, I'll say it. But if that's what praise is, whatever philosophers mean by the word "good," what do I have to praise in you? If it's good to speak well, teach me, and I'll praise you. "What then? Shouldn't a person listen to such things without pleasure?" I hope not. For my part, I don't even listen to a musician without pleasure. But should I stand and play the lute just because of that? Listen to what Socrates says: "Nor would it be appropriate for a man of my age, like a young man composing speeches, to appear before you." Like a young man, he says. Because, in truth, this small art is a delicate thing: to choose words, put them together, and present them gracefully, and while doing so, to think, "There aren't many who can do these things." I swear by all that you value.

Does a philosopher invite people to hear him? Just as the sun draws people to it, or as food does, doesn't a philosopher also attract those who will benefit? What doctor invites a patient to be treated? Actually, I've heard that even doctors in Rome now invite patients, but when I lived there, patients invited the doctors. I invite you to come and hear that things are going badly for you, that you're taking care of everything except what you should be taking care of, and that you don't know what's good and bad and are unlucky and unhappy. A fine kind of invitation: and yet, if the philosopher's words don't have this effect on you, he might as well be dead, and so is the speaker. Rufus used to say, "If you have time to praise me, I'm speaking to no purpose." He used to speak in such a way that every one of us sitting there thought someone had accused him before Rufus: he touched on what was happening, and he showed every man's faults right in front of their eyes.

The philosopher's school, men, is like a doctor's office: you shouldn't leave it feeling pleased, but in pain. Because you're not in good health when you enter: one person has a dislocated shoulder, another has an abscess, a third has a fistula, and a fourth has a headache. Should I sit here and share little thoughts and exclamations so that you can praise me and then leave, one with his shoulder still dislocated, another with his head still aching, and a third with his fistula or abscess just as it was before? Is this why young men should leave home, leave their parents, friends, relatives, and property, just so they can say to you, "Wonderful!" when you're speaking? Did Socrates do this, or Zeno, or Cleanthes?

"What then? Isn't there a style of speaking that encourages people?" Who denies that? Just like there's a style for refuting arguments and teaching. But who ever added a fourth style to these, the style of showing off? What is the style of encouragement? It's the ability to show both one person and many the struggle they're engaged in, and that they're focusing on anything but what they truly want. Because they want things that lead to happiness, but they're looking for them in the wrong place. To do this, you don't need a thousand seats and a fancy pulpit, nor do you need to dress up in a fine robe or cloak and describe the death of Achilles. Stop, I beg you by the gods, stop ruining good words and good actions as much as you can. Nothing is more powerful in encouragement than when the speaker shows the listeners that they need him. But tell me, who, when they hear you preaching or speaking, becomes anxious about themselves or starts reflecting on their own life? Or, after leaving, says, "The philosopher really struck a chord with me; I must stop doing these things." Instead, don't they just say to someone else, "He spoke beautifully about Xerxes;" and another person says, "No, he spoke better about the battle of Thermopylae." Is this what it means to listen to a philosopher?

Chapter 24
We Should Not Be Moved by a Desire for Things Beyond Our Control

Don't let something that is against nature in someone else be a problem for you. You weren't made by nature to be sad because of others or to be unhappy because of others, but to be happy with them. If someone is unhappy, remember that it's their own fault. God made all people to be happy and free from disturbances. He gave each person certain things that are their own and other things that are not. Some things are subject to being blocked, forced, or taken away, and these things are not truly ours. But the things that can't be hindered are truly ours. God, like a caring father, made the nature of good and evil something that belongs to us.

But you might say, "I've parted from someone, and they are sad." Why did they think something that belonged to someone else was their own? Why, when they looked at you and felt joy, didn't they also realize that you are mortal and that it's natural for you to leave them or travel far away? Because they didn't think about these things, they now suffer the consequences of their own foolishness. But why do you, or for what reason, feel sorry for yourself? Is it because you didn't think about these things either? Have you, like people who don't think deeply, enjoyed everything as if you would always have them, whether it's places, people, or conversations? And now you're sitting and crying because you don't see the same people or live in the same places. Indeed, you deserve this, to be more miserable than crows and ravens who can fly wherever they want, change their nests, and cross the seas without crying or regretting their past conditions. "But they do this because they are irrational creatures," you might say. Was reason then given to us by the gods so that we could be unhappy and miserable, living our lives in sorrow and tears? Should all people be immortal? Should no one ever travel? Should we never leave our homes, but instead stay rooted like plants? And if any of our friends go away, should we just sit and cry? And when they come back, should we dance and clap our hands like little children?

Shouldn't we grow up now and remember what we've heard from the philosophers? If we didn't listen to them like they were just entertainers, they told us that this world is one city, that we are all made from the same substance, and that things must change over time. Some things must give way to others, some must dissolve, and others take their place. Some stay in the same place, and others move. All things are full of harmony, first with the gods and then with people, who are naturally meant to be one family. Some people must stay together, and others must be separated, finding joy in those who are with them and not grieving for those who are away. Besides having a noble character and disregarding things beyond his control, man also has the ability not to be fixed to one place but to go to different places at different times, sometimes out of necessity and other times just to see new things.

This is how it was for Ulysses, who saw "the cities of many men and learned their ways" (Iliad vi 490). Even before him, Hercules traveled the world, seeing both the lawless deeds and the good laws of people, casting out lawlessness and introducing good laws. And yet, how many friends do you think he had in Thebes, in Argos, in Athens? And how many friends did he make as he traveled? He even married when it seemed right to him, had children, and left them without regret or sadness because he knew that no one is truly an orphan. The true father, who cares for everyone, is always there. Hercules didn't just hear that Zeus was the father of men; he believed it deeply. He called Zeus his own father and looked to him in everything he did. Because of this, Hercules was able to live happily wherever he was. Happiness and longing for what isn't present can never go together. A happy person must have everything they desire, like someone who is full of food and has no thirst or hunger.

"But Ulysses longed for his wife and cried as he sat on a rock," you might say. Do you follow Homer and his stories in everything? Or if Ulysses did cry, then what was he but an unhappy man? And what good person is unhappy? If Zeus doesn't take care of his own citizens, making sure they are happy like himself, then everything is poorly managed. But it's not right to think this way. If Ulysses did weep and lament, then he wasn't a good man. For who is good if they don't know who they are? And who knows what they are if they forget that all things made by nature are perishable and that it's impossible for one person to always be with another? To desire impossible things is foolish and shows a slavish character, someone who is fighting against God in the only way they can—through their opinions.

"But my mother cries when she doesn't see me," you might say. Why hasn't she learned these principles? I'm not saying we shouldn't care that she's crying, but we shouldn't desire things that aren't ours. Another person's sorrow is their own, but my sorrow is mine. I will do everything in my power to stop my own sorrow, but I won't try to stop someone else's by all means. If I did, I would be fighting against God, opposing Zeus, and placing myself against his plan for the universe. The punishment for this disobedience isn't just something my children will pay for; I will pay for it too, by being disturbed, frightened by dreams, anxious at every piece of news, and having my peace depend on letters from others.

"Someone has arrived from Rome. I just hope there's no bad news." But what harm can happen to you where you are not? "Someone has come from Greece. I hope there's no bad news." This way, every place can be a source of trouble for you. Isn't it enough to be unfortunate where you are? Must you also be miserable about places across the sea, based on letters? Is this how your life is secure? "Well then, what if my friends have died in places far from me?" What have they suffered other than the natural fate of mortals? How can you want to live to old age and not see the death of anyone you love? Don't you know that over a long time, many different things must happen? One person will die of fever, another will be killed by a robber, and another will be taken by a tyrant. Such is the nature of life, and these are the people we live with in the world. Cold, heat, bad living conditions, travel, sea voyages, winds, and other circumstances can destroy one person, banish another, and send one on an embassy and another into an army. Will you sit there, anxious about all these things, lamenting, unhappy, and dependent on others—not just one or two people, but thousands upon thousands?

Did you learn this when you were with the philosophers? Didn't you learn that human life is like a battle, where one person must keep watch, another must go on reconnaissance, and another must fight? It's impossible for everyone to be in one place, nor would it be better if they were. But you neglect the orders of the general and complain when something harder than usual is asked of you. You don't realize what you're doing to the army by your actions. If everyone acted like you, no one would dig a trench, build a wall, keep watch, or expose themselves to danger, and the army would be useless. Similarly, if you're on a ship as a sailor, you should stick to your assigned place. If you're told to climb the mast, don't refuse. If you're told to go to the front of the ship, don't refuse. What captain would tolerate you? Wouldn't he throw you overboard as useless, an obstacle and a bad example to the other sailors? It's the same in life. Every person's life is like a battle, and it's long and varied. You must act like a soldier and follow the general's orders, even trying to anticipate what he wants. There's no comparison between this general and any other, neither in strength nor in superiority of character. You are in a high position, not a low one; you are always a senator. Don't you know that someone in such a position must spend little time on personal matters and often be away from home, either governing or being governed, fulfilling some duty, serving in war, or acting as a judge? And yet you tell me that you want to be like a plant, fixed to one place and rooted there? "Yes, because it's pleasant," you might say. Who says it isn't? But so is a good meal, or a beautiful woman. What else do those who seek pleasure as their end goal say? Don't you see what kind of people you're imitating? You're speaking like Epicureans and people who live only for pleasure. Yet, while you act like them and share their opinions, you still want to talk like Zeno and Socrates? Won't you stop borrowing from others things that don't suit you at all?

For what do they desire other than to sleep without disturbance, to yawn at their leisure when they wake up, to wash their face, to write and read whatever they like, to talk about trivial matters while being praised by their friends for anything they say, then to go for a short walk, bathe, eat, and sleep again in their usual way? Why should we even describe it further? You can easily imagine it. Now tell us how you want to spend your time, you who admire truth, Socrates, and Diogenes. What do you wish to do in Athens—the same as others, or something different? If so, why do you call yourself a Stoic? People who falsely claim to be Roman citizens are punished severely, and should those who falsely claim to follow something so great and honorable get away with it? No, this is not possible. The divine law is strong and inevitable, and it punishes the greatest crimes most severely. What does this law say? Let the person who pretends to be something they are not be a braggart, a vain person. Let the person who disobeys the divine order be base and a slave. Let them suffer grief, envy, and pity, and, in short, let them be unhappy and full of lament.

"Well then, do you want me to flatter a certain person? To go to their door?" If reason requires this for the sake of your country, family, or humanity, then why not go? You're not ashamed to go to the shoemaker when you need shoes or to the gardener when you need vegetables. Why should you be ashamed to go to a wealthy person when you need something? "But I don't feel any awe of a shoemaker," you might say. Then don't feel awe of the rich. "But I won't flatter the gardener," you might add. And don't flatter the rich. "How then shall I get what I want?" Do I tell you to go as if you're sure to get what you want? No, I only tell you to do what is fitting for you. "Then why should I still go?" So that you can say you've done your duty as a citizen, a brother, a friend. Remember, you went to the shoemaker and the vegetable seller, who have no power in anything great or noble, even if they charge a high price. You go to buy lettuce; it costs a penny, not a fortune. So it is here. The matter is worth going to the rich man's door for. Fine, I'll go. It's worth talking to him about. Fine, I'll talk with him. But do you also have to kiss his hand and flatter him with praise? No, that's not worth it. It's not good for me, the state, or my friends to do something that ruins a good citizen and a friend. "But you'll seem uninterested in the matter if you don't succeed." Have you forgotten why you went? Don't you know that a good person does nothing for appearances but only for doing what's right? "What's the benefit of doing right, then?" And what's the benefit of a man writing the name "Dion" correctly? The benefit is having written it correctly. "Is there no reward, then?" Do you seek a reward for doing what's right beyond the act itself? In the Olympic Games, you wish for nothing more, but it seems enough to be crowned. Does it seem so small and worthless to be good and happy? For these purposes, being introduced by the gods into this world, and it being your duty to undertake the work of a man, do you still need a nurse or a mother to care for you? Are you so easily influenced by the tears of foolish women, and do you become weak because of them? Will you never stop being a foolish child? Don't you know that the older a person is when they act like a child, the more ridiculous they are?

In Athens, did you visit anyone you wanted to? "Yes, I visited anyone I pleased." Then here too, be ready to see whom you please, but do it without being mean, neither with desire nor aversion, and your affairs will be well managed. But this doesn't depend on whether you go or stand at doors; it depends on what's inside you, on your opinions. When you've learned not to value external things that aren't under your control and to consider that none of them is truly yours, but that only your own judgments, opinions, and actions are yours, where is there any room left for flattery or meanness? Why do you still long for the peace of Athens and the familiar places? Wait a little, and you will become familiar with these new places too. Then, if you're so weak-minded, when you leave these places again, you'll cry and lament once more.

"How then shall I become kind-hearted?" By being noble and happy. It's not reasonable to be mean-spirited or to cry for yourself, or to depend on others, or to blame God or people. I urge you to become kind-hearted in this way, by following these rules. But if, because of what you call affection, you become a slave and wretched, there's no benefit in being affectionate. What stops you from loving someone as a person who is mortal, someone who might leave you? Didn't Socrates love his own children? He did, but as a free man, someone who remembered that he must first be a friend to the gods. Because of this, he didn't do anything unworthy of a good man, not even in his defense, nor when deciding his penalty, nor at any other time in his life as a senator or soldier. Yet we always find excuses for being weak, some for the sake of a child, others for a mother, or brothers. But it's not right for us to be unhappy because of any person.

Instead, we should be happy because of all people, but especially because of God, who made us for this purpose.

Well, did Diogenes love no one? He was so kind and cared so much for all people that he willingly took on many labors and hardships for humanity. He did love people, but how? As a servant of God, caring for people but also being subject to God. Because of this, the whole world was his home, not just one place. When he was captured, he didn't regret leaving Athens or his friends there. He even became familiar with the pirates and tried to help them. Later, when he was sold, he lived in Corinth just as he had lived in Athens. He would have done the same if he had gone to another country. This is how freedom is acquired. For this reason, he used to say, "Ever since Antisthenes made me free, I have not been a slave." How did Antisthenes make him free? Listen to what Diogenes says: "Antisthenes taught me what is mine and what is not mine. Possessions are not mine, nor are family, servants, friends, reputation, familiar places, or way of life—all these belong to others. What then is truly mine? The use of appearances. This Antisthenes showed me, and I possess it free from any hindrance or compulsion. No person can block my way, no person can force me to use appearances in a way I don't choose." Who then has power over me? Is it Philip or Alexander, or the great king? How could they have power over me? For if a person is going to be overpowered by another, they must first be overpowered by things. If pleasure doesn't have power over someone, nor pain, nor fame, nor wealth, but that person is willing to spit out their own poor body and leave life when they choose, whose slave can they still be? But if Diogenes had loved living in Athens and was overpowered by that life, his affairs would have been at everyone's command. The stronger would have had the power to make him suffer. Do you think Diogenes would have flattered the pirates so that they might sell him to an Athenian, just so he could see the beautiful Piraeus, the Long Walls, and the Acropolis? In what condition would he have seen them? As a captive, a slave, and a weak person. And what good would that have done him? "No," you might say, "I would see them as a free man." Show me how you would be free. Imagine someone has caught you, takes you away from your familiar place, and says, "You are my slave because I can stop you from living as you wish. I can treat you harshly or kindly as I choose." On the other hand, you are cheerful and eager to return to Athens. What would you say to the person who treats you as a slave? What would you do to find someone to free you from slavery? Could you even look him in the face, or would you just beg to be set free? Man, you should go gladly to prison, eager to go before those who lead you there. Then I ask you, are you unwilling to live in Rome and desire to live in Greece? And when you must die, will you then also fill us with your tears because you won't see Athens or walk in the Lyceum? Did you go abroad for this? Was this why you sought someone to help you? What kind of help? To solve logical puzzles more quickly or to handle complex arguments? Is this why you left your brother, your country, your friends, and your family? So that you could return after learning these things? So you didn't go abroad to gain a steady mind, to be free from disturbance, to be safe from harm, to never complain about anyone, to accuse no one, and to ensure no one could wrong you, and so you could maintain your place in life without obstacles? This is a fine goal you've gone abroad for—logical puzzles and sophistry. If you like, take your place in the marketplace and sell them like medicines. Won't you even deny everything you've learned so that you don't give a bad name to your teachings as useless? What harm has philosophy done you? How has Chrysippus harmed you that you would prove through your actions that his teachings are useless? Were the troubles you had at home not enough, the ones that caused your pain and complaints, even if you hadn't gone abroad? Have you added more to the list? And if you make new friends, you'll have more reasons to complain, and the same if you grow attached to another country. Why then do you live just to surround yourself with new sorrows that make you unhappy? Then, I ask you, do you call this affection? What affection, man! If it's a good thing, it causes no harm; if it's bad, I have nothing to do with it. I'm made by nature for my own good, not for my own harm.

What then is the training for this? First and foremost, the highest and most important is this: when you enjoy something, enjoy it as if it's not one of those things that can't be taken away, but as something fragile, like a clay pot or a glass cup. That way, if it breaks, you'll remember what it was and won't be troubled. The same applies to people. If you kiss your child, your brother, or your friend, don't let your pleasure go unchecked. Hold it back, just like those who stand behind victorious generals and remind them they are mortal. You, too, remind yourself that the one you love is mortal and that what you love isn't truly yours. It has been given to you for the moment, not to be kept forever. It's like a fig or a bunch of grapes given to you at the right season. But if you want these things in the winter, you're a fool. So, if you long for your son or friend when it's not possible, know that you're wishing for a fig in winter. For just as winter comes to figs, so do all things in life come to an end according to nature. And further, when you're enjoying something, consider the opposite. What harm is there in saying to yourself while you kiss your child, "Tomorrow you will die," or to a friend, "Tomorrow you will leave, or I will, and we will never see each other again?" "But these are words of bad omen," you might say. And some charms are also considered bad omens, but because they're useful, I don't care. Let them be useful. But do you call something a bad omen just because it signifies something natural? Cowardice is a bad omen, so is a weak spirit, sorrow, grief, and shamelessness. These are bad omens, yet we shouldn't hesitate to speak them to protect ourselves from these things. Do you tell me that a name that signifies something natural is a bad omen? Then say that the reaping of grain is a bad omen, for it means the destruction of the grain, but not of the world. Say that the falling of leaves is a bad omen, and that it's bad for dried figs to replace fresh ones, and for grapes to turn into raisins. All these things are just changes from one state to another, not destruction, but part of a fixed plan and order. Leaving home is a small change. Death is a bigger change, not from being to nothingness, but to something that isn't now. "Shall I then no longer exist?" you might ask. No, you won't exist in the same way, but you'll become something else that the world now needs. For you came into existence not when you chose, but when the world needed you.

The wise and good person, remembering who they are, where they came from, and who created them, focuses only on this: how to fulfill their role according to the order of things and in obedience to God. Do you still want me to live? I will continue to live as free and noble as you intended. For you have made me free from obstacles in what is truly mine. But if you no longer need me, I thank you for the time I have stayed in your service, and now I leave, still obedient to you. How do I leave? As you please, as a free person, as your servant, as someone who understands your commands and prohibitions. And as long as I stay in your service, who do you want me to be? A prince or a private person, a senator or a commoner, a soldier or a general, a teacher or the head of a household? Whatever place and position you assign to me, as Socrates says, I will die ten thousand times rather than abandon it. And where do you want me to be? In Rome, Athens, Thebes, or Gyara? Just remember me wherever I am. If you send me to a place where I can't live according to nature, I will not leave life in disobedience to you, but as if you were giving me the signal to retreat. I do not leave you, far from it, but I see that you no longer need me. If I can live according to nature, I will seek no other place than where I am, or other people than those among whom I am.

Let these thoughts be with you day and night. Write them down, read them, talk about them with yourself and others. Ask someone, "Can you help me with this?" and then go to another and another. Then, if something happens that is against your wish, this thought will immediately comfort you: that it is not unexpected. It is a great thing to say in all situations, "I knew that I brought a mortal child into the world." For so you will also say, "I knew that I am mortal, I knew that I could leave my home, I knew that I could be thrown out, I knew that I could be imprisoned." Then if you turn to yourself and ask where the event came from, you will immediately remember that it came from the world of things outside your control, things that are not yours. Then you will ask, "And who sent it?" The leader, the general, the state, the law. Give it to me, then, for I must always obey the law in everything. Then, when the thought of the situation pains you, for it is not within your power to prevent this, fight against it with reason and overcome it. Don't let it grow stronger or lead you to conclusions by creating images in your mind as it pleases. If you are in Gyara, don't imagine life in Rome, and how many pleasures were there for those who lived there, and how many there would be for those who returned to Rome. Instead, focus on how a person who lives in Gyara ought to live in Gyara like a person of courage. And if you are in Rome, don't imagine what life in Athens is like, but think only of life in Rome.

Then, instead of all other pleasures, substitute this one: the pleasure of knowing that you are obeying God, that not just in words but in actions, you are living as a wise and good person. What a thing it is to be able to say to yourself, "Now, whatever others may say solemnly in schools and may be judged to be saying in a strange way, this I am doing; and they are sitting and talking about my virtues,

221

inquiring about me, and praising me. And of this, Zeus has willed that I shall receive proof from myself and shall know if he has a soldier such as he ought to have, a citizen such as he ought to have, and if he has chosen to show me to others as a witness of things beyond their control: Look, you fear without reason, you foolishly desire what you desire. Don't seek the good in things outside yourself; seek it within, or you won't find it." For this purpose, he leads me here and sends me there, shows me to people as poor, without power, and sick; sends me to Gyara, leads me to prison—not because he hates me, far from it, for who hates his best servants? Nor because he doesn't care about me, for he doesn't neglect even the smallest things. But he does this to exercise me and use me as an example to others. Being given such a task, do I still care about where I am, who I am with, or what people say about me? Should I not focus entirely on God and his instructions and commands?

With these thoughts always in mind, practicing them yourself, and keeping them ready, you will never lack comfort and strength. For it is not shameful to be without food, but it is shameful not to have enough reason to keep away fear and sorrow. Once you've freed yourself from fear and sorrow, will there be any tyrant for you, or a tyrant's guard, or attendants on Caesar? Or will any appointment to high office trouble you, or those who sacrifice in the Capitol when given important roles? How could these things bother you who have received such great authority from Zeus? Only, don't boast about it or make a show of it, but show it through your actions. And if no one notices, be satisfied that you are yourself in a healthy state and happy.

Chapter 25
To Those Who Stray From Their Purpose

Think about the goals you set for yourself at the beginning. Consider which ones you've achieved and which ones you haven't. Notice how you feel happy when you remember the goals you've met and feel upset about the ones you've missed. If it's possible, try to regain what you've lost. We shouldn't give up when we're in the middle of a big challenge; we must even be willing to take hits. The struggle we're facing isn't like wrestling or the Pancration, where both winners and losers can still have some merit or luck. No, this battle is for good fortune and happiness themselves.

Even if you've stepped out of the fight for good fortune and happiness, nothing stops you from getting back in. You don't have to wait four more years for the next Olympic Games. As soon as you're ready and motivated again, you can jump back into the fight. And if you give up again, you can still return to it once more. If you finally win, it's as if you've never given up. Just don't get into the habit of quitting so often that you start to enjoy it, like a bad athlete who goes around, defeated in every game, like quails who've run away from a fight.

If the sight of a beautiful young girl tempts me, well, hasn't that happened before? If I feel an urge to criticize someone, haven't I done that before, too? You talk as if you've escaped unharmed, just like someone who might say to a doctor who advises against bathing, "But haven't I bathed before?" If the doctor could respond, he might ask, "And what happened after your bath? Didn't you get a fever or a headache?" Likewise, when you recently criticized someone, didn't you act like a mean-spirited person, like a petty gossip? Didn't you reinforce that habit in yourself by repeating it? And when you were overpowered by that young girl's beauty, did you really come away unharmed? So, why do you bring up what you did before?

You should remember your past mistakes, just like a slave remembers the beatings they've received, and you should avoid making the same errors again. But unlike slaves, who remember because of the pain, what causes you to remember your mistakes?

What punishment do you face for your faults? When have you ever been in the habit of avoiding bad behavior? Painful experiences, whether we like it or not, can be helpful to us.

Chapter 26
To Those Who Fear Want

Are you not embarrassed to be more fearful and cowardly than runaway slaves? When they escape from their masters, what do they depend on? What property do they have? What servants do they rely on? Don't they just steal a little to survive the first few days, and then figure out ways to keep themselves alive as they move from place to place, whether by land or sea? And have you ever heard of a runaway slave dying of hunger? But here you are, worried that you might run out of the things you need and staying awake at night because of it. How blind are you that you can't see where the lack of necessities leads?

"Well, where does it lead?" you ask. It leads to the same place that a fever or a falling rock would lead you—to death. Haven't you told your friends many times that you're not afraid of death? Haven't you read about it and even written about it? And how many times have you bragged that you were okay with the idea of dying?

"Yes, but my wife and children might go hungry too," you say. And where does their hunger lead them? Isn't it the same place? Don't they also face the same end? So why not look at that final destination with courage, knowing that both the richest people and the poorest people, kings and even tyrants, must all end up there? You might arrive at that place hungry, while they might arrive there stuffed from overeating and drinking.

Have you ever seen a beggar who wasn't old, even very old? They sleep outside in the cold, day and night, lying on the ground, eating only what's absolutely necessary, and somehow, they almost never die. Can't you write? Can't you teach children? Can't you be a guard at someone's door?

"But it's shameful to be in such a position," you say. Then first learn what things are truly shameful and then tell us that you're a philosopher. But until then, don't let anyone call you a philosopher.

Is it shameful for you to experience something that's not your fault, something you didn't cause, something that happened by chance, like a headache or a fever? If your parents were poor and didn't leave you anything, or if they're still alive but don't help you, is that shameful for you? Is this what you learned from philosophers? Didn't you learn that only the things that are truly shameful should be blamed, and only what's blameworthy deserves blame? Who do you blame for something that's not their fault, something they didn't do themselves? Did you make your father the way he is? Can you change him? Is that within your power? Then why should you wish for things that aren't within your control, or feel ashamed if you don't get them? Have you really spent your time studying philosophy by looking to others and hoping for things outside yourself?

Then go ahead and complain, cry, and worry that you won't have food tomorrow. Worry about your poor servants stealing from you, running away, or dying. Live your life in constant fear, you who have only approached philosophy in name and have shown by your actions that its teachings are useless and unprofitable. You've never sought stability, freedom from disturbance, or control over your emotions. You've never sought out a teacher for these purposes, but you've looked for many just to learn arguments. You've never truly asked yourself, "Can I handle this, or can't I? What should I do next?" Instead, you've acted as if all your affairs were secure and you could just sit back and focus on intellectual exercises.

Shouldn't you have gained something more from philosophy, and then protected it? Have you ever seen someone build a wall without also building a fort around it? Have you ever seen a guard posted with no door to watch? But you practice philosophy to prove—what? That you won't be confused by tricky arguments and won't be swayed— by what? Show me first what you hold onto, what you measure, or what you weigh. Show me the scales or the measuring stick you use. Or how long will you keep measuring dust? Shouldn't you be showing people the things that make them happy, the things that help them achieve their goals, and why we shouldn't blame anyone or complain about anything, but instead accept the way the universe works? Show me these things.

"Look, I'll show you: I'll solve some logical puzzles for you," you say. But that's just a tool, not the real measure. That's why you're now paying the price for neglecting true philosophy. You're trembling with fear, lying awake at night, consulting everyone for advice. And if your plans don't please everyone, you think you've done something wrong.

You're afraid of hunger, but it's not really hunger that you fear. You're afraid that you won't have someone to cook for you, someone to shop for you, someone to take off your shoes, someone to dress you, others to rub you down, and to follow you around. You're afraid that you won't have the life of a sick person who's pampered and waited on. But learn how healthy people live, how slaves live, how laborers live, how true philosophers live. Learn how Socrates lived, who had a wife and children. Learn how Diogenes lived, and how Cleanthes lived, who ran a school and also drew water for a living. If you want to live like them, you can do it anywhere and live with full confidence.

What should you have confidence in? In what's truly secure, in what can't be taken away: your own will. Why have you made yourself so useless that no one wants to take you into their home, no one wants to care for you? If someone found a useful and intact tool on the street, they would pick it up and consider it a valuable find. But no one will pick you up, and everyone will see you as a burden. Can't you even do the job of a dog or a rooster? Why do you want to keep living if this is what you are?

Does a good person worry that they won't have food? Blind people don't starve, neither do lame people. Should a good person starve? And a good soldier will always find someone to pay him, just like a laborer or a shoemaker does. So, will a good person be lacking in anything? Does God really neglect the things he's created—his servants, his witnesses—who he uses as examples for others to show that he exists and that he takes care of the world? Doesn't he show that a good person faces no real evil, whether in life or in death?

What if God doesn't provide a good person with food? What else is he doing but, like a good general, giving the signal to retreat? I obey, I follow, agreeing with the commander's orders and praising his actions. I came when he called me, and I will go when he tells me to leave. And while I'm alive, it's my duty to praise God by myself, with others, and with many people. God doesn't give me many things or an abundance of wealth. He doesn't want me to live luxuriously. He didn't even give that to Hercules, who was his own son. Another person, Eurystheus, was king of Argos and Mycenae, and Hercules obeyed orders, worked hard, and was tested. And what was Eurystheus in the end? He wasn't even king of himself, while Hercules was the ruler and leader of the whole earth and sea. He purified the world of lawlessness and brought in justice and holiness, and he did all this both naked and alone.

And when Ulysses was shipwrecked, did he lose hope? Did it break his spirit? No. How did he go to the maidens to ask for help, to beg—something that most people consider shameful?

"Like a lion bred in the mountains, trusting in his strength" —
Odyssey vi 130

What was he relying on? Not on his reputation, wealth, or power, but on his own strength, which is his understanding of what's within our control and what's not. These are the only things that make people truly free, that free them from obstacles, that allow them to look confidently at the rich and powerful. This is the gift given to philosophers. But you won't come out strong and bold; instead, you'll be trembling over your trivial possessions and silverware.

Unhappy man, is this how you've spent your time until now?

"What if I get sick?" you ask. You will be sick in the way you ought to be.

"Who will take care of me?" you ask. God and your friends.

"I will lie on a hard bed," you say. But you will lie there like a man.

"I won't have a comfortable room," you complain. You will be sick in an uncomfortable room.

"Who will provide me with the necessary food?" you wonder. The same people who provide for others.

You will be sick like everyone else. And what will be the end of your sickness? Anything other than death?

Do you think that death is the worst thing that can happen to a person, or is it the fear of death that's truly terrifying? To overcome this fear, I advise you to practice reasoning, exercises, and reading. Only then will you understand that this is the way to become truly free.

Book IV

Chapter 1
On Freedom

Aperson is free who lives as they wish to live; who is neither subject to compulsion, nor to hindrance, nor to force; whose movements towards action are not impeded, whose desires reach their goal, and who does not fall into what they wish to avoid. Who, then, chooses to live in error? No one. Who chooses to live deceived, prone to mistake, unjust, unrestrained, or discontented? No one. Not one of the bad lives as they wish; nor are they then free. And who chooses to live in sorrow, fear, envy, pity, desiring and failing in their desires, attempting to avoid something but falling into it? Not one. Do we then find any of the bad free from sorrow, free from fear, who does not fall into what they wish to avoid, and who does not fail in what they wish to achieve? Not one; nor do we find any bad person free.

If a person who has been twice consul hears this, and if you add, "But you are a wise person; this is nothing to you," they will forgive you. But if you tell them the truth, and say, "You are no different from those who have been sold three times as far as not being a slave," what else should you expect but blows? For they will say, "What? I, a slave, I whose father was free, whose mother was free? I, who no man can purchase? I, who am of senatorial rank, a friend of Caesar, who have been consul, and who own many slaves?"—In the first place, most excellent senator, perhaps your father was also a slave in the same kind of servitude, and your mother, and your grandfather, and all your ancestors as well. But even if they were as free as possible, what is that to you? What if they were noble, and you are of a mean nature; if they were fearless, and you are a coward; if they had the power of self-restraint, and you do not?

"And what," you may say, "has this to do with being a slave?" Does it seem to you to be nothing to act unwillingly, under compulsion, with groans—does this have nothing to do with being a slave? "It is something," you say: "but who can compel me except Caesar, the lord of all?" Then even you have admitted that you have one master. But that he is the common master of all, as you say, should not console you at all: but know that you are a slave in a great household. So also, the people of Nicopolis are accustomed to exclaim, "By the fortune of Caesar, we are free."

However, if you please, let us not speak of Caesar for the moment. But tell me this: have you never loved anyone, a young girl, a slave, or someone free? "What does this have to do with being a slave or free?" Were you never commanded by the person you loved to do something you did not wish to do? Have you never flattered your little slave? Have you never kissed her feet? And yet, if someone compelled you to kiss Caesar's feet, you would think it an insult and excessive tyranny. What else, then, is slavery? Have you never gone out by night to some place you did not wish to go, spent money you did not wish to spend, uttered words with sighs and groans, or submitted to abuse and exclusion? But if you are ashamed to confess your own actions, look at what Thrasonides says and does, who, after having served in the military, perhaps more than you, went out by night, when Geta (a slave) does not venture out. But if Geta were compelled by his master, he would have cried out and gone out, lamenting his bitter slavery. Next, what does Thrasonides say? "A worthless girl has enslaved me, me whom no enemy ever did." Unhappy man, you are the slave of a girl, and a worthless girl at that. Why do you still call yourself free? Why do you talk of your military service? Then he calls for a sword and is angry with the person who, out of kindness, refuses it; and he sends presents to the girl who hates him, entreats, and weeps, and on the other hand, after having a little success, he is elated. But even then, how? Was he free enough neither to desire nor to fear?

Now consider the case of animals, how we apply the notion of liberty. People keep tame lions shut up and feed them, and some take them around; and who will say that this lion is free? Isn't it the fact that the more he lives at ease, the more he is in a slavish condition? And who, if they had perception and reason, would wish to be one of these lions? Well, when birds are caught and kept shut up, how much do they suffer in their attempts to escape? And some of them die of hunger rather than submit to such a life. And as many of them as live, barely live and with suffering waste away; and if they ever find any opening, they make their escape. So much do they desire their natural liberty, to be independent and free from hindrance. And what harm is there in this? What do you say? I am made by nature to fly where I choose, to live in the open air, to sing when I choose: you deprive me of all this, and say, what harm is it to you? For this reason, we shall say that only those animals are free which cannot endure capture but escape from captivity by death as soon as they are caught. So Diogenes also somewhere says that there is only one way to freedom, and that is to die content. And he writes to the Persian king, "You cannot enslave the Athenian state any more than you can enslave fish." How is that? Cannot I catch them? "If you catch them," says Diogenes, "they will immediately leave you, just like fish; for if you catch a fish, it dies; and if these men are caught, they will die too. What use, then, is the preparation for war?" These are the words of a free man who had carefully examined the matter, and, as was natural, had discovered it. But if you look for it in a different place than where it is, what wonder is it that you never find it?

The slave wishes to be set free immediately. Why? Do you think he wishes to pay money to the collectors of the twentieth tax? No; but because he imagines that so far, through not obtaining this, he is hindered and unfortunate. "If I shall be set free, immediately it is all happiness, I care for no one, I speak to all as an equal and like them,

I go where I choose, and I come from any place I choose, and go where I choose." Then he is set free, and forthwith, having no place where he can eat, he looks for someone to flatter, someone with whom he shall sup. Then he either works with his body and endures the most dreadful things; and if he can obtain a manger, he falls into a slavery much worse than his former slavery. Or even if he becomes rich, being a man without any knowledge of what is good, he loves some little girl, and in his unhappiness laments and desires to be a slave again. He says, "What evil did I suffer in my state of slavery? Another clothed me, another gave me shoes, another fed me, another looked after me when I was sick; and I only did a few services for him. But now, wretched man that I am, what things I suffer, being a slave to many instead of to one. But however," he says, "if I shall acquire rings, then I shall live most prosperously and happily." First, to acquire these rings, he submits to what he is worthy of; then, when he has acquired them, it is again all the same. Then he says, "If I shall be engaged in military service, I will be free from all evils." He obtains military service. He suffers as much as a flogged slave, and nevertheless, he asks for a second service and a third. After this, when he has completed his career, and is made a senator, then he becomes a slave by entering the assembly, and he serves the finer and most splendid slavery—not to be a fool, but to learn what Socrates taught, what is the nature of each thing that exists, and that a man should not rashly adapt preconceptions to the various things that are. For this is the cause of all men's evils—their inability to adapt their general preconceptions to particular things. But we have different opinions about the cause of our evils. One man thinks that he is sick—not so, however, but the fact is that he does not adapt his preconceptions correctly. Another thinks that he is poor; another that he has a severe father or mother; and another again that Caesar is not favorable to him. But all this is one and only one thing—the inability to adapt preconceptions correctly. For who does not have a preconception of what is bad: that it is harmful, that it should be avoided, that it should in every way be guarded against? One preconception is not opposed to another, except when it comes to the matter of adaptation. What then is this evil, which is both harmful and something to be avoided? He answers, "Not being Caesar's friend." He has missed the mark; he has failed to adapt correctly, and is confused, seeking things that are not relevant to the matter. For when he has succeeded in being Caesar's friend, he still has not found what he was looking for. For what is it that everyone seeks? To live securely, to be happy, to do everything as they wish, not to be hindered, nor compelled. When then he has become Caesar's friend, is he free from hindrance? Free from compulsion? Is he tranquil? Is he happy? Of whom shall we inquire? What more trustworthy witness have we than this very man who has become Caesar's friend? Come forward and tell us: When did you sleep more quietly, now or before you became Caesar's friend? Immediately, you hear the answer, "Stop, I beg you, do not mock me; you do not know what miseries I suffer, and sleep does not come to me. One comes and says, 'Caesar is already awake, he is now going forth'; then come troubles and cares." Well, when did you dine with more pleasure, now or before? Hear what he says about this too. He says that if he is not invited, he is pained; and if he is invited, he dines like a slave with his master, all the while being anxious that he does not say or do anything foolish. And what do you suppose he is afraid of? Being beaten like a slave? How could he expect anything so good? No, but as befits so great a man, Caesar's friend, he is afraid that he may lose his head. And when did you bathe more freely, and exercise more peacefully? Finally, which life do you prefer, your present or your former life? I swear that no one is so foolish or so ignorant of truth as not to lament his own misfortunes the closer he is in friendship to Caesar. Since then, neither those who are called kings live as they wish, nor the friends of kings, who then are truly free? Seek, and you will find; for you have aids from nature to discover the truth. But if you are not able to discover it by yourself, listen to those who have made the inquiry. What do they say? Does freedom seem to you a good thing? "The greatest good." Is it possible then for someone who possesses the greatest good to be unhappy or suffer misfortune? "No." Whomever you see unhappy, unfortunate, or lamenting, confidently declare that they are not free. "I do declare it." We have now moved away from buying and selling and similar arrangements concerning property: for if you have rightly agreed to these matters, if the great king (the Persian king) is unhappy, he cannot be free, nor can a minor king, nor a man of consular rank, nor one who has been twice consul. So be it.

Further, answer me this question too: does freedom seem to you something great, noble, and valuable? "How could it not?" Is it possible then that someone who possesses something so great, valuable, and noble can be mean? "It is not possible." When you see someone subject to another or flattering them against their own judgment, confidently declare that this person is not free; not only if they do this for a bit of supper but also if they do it for a governorship or a consulship. And call those who do these things for small matters little slaves, and those who do them for great matters great slaves, as they deserve to be called. "This is agreed upon." Do you think that freedom is independent and self-governing? "Certainly." Then, whoever it is in another's power to hinder or compel, declare that person is not free. And do not look, I beg you, at his grandfathers and great-grandfathers, or inquire about whether he was bought or sold. But if you hear him saying from his heart and with feeling, "Master," even if the twelve fasces precede him (as consul), call him a slave. And if you hear him say, "Wretch that I am, how much I suffer," call him a slave. If finally, you see him lamenting, complaining, or unhappy, call him a slave, even though he wears a praetexta. If he is doing none of these things, do not yet say he is free, but learn his opinions. Are they subject to compulsion or hindrance, or bad fortune? If you find them so, call him a slave who has a holiday during the Saturnalia: say that his master is away; he will return soon, and you will know what he suffers. "Who will return?" Whoever has power over anything the man desires, either to give it to him or take it away. "So then we have many masters?" We do: for we have circumstances as masters before our present masters, and these circumstances are many. Therefore, it is necessary that those who have power over any of these circumstances must be our masters. For no one fears Caesar himself, but they fear death, banishment, loss of property, prison, and disgrace. Nor does anyone love Caesar unless Caesar is a person of great merit, but they love wealth, the office of tribune, praetor, or consul. When we love, hate, and fear these things, those who have power over them must be our masters. Therefore, we adore them even as gods; for we think that what can give us the greatest benefit is divine. Then we wrongly assume that a certain person has the power of conferring the greatest benefits; therefore, he is something divine. For if we wrongly assume that a certain person has the power of conferring the greatest benefits, it is a necessary consequence that the conclusion from these premises must be false.

What then makes a person free from hindrance and makes them their own master? For wealth does not do it, nor consulship, nor provincial government, nor royal power; but something else must be found. What then is it that, when we write, makes us free from hindrance and unimpeded? The knowledge of the art of writing. What then is it in playing the lute? The science of playing the lute. Therefore in life also, it is the science of life. You have heard this in a general way, but examine it in parts. Is it possible for someone who desires things that depend on others to be free from hindrance? No. Is it possible for them to be unimpeded? No. Therefore, they cannot be free. Consider this: do we have nothing in our power, or do we have all things, or are some things in our power and others in the power of others? "What do you mean?" When you want your body to be whole, is it in your power or not? "It is not in my power." When you want it to be healthy? "Neither is this in my power." When you want it to be beautiful? "Nor is this." Life or death? "Neither is this in my power." Your body, then, belongs to another, subject to anyone stronger than yourself. "It does." But your estate, is it in your power to have it when you please, as long as you please, and in the way you please? "No." And your slaves? "No." And your clothes? "No." And your house? "No." And your horses? "Not one of these things." And if you wish for your children to live, or your wife, or your brother, or your friends, is it in your power? "This too is not in my power."

So, do you have nothing that is your own, nothing that depends on you alone and cannot be taken away, or do you have something of the kind? "I do not know." Look at the matter this way and examine it. Can anyone make you agree with something false? "No one." In the matter of agreement, then, you are free from hindrance and obstruction. "Agreed." Well, and can anyone force you to desire something you do not wish? "He can, for when he threatens me with death or imprisonment, he compels me to desire to avoid it." If you despise death and imprisonment, do you still care what he says? "No." Is then the despising of death your own act or not? "It is my act." It is your own act then to desire to move toward something: or is it not so? "It is my own act." But to desire to avoid something, whose act is that? This too is your act. "What if I try to walk, but someone stops me?" What part of you does he stop? Does he stop your power of agreeing? "No, but he stops my poor body." Yes, as he would stop a stone. "Agreed, but I no longer walk." And who told you that walking is your own act, free from hindrance? I said that this only was free from hindrance: the desire to move, but where there is a need for the body and its cooperation, you heard long ago that nothing is your own. "Agreed to this also." And who can compel you to desire what you do not wish? "No one." And to plan or decide, or in short, to use the appearances that present themselves—can anyone compel you? "He cannot do this, but he will stop me from obtaining what I desire." If you desire something that is your own, and one of the things that cannot be stopped, how will he stop you? "He cannot in any way." Who then tells you that he who desires things that belong to others is free from hindrance?

"Must I then not desire health?" By no means, nor anything else that belongs to another: for what is not in your power to obtain or keep when you wish, belongs to another. Keep, then, not only your hands but even your desires far from it. If you do not, you have surrendered yourself as a slave; you have subjected your neck, if you admire anything that is not your own, to everything that depends on others' power and is perishable, to which you have conceived a liking. "Is not my hand my own?" It is a part of your own body, but it is by nature earth, subject to hindrance, compulsion, and the slave of everything stronger. And why do I say your hand? You should hold your entire body as a poor ass loaded, as long as it is possible, as long as you are allowed. But if there is pressure and a soldier seizes it, let it go, do not resist, nor complain; if you do, you will be beaten, and still lose the ass. But when you should feel this way about the body, consider what remains to be done about everything else provided for the body's sake. When the body is an ass, all other things are bits belonging to the ass: packsaddles, shoes, barley, fodder. Let these also go: get rid of them faster and more readily than the ass.

When you have prepared yourself this way, and practiced this discipline—to distinguish what belongs to another from what is your own, what is subject to hindrance from what is not, to concern yourself with the things free from hindrance, and not concern yourself with the things that are not free—do you still fear any man? No one. For what will you be afraid of? About the things that are your own, in which the nature of good and evil consists? And who has power over these things? Who can take them away? Who can impede them? No one can, no more than they can impede God. But will you be afraid about your body and possessions, things that are not yours, things that in no way concern you? And what else have you been studying from the beginning but to distinguish between your own and not your own, the things that are in your power and not in your power, the things subject to hindrance and not subject? Why did you come to the philosophers? Was it so that you may still be unfortunate and unhappy? You will then, as I have supposed you to do, be without fear and disturbance. And what is grief to you? For fear comes from what you expect, but grief from what is present. But what more will you desire? For of the things that are within the power of the will, as being good and present, you have a proper and regulated desire: but of the things that are not in the power of the will, you do not desire any one, and so you do not allow any place for what is irrational, impatient, or excessively hasty.

When you are this way towards things, what man can still be formidable to you? For what has a man that is formidable to another, either when you see him or speak to him or finally are conversant with him? Not more than one horse has with respect to another, or one dog to another, or one bee to another bee. Things indeed are formidable to every man, and when any man can give these things to another or take them away, then he too becomes formidable. How then is a fortress demolished? Not by the sword, not by fire, but by opinion. For if we demolish the fortress within the city, can we also demolish the one of fever, or that of beautiful women? Can we, in a word, demolish the fortress within us and cast out the tyrants within us, whom we have daily over us, sometimes the same tyrants, other times different tyrants? But with this, we must begin, and with this, we must demolish the fortress and eject the tyrants by giving up the body, the parts of it, the faculties of it, the possessions, the reputation, magisterial offices, honors, children, brothers, friends, by considering all these things as belonging to others. And if tyrants have been ejected from us, why do I still enclose the fortress by a wall of circumvallation, at least on my account; for if it still stands, what does it do to me? Why do I still eject the guards? For where do I perceive them? Against others, they have their fasces, and their spears, and their swords. But I have never been hindered in my will, nor compelled when I did not will. And how is this possible? I have placed my actions in obedience to God. Is it his will that I shall have a fever? It is my will also. Is it his will that I should move toward something? It is my will also. Is it his will that I should obtain something? It is my wish also. Does he not will? I do not wish. Is it his will that I die, that I be put to the rack? It is my will then to die, it is my will then to be put to the rack. Who then can still hinder me contrary to my judgment, or compel me? No one more than they can hinder or compel Zeus.

This is how the more cautious travelers act. A traveler has heard that the road is infested by robbers; he does not venture to enter it alone but waits for the companionship on the road either of an ambassador, a quaestor, or a proconsul, and when he has attached himself to such persons, he goes along the road safely. So in the world, the wise man acts. There are many bands of robbers, tyrants, storms, difficulties, losses of what is dearest. Where is there any place of refuge? How shall he pass along without being attacked by robbers? What company shall he wait for to pass along safely? To whom shall he attach himself? To what person generally? To the rich man, to the man of consular rank? And what is the use of that to me? Such a man is stripped himself, groans, and laments. But what if the fellow companion himself turns against me and becomes my robber? What shall I do? I will be a friend of Caesar: when I am Caesar's companion, no one will wrong me. First, to become illustrious, what things must I endure and suffer? How often and by how many must I be robbed? Then, if I become Caesar's friend, he too is mortal. And if Caesar, from any circumstance, becomes my enemy, where is it best for me to retire? Into a desert? Well, does fever not come there? What shall be done then? Is it not possible to find a safe companion, a faithful one, strong, secure against all surprises? Thus he considers and perceives that if he attaches himself to God, he will make his journey safely.

How do you understand "attaching yourself to God?" In this sense: that whatever God wills, a man also shall will; and what God does not will, a man also shall not will. How then shall this be done? In what other way than by examining the actions and administration of God? What has he given to me as my own and in my power? What has he reserved to himself? He has given me the things that are in the power of the will: he has put them in my power free from impediment and hindrance. How was he able to make the earthy body free from hindrance? He could not, and so he subjected to the revolution of the whole possessions, household things, house, children, wife. Why then do I fight against God? Why do I will what does not depend on the will? Why do I will to have absolutely what is not granted to me? But how should I will to have things? In the way, they are given and as long as they are given. But he who has given takes away. Why then do I resist? I do not say I will be a fool if I use force against one who is stronger, but I will first be unjust. For whence had I things when I came into the world? My father gave them to me. And who gave them to him? And who made the sun? And who made the fruits of the earth? And who made the seasons? And who made the connection of men with one another and their fellowship?

Then after receiving everything from another and even yourself, are you angry and do you blame the giver if he takes anything from you? Who are you, and for what purpose did you come into the world? Did he not introduce you here, did he not show you the light, did he not give you fellow workers, and perceptions and reason? And as who did he introduce you here? Did he not introduce you as subject to death, and as one to live on the earth with a little flesh, to observe his administration, and to join him in the spectacle and the festival for a short time? Will you not then, as long as you have been permitted, after seeing the spectacle and the solemnity, when he leads you out, go with adoration of him and thanks for what you have heard and seen? "No; but I would still enjoy the feast." The initiated too would wish to be longer in the initiation; and perhaps also those at Olympia to see other athletes; but the solemnity is ended: go away like a grateful and modest man; make room for others: others also must be born, as you were, and being born, they must have a place, and houses, and necessary things. And if the first do not retire, what remains? Why are you insatiable? Why are you not content? Why do you contract the world? "Yes, but I would have my little children with me and my wife." What, are they yours? Do they not belong to the giver and to him who made you? Will you not give up what belongs to others? Will you not give way to him who is superior? "Why then did he introduce me into the world on these conditions?" And if the conditions do not suit you, depart. He has no need of a spectator who is not satisfied. He wants those who join the festival, those who take part in the chorus, so they may rather applaud, admire, and celebrate with hymns the solemnity. But those who cannot bear trouble, and the cowardly, he will not unwillingly see absent from the great assembly; for they did not, when they were present, behave as they ought to at a festival nor fill up their place properly, but they lamented, found fault with the deity, fortune, their companions; not seeing both what they had and their powers, which they received for contrary purposes, the powers of magnanimity, of a generous mind, manly spirit, and what we are now inquiring about—freedom. "For what purpose then have I received these things?" To use them. "How long?" As long as he who has lent them chooses. "What if they are necessary to me?" Do not attach yourself to them, and they will not be necessary: do not say to yourself that they are necessary, and they are not necessary.

This study you ought to practice from morning to evening, beginning with the smallest things and those most liable to damage: with an earthen pot, with a cup. Then proceed in this way to a tunic, a little dog, a horse, a small estate in land; then to yourself, your body, the parts of your body, your children, your wife, your brothers. Look all around and throw these things from you (which are not yours). Purge your opinions so that nothing clings to you of the things that are not your own, that nothing grows to you, that nothing gives you pain when it is torn from you; and say, while you are daily exercising yourself as you do in the school, not that you are philosophizing, for this is an arrogant expression, but that you are presenting as an asserter of freedom: for this is really freedom. To this freedom, Diogenes was called by Antisthenes, and he said that he could no longer be enslaved by anyone. For this reason, when he was taken prisoner, how did he behave towards the pirates? Did he call any of them master? And I do not speak of the name, for I am not afraid of the word, but of the state of mind by which the word is produced. How did he reprove them for feeding their captives badly? How was he sold? Did he seek a master? No, but a slave. And when he was sold, how did he behave towards his master? Immediately he argued with him and told his master that he should not be dressed as he was, nor shaved in such a way; and about the children, he told them how they should be raised. And what was strange about this? For if his master had bought a wrestling teacher, would he have employed him in the exercises of the palestra as a servant or as a master? And so if he had bought a physician or an architect. And so in every matter, it is absolutely necessary that he who has skill must be the superior of him who does not. Whoever then generally possesses the science of life, what else must he be than a master? For who is the master on a ship? The person who steers the helm. Why? Because the person who does not obey him suffers for it. "But a master can give me stripes." Can he do it then without suffering for it? So I also used to think. But because he cannot do it without suffering for it, for this reason, it is not in his power: and no one can do what is unjust without suffering for it. And what is the penalty for someone who puts their slave in chains? What do you think that is? The fact of putting the slave in chains; and you will also admit this if you choose to maintain the truth, that man is not a wild beast, but a tame animal. For when is a vine doing badly? When it is in a condition contrary to its nature. When is a rooster? Just the same. Therefore a man also is so. What then is a man's nature? To bite, to kick, to throw into prison, and behead? No; but to do good, to cooperate with others, to wish them well. At that time then, he is in a bad condition, whether you choose to admit it or not, when he is acting foolishly.

"Socrates then did not fare badly?" No, but his judges and his accusers did. "Nor did Helvidius at Rome fare badly?" No, but his murderer did. "How do you mean?" The same as you do when you say that a rooster has not fared badly when he has gained the victory and been severely wounded; but that the rooster has fared badly when he has been defeated and is unhurt; nor do you call a dog fortunate, who neither pursues game nor works, but when you see him sweating, when you see him in pain and panting violently after running. What paradox (unusual thing) do we utter if we say that the evil in everything is what is contrary to its nature? Is this a paradox? Do you not say this in the case of all other things? Why then, in the case of man only, do you think differently? But because we say that the nature of man is tame (gentle), social, and faithful, you will not say that this is a paradox. It is not. What then is it a paradox to say that a man is not hurt when he is whipped, put in chains, or beheaded? Does he not, if he suffers nobly, come off even with increased advantage and profit? But is he not hurt, who suffers most pitifully and disgracefully, who in place of a man becomes a wolf, or viper, or wasp?

Well then, let us summarize the things that have been agreed on. The person who is not restrained is free, to whom things are exactly as they wish them to be; but one who can be restrained, compelled, hindered, or thrown into any circumstances against their will, is a slave. But who is free from restraint? One who desires nothing that belongs to others. And what are the things that belong to others? Those that are not in our power either to have or not to have, or to have of a certain kind or in a certain manner. Therefore, the body belongs to another, the parts of the body belong to another, possession (property) belongs to another. If then you are attached to any of these things as your own, you will pay the penalty, which is proper for someone who desires what belongs to another. This road leads to freedom; this is the only way of escaping from slavery, to be able to say at last with all your soul:

"Lead me, O Zeus, and thou, O destiny,
The way that I am bid by you to go."
— Iliad vi 490

But what do you say, philosopher? The tyrant summons you to say something that does not suit you. Do you say it or not? Answer me. "Let me consider." Will you consider now? But when you were in the school, what was it that you used to consider? Did you not study what things are good and what are bad, and what things are neither one nor the other? "I did." What then was our opinion? "That just and honorable acts were good; and that unjust and disgraceful acts were bad." Is life a good thing? "No." Is death a bad thing? "No." Is prison? "No." But what did we think about mean and faithless words and betrayal of a friend and flattery of a tyrant? "That they are bad." Well then, you are not considering, nor have you considered nor deliberated. For what is the matter for consideration? Is it whether it is appropriate for me, when I have the power, to secure for myself the greatest of good things and not avoid the greatest evils? A fine inquiry indeed, and necessary, and one that demands much deliberation. Man, why do you mock us? Such an inquiry is never made. If you really imagined that base things were bad and honorable things were good, and that all other things were neither good nor bad, you would not even have approached this inquiry, nor have come near it; but immediately you would have been able to distinguish them by the understanding as you would do (in other cases) by the vision. For when do you inquire if black things are white, if heavy things are light, and do not comprehend the manifest evidence of the senses? How then do you now say that you are considering whether things that are neither good nor bad ought to be avoided more than things that are bad? But you do not possess these opinions, and neither do these things seem to you to be neither good nor bad, but you think that they are the greatest evils; nor do you think those other things (mean and faithless words, etc.) to be evils, but matters which do not concern us at all. For thus, from the beginning, you have accustomed yourself. "Where am I? In the schools: and are any listening to me? I am discoursing among philosophers." But I have gone out of the school. Away with this talk of scholars and fools. Thus a friend is overpowered by the testimony of a philosopher; thus a philosopher becomes a parasite; thus he lets himself for hire for money; thus, in the senate, a person does not say what he thinks; in private (in the school), he proclaims his opinions. You are a cold and miserable little opinion, suspended from idle words as from a hair. But keep yourself strong and fit for the uses of life, and be initiated by being exercised in action. How do you hear (the report)? I do not say that your child is dead, for how could you bear that? But that your oil is spilled, your wine drunk up? Do you act in such a way that one standing by you while you are making a great noise, may say this only: "Philosopher, you say something different in the school. Why do you deceive us? Why, when you are only a worm, do you say that you are a man?" I should like to be present when some philosophers lie with a woman, that I might see how they are exerting themselves, and what words they are uttering, and whether they remember their title of philosopher, and the words they hear, say, or read.

And what is this to liberty? Nothing else than this: whether you who are rich choose or not. And who is your evidence for this? Who else than yourselves? Who have a powerful master (Caesar), and who live in obedience to his nod and motion, and who faint if he only looks at you with a scowling countenance; you who court old women and old men, and say, "I cannot do this: it is not in my power." Why is it not in your power? Did you not lately contend with me and say that you are free? "But Aprulla has hindered me." Tell the truth then, slave, and do not run away from your masters, nor deny, nor venture to produce anyone to assert your freedom, when you have so many evidences of your slavery. And indeed, when a man is compelled by love to do something contrary to his opinion (judgment), and at the same time sees the better, but has not the strength to follow it, one might consider him still more worthy of excuse as being held by a certain violent and in a manner a divine power. But who could endure you who are in love with old women and old men, and wipe the old women's noses, and wash them and give them presents, and also wait on them like a slave when they are sick, and at the same time wish them dead, and question the physicians whether they are sick unto death? And again, when to obtain these great and much admired magistracies and honors, you kiss the hands of these slaves of others, so you are not the slave even of free men. Then you walk about before me in stately fashion as a praetor or a consul. Do I not know how you became a praetor, by what means you got your consulship, who gave it to you? I would not even choose to live, if I must live by help of Felicion and endure his arrogance and servile insolence; for I know what a slave is, who is fortunate, as he thinks, and puffed up by pride.

"You then," someone may say, "are you free?" I wish, by the Gods, and pray to be free; but I am not yet able to face my masters; I still value my poor body; I value greatly the preservation of it entire, though I do not possess it entirely. But I can point out to you a free man so that you may no longer seek an example. Diogenes was free. How was he free? Not because he was born of free parents, but because he was himself free because he had cast off all the handles of slavery, and it was not possible for any man to approach him, nor had any man the means of laying hold of him to enslave him. He had everything easily loosed, everything only hanging to him. If you laid hold of his property, he would have rather let it go and be yours than he would have followed you for it; if you had laid hold of his leg, he would have let go his leg; if of all his body, all his poor body; his intimates, friends, country, just the same. For he knew from whence he had them and from whom, and on what conditions. His true parents indeed, the Gods, and his real country he would never have deserted, nor would he have yielded to any man in obedience to them and their orders, nor would any man have died for his country more readily. For he was not used to inquire when he should be considered to have done anything on behalf of the whole of things (the universe, or all the world), but he remembered that everything that is done comes from there and is done on behalf of that country and is commanded by him who administers it. Therefore see what Diogenes himself says and writes: "For this reason, he says, Diogenes, it is in your power to speak both with the King of the Persians and with

Archidamus the king of the Lacedaemonians, as you please." Was it because he was born of free parents? I suppose all the Athenians and all the Lacedaemonians because they were born of slaves, could not talk with them (these kings) as they wished, but feared and paid court to them. Why then does he say that it is in his power? Because I do not consider the poor body to be my own, because I want nothing, because law is everything to me, and nothing else is. These were the things that permitted him to be free.

And that you may not think that I show you the example of a man who is a solitary person, who has neither wife nor children, nor country, nor friends, nor kinsmen, by whom he could be bent and drawn in various directions, take Socrates and observe that he had a wife and children, but he did not consider them as his own; that he had a country, as long as it was fit to have one, and in such a manner as was fit; friends and kinsmen also, but he held all in subjection to law and obedience to it. For this reason, he was the first to go out as a soldier, when it was necessary, and in war, he exposed himself to danger most unsparingly; and when he was sent by the tyrants to seize Leon, he did not even deliberate about the matter, because he thought it was a base action, and he knew he must die (for his refusal), if it so happened. And what difference did that make to him? For he intended to preserve something else, not his poor flesh, but his fidelity, his honorable character. These are things that could not be assailed nor brought into subjection. Then when he was obliged to speak in defense of his life, did he behave like a man who had children, who had a wife? No, but he behaved like a man who has neither. And what did he do when he was ordered to drink the poison, and when he had the power of escaping from prison, and when Crito said to him, "Escape for the sake of your children," what did Socrates say? Did he consider the power of escape as an unexpected gain? By no means: he considered what was fit and proper; but the rest he did not even look at or take into the reckoning. For he did not choose, he said, to save his poor body, but to save that which is increased and saved by doing what is just, and is impaired and destroyed by doing what is unjust. Socrates will not save his life by a base act; he who would not put the Athenians to the vote when they clamored that he should do so, he who refused to obey the tyrants, he who discoursed in such a manner about virtue and right behavior. It is not possible to save such a man's life by base acts, but he is saved by dying, not by running away. For the good actor also preserves his character by stopping when he ought to stop, better than when he goes on acting beyond the proper time. What then shall the children of Socrates do? "If," said Socrates, "I had gone off to Thessaly, would you have taken care of them; and if I depart to the world below, will there be no man to take care of them?" See how he gives death a gentle name and mocks it. But if you and I had been in his place, we should have immediately answered as philosophers that those who act unjustly must be repaid in the same way, and we should have added, "I shall be useful to many, if my life is saved, and if I die, I shall be useful to no one." For, if it had been necessary, we should have made our escape by slipping through a small hole. And how in that case should we have been useful to anyone? Where would they have been staying? Or if we were useful to people while we were alive, should we not have been much more useful to them by dying when we ought to die, and as we ought? And now Socrates, being dead, is no less useful to people, and even more useful, by the memory of what he did or said when he was alive.

Think of these things, these opinions, these words: look at these examples if you want to be free if you desire the thing according to its worth. And what is the wonder if you buy so great a thing at the price of so many and so great things? For the sake of what is called liberty, some hang themselves, others throw themselves down precipices, and sometimes even whole cities have perished. And will you not, for the sake of true, unassailable, and secure liberty, give back to God the things he has given when he demands them? Will you not, as Plato says, study not to die only, but also to endure torture, exile, and scourging, and in a word to give up all that is not your own? If you do not, you will be a slave among slaves, even if you are ten thousand times a consul; and if you make your way up to the Palace (Caesar's residence), you will still be a slave; and you will feel that perhaps philosophers speak words that are contrary to common opinion (paradoxes), as Cleanthes also said, but not words contrary to reason. For you will know by experience that the words are true and that there is no profit from the things that are valued and eagerly sought by those who have obtained them; and to those who have not yet obtained them, there is an imagination that when these things come, all that is good will come with them. Then, when they come, the feverish feeling is the same, the tossing to and fro is the same, the satiety, the desire for things that are not present; for freedom is acquired not by the full possession of the things that are desired, but by removing the desire. And that you may know that this is true, as you have labored for those things, so transfer your labor to these; be vigilant for the purpose of acquiring an opinion that will make you free; pay court to a philosopher instead of to a rich old man; be seen about a philosopher's doors: you will not disgrace yourself by being seen; you will not go away empty nor without profit if you go to the philosopher as you ought, and if not (if you do not succeed), try at least: the attempt is not disgraceful.

Chapter 2
On Familiar Intimacy

First of all, make sure you never get so close to your old friends or anyone you used to hang out with that you start doing the same things they do again. If you don't stick to this, you'll end up hurting yourself. But if you start to think, "They might think I'm being unfriendly, and they won't like me as much," remember that everything has a price. You can't stay the same person if you stop doing what they do. So, you have to choose: do you want to stay as you were and keep their affection, or do you want to grow and be different, even if it means they don't treat you the same?

If you think it's better to improve yourself, then focus on that and don't let anything else distract you. No one can make real progress if they're always torn between two choices. But if you decide to stick to your old ways, then you'll miss out on both— you won't get better, and you won't keep what you had before. When you used to care about things that weren't important, you pleased your friends. But you can't be the best at both, and the more you focus on one, the more you'll fall behind in the other.

For example, if you stop drinking with your old drinking buddies, you won't be as fun for them as you used to be. So, you have to choose: do you want to be a heavy drinker and keep their friendship, or do you want to be sober and maybe lose their affection? You also can't expect to be as well-liked as before if you stop singing with the same people you used to sing with. Here too, you have to decide which you prefer. If you think it's better to be modest and behave properly, then let go of the other stuff—don't engage with those people anymore. But if you find that this doesn't suit you, then go all in the other way: become someone who chases after pleasure and acts accordingly, and you'll get what you want.

You might even jump up in the theater and shout out praise for the dancer. But remember, you can't be two completely different characters at once. You can't be both Thersites, who was known for being ugly and mean, and Agamemnon, who was tall, handsome, and respected by others. If you choose to be like Thersites, then you have to accept being unattractive and bald. If you want to be like Agamemnon, then you have to be noble, strong, and care for those who follow you.

Chapter 3
What To Aim at in Exchange

Keep this idea in mind whenever you lose something that's outside of your control: think about what you gain in return. If what you gain is more valuable, never say, "I've lost something." For example, if you get a horse instead of a donkey, or an ox instead of a sheep, or if you gain the chance to do a good deed instead of receiving money, or if you gain peace of mind instead of idle gossip, or if you gain modesty instead of crude talk. If you remember this, you will keep your character the way it should be. But if you don't, you'll lose important opportunities, and no matter how hard you work on yourself, you'll end up wasting your efforts and destroying what you've built. It only takes a small mistake to lose everything, just like a ship captain only needs to turn the ship slightly the wrong way to cause it to crash, even if he didn't do it on purpose but just wasn't paying enough attention. The same thing can happen with your life: if you just "fall asleep" on your duties for a moment, everything you've worked on can disappear.

So, pay attention to what's happening around you, and stay alert. What you're trying to protect is no small thing. It's your modesty, honesty, consistency, freedom from emotions, calmness, and in short, your liberty. Ask yourself, "What will I trade these things for? Is it worth it?" If you do give them up, see what you're getting in return. Maybe I have decency, and someone else has a powerful job like being a tribune or a praetor. But I don't cheer when it's not appropriate, and I won't stand up where I shouldn't, because I'm free and I follow God willingly. I don't seek anything else—not my body, not possessions, not a high position, not even a good reputation.

Because God doesn't want me to seek those things. If He wanted them to be good for me, He would have made them so. But since He didn't, I can't go against His will.

Always protect what is truly good for you, and in everything else, behave in a way that's reasonable and consistent. If you don't, you'll be unhappy, you'll fail at everything, and you'll face obstacles. These are the laws given by God, and we should follow them—not the laws made by people like Masurius and Cassius.

Chapter 4
To Those Who Want to Live a Peaceful Life

Remember that not only the desire for power and wealth makes us lowly and dependent on others, but even the desire for peace, free time, travel, and learning can do the same.

Always keep in mind that it's not just wanting power and riches that can make us feel weak and controlled by others, but even wanting peace, leisure, travel, or learning can also put us in the same position.

For to speak plainly, whatever the external thing may be, the value which we set upon it places us in subjection to others.

To put it simply, whatever external thing we place high value on makes us dependent on others.

What then is the difference between desiring to be a senator or not desiring to be one; what is the difference between desiring power or being content with a private station; what is the difference between saying, "I am unhappy, I have nothing to do, but I am bound to my books as a corpse"; or saying, "I am unhappy, I have no leisure for reading"?

So, what's the difference between wanting to be a senator or not wanting to be one? What's the difference between wanting power or being content with a simple life? What's the difference between saying, "I'm unhappy because I have nothing to do but read," or saying, "I'm unhappy because I don't have time to read"?

For as salutations and power are things external and independent of the will, so is a book.

Just like greetings and power are external things beyond our control, so is a book.

For what purpose do you choose to read? Tell me.

Why do you choose to read? Tell me.

For if you only direct your purpose to being amused or learning something, you are a silly fellow and incapable of enduring labor.

If your purpose is just to amuse yourself or learn something, you're being foolish and unable to handle real effort.

But if you refer reading to the proper end, what else is this than a tranquil and happy life?

But if you read to achieve a peaceful and happy life, what else could it be?

But if reading does not secure for you a happy and tranquil life, what is the use of it?

If reading doesn't bring you peace and happiness, what's the point of it?

"But it does secure this," the man replies, "and for this reason I am vexed that I am deprived of it."

You might say, "But it does bring me peace and happiness, and that's why I'm upset when I can't read."

And what is this tranquil and happy life, which any man can impede, I do not say Caesar or Caesar's friend, but a crow, a piper, a fever, and thirty thousand other things?

But what kind of peaceful and happy life can be so easily disturbed—not just by Caesar or Caesar's friend, but by something as small as a crow, a noisy musician, a fever, or any number of little things?

But a tranquil and happy life contains nothing so sure as continuity and freedom from obstacle.

True peace and happiness should be steady and uninterrupted.

Now I am called to do something: I will go then with the purpose of observing the measures (rules) which I must keep, of acting with modesty, steadiness, without desire and aversion to things external;

If I'm called to do something else, I'll go and do it, keeping in mind the rules I must follow, acting with modesty, calmness, without strong desires or dislikes for external things;

and then that I may attend to men, what they say, how they are moved;

I'll pay attention to what people say and how they react;

and this not with any bad disposition, or that I may have something to blame or to ridicule;

but I won't do this with a bad attitude or just to find something to blame or mock;

but I turn to myself, and ask if I also commit the same faults.

Instead, I'll turn inward and ask if I make the same mistakes.

How then shall I cease to commit them?

How can I stop making these mistakes?

Formerly I also acted wrong, but now I do not: thanks to God.

I used to do wrong too, but now I don't, thanks to God.

Come, when you have done these things and have attended to them, have you done a worse act than when you have read a thousand verses or written as many?

So, after you've done all this and paid attention to it, have you really done something worse than when you've read or written a thousand verses?

For when you eat, are you grieved because you are not reading?

When you eat, do you get upset because you're not reading?

Are you not satisfied with eating according to what you have learned by reading, and so with bathing and with exercise?

Aren't you content with just eating as you've learned from reading, and the same goes for bathing and exercising?

Why then do you not act consistently in all things, both when you approach Caesar, and when you approach any person?

Why not act the same way in all things, whether you're meeting with Caesar or anyone else?

If you maintain yourself free from perturbation, free from alarm, and steady; if you look rather at the things which are done and happen than are looked at yourself;

If you stay calm, free from fear, and steady; if you focus more on what's being done and happening rather than on yourself;

if you do not envy those who are preferred before you; if surrounding circumstances do not strike you with fear or admiration, what do you want? Books?

If you don't envy those who are ahead of you; if the things around you don't make you feel fear or awe, what more do you need? Books?

How or for what purpose? for is not this (the reading of books) a preparation for life? and is not life itself (living) made up of certain other things than this?

Why? What for? Isn't reading books just preparation for life? And isn't life itself made up of more than just this?

This is just as if an athlete should weep when he enters the stadium, because he is not being exercised outside of it.

This is like an athlete crying when he enters the stadium because he's not still training outside.

It was for this purpose that you used to practice exercise; for this purpose were used the halteres (weights), the dust, the young men as antagonists; and do you seek for those things now when it is the time of action?

You trained for this moment; you used weights, dust, and sparring partners for this; and now, when it's time to act, do you still want those things?

This is just as if in the topic (matter) of assent when appearances present themselves, some of which can be comprehended, and some cannot be comprehended, we should not choose to distinguish them but should choose to read what has been written about comprehension (κατάληψις).

It's like in matters of understanding when some things can be grasped and others can't, instead of trying to figure them out, you'd rather just read about comprehension.

What then is the reason of this? The reason is that we have never read for this purpose, we have never written for this purpose, so that we may in our actions use in a way conformable to nature the appearances presented to us;

Why is this? It's because we've never read or written with the purpose of using what we learn in our actions, in a way that aligns with nature;

but we terminate in this, in learning what is said, and in being able to expound it to another, in resolving a syllogism, and in handling the hypothetical syllogism.

instead, we stop at just learning what's said, being able to explain it to others, solving a logical problem, and handling a hypothetical situation.

For this reason where our study (purpose) is, there alone is the impediment.

That's why, wherever our study is focused, that's where the obstacles are.

Would you have by all means the things which are not in your power?

Do you want to have things that aren't within your control?

Be prevented then, be hindered, fail in your purpose.

Then be ready to be blocked, hindered, and fail in your purpose.

But if we read what is written about action (efforts), not that we may see what is said about action, but that we may act well:

But if we read what's written about action not just to see what's said, but to actually act well:

if we read what is said about desire and aversion (avoiding things), in order that we may neither fail in our desires, nor fall into that which we try to avoid;

if we read about desire and avoiding things so that we neither fail in our desires nor fall into what we try to avoid;

if we read what is said about duty, in order that remembering the relations (of things to one another) we may do nothing irrationally nor contrary to these relations;

if we read about duty so that, by remembering how things are related, we don't do anything irrational or contrary to these relations;

we should not be vexed in being hindered as to our readings, but we should be satisfied with doing the acts which are conformable (to the relations),

then we wouldn't be upset about being hindered from reading, but we would be content with doing actions that are in line with these relations,

and we should be reckoning not what so far we have been accustomed to reckon: "Today I have read so many verses, I have written so many;"

and we wouldn't be counting how many verses we've read or written today;

but (we should say), "Today I have employed my action as it is taught by the philosophers; I have not employed my desire; I have used avoidance (ἐκκλίσει) only with respect to things which are within the power of my will;

but instead, we'd say, "Today I've acted according to what the philosophers teach; I haven't let desire control me; I've only avoided things that are within my control;

I have not been afraid of such a person, I have not been prevailed upon by the entreaties of another; I have exercised my patience, my abstinence, my cooperation with others;"

259

I haven't been afraid of anyone, I haven't given in to anyone's pleas; I've practiced patience, self-control, and cooperation with others;"

and so we should thank God for what we ought to thank him.

and so we should thank God for the things we should be thankful for.

But now we do not know that we also in another way are like the many.

But right now, we don't realize that in another way, we're just like everyone else.

Another man is afraid that he shall not have power: you are afraid that you will.

Another person fears they won't have power, while you fear that you will.

Do not do so, my man; but as you ridicule him who is afraid that he shall not have power, so ridicule yourself also.

Don't be like that, my friend; and just as you might laugh at someone who fears not having power, you should also laugh at yourself.

For it makes no difference whether you are thirsty like a man who has a fever, or have a dread of water like a man who is mad.

Because it doesn't matter if you're thirsty like someone with a fever or if you're afraid of water like someone who's mad.

Or how will you still be able to say as Socrates did, "If so it pleases God, so let it be?"

How will you be able to say, like Socrates did, "If it pleases God, then let it be?"

Do you think that Socrates if he had been eager to pass his leisure in the Lyceum or in the Academy and to discourse daily with the young men, would have readily served in military expeditions so often as he did;

Do you think Socrates, if he had been eager to spend his free time in the Lyceum or the Academy talking with young men every day, would have so easily gone on military expeditions as often as he did?

and would he not have lamented and groaned, "Wretch that I am; I must now be miserable here, when I might be sunning myself in the Lyceum?"

And wouldn't he have complained and groaned, saying, "Poor me, I have to suffer here when I could be relaxing in the Lyceum?"

Why, was this your business, to sun yourself? And is it not your business to be happy, to be free from hindrance, free from impediment?

But was it really his job to just sun himself? Isn't it more important to be happy, free from obstacles, and free from hindrances?

And could he still have been Socrates, if he had lamented in this way: how would he still have been able to write Paeans in his prison?

And could he still be Socrates if he complained like that? How would he have been able to write hymns in his prison?

In short remember this, that what you shall prize which is beyond your will, so far you have destroyed your will.

In short, remember this: if you value anything beyond your control, you've already destroyed your will.

But these things are out of the power of the will, not only power (authority), but also a private condition: not only occupation (business), but also leisure.

But these things—power, a private life, work, and leisure—are all beyond your control.

"Now then must I live in this tumult?"

"So now do I have to live in this chaos?"

Why do you say tumult?

Why do you call it chaos?

"I mean among many men."

"I mean among many people."

Well what is the hardship?

But what's so hard about that?

Suppose that you are at Olympia: imagine it to be a panegyris (public assembly), where one is calling out one thing, another is doing another thing, and a third is pushing another person; in the baths there is a crowd: and who of us is not pleased with this assembly, and leaves it unwillingly?

Imagine you're at Olympia, at a public gathering where one person is shouting one thing, another person is doing something else, and someone else is pushing people around; in the baths, there's a crowd: but who among us doesn't enjoy this kind of gathering and leaves it reluctantly?

Be not difficult to please nor fastidious about what happens.

Don't be hard to please or picky about what happens.

"Vinegar is disagreeable, for it is sharp; honey is disagreeable, for it disturbs my habit of body. I do not like vegetables.

"Vinegar is unpleasant because it's sharp; honey is unpleasant because it upsets my stomach. I don't like vegetables.

262

So also I do not like leisure; it is a desert: I do not like a crowd; it is confusion."

In the same way, I don't like leisure; it's boring: I don't like crowds; they're chaotic."

But if circumstances make it necessary for you to live alone or with a few, call it quiet, and use the thing as you ought: talk with yourself, exercise the appearances (presented to you), work up your preconceptions.

But if you have to live alone or with just a few people, call it peace and use it as you should: talk with yourself, think about the things that appear to you, and challenge your assumptions.

If you fall into a crowd, call it a celebration of games, a panegyris, a festival: try to enjoy the festival with other men.

If you find yourself in a crowd, call it a celebration, a festival: try to enjoy the festival with others.

For what is a more pleasant sight to him who loves mankind than a number of men?

Because what's more pleasant to someone who loves people than seeing a lot of people?

We see with pleasure herds of horses or oxen: we are delighted when we see many ships: who is pained when he sees many men?

We enjoy watching herds of horses or oxen, and we're happy when we see many ships: who gets upset when they see a lot of people?

"But they deafen me with their cries."

"But their noise deafens me."

Then your hearing is impeded. What then is this to you?

So your hearing is blocked. But what does that have to do with you?

Is then the power of making use of appearances hindered?

Is your ability to make use of what appears to you hindered?

And who prevents you from using according to nature inclination to a thing and aversion from it; and movement towards a thing and movement from it?

Who's stopping you from naturally being drawn to or away from something; from moving toward or away from it?

What tumult (confusion) is able to do this?

What chaos can stop you from doing this?

Do you only bear in mind the general rules: what is mine? what is not mine? what is given (permitted) to me? what does God will that I should do now? what does he not will?

Just keep in mind the general rules: What's mine? What isn't mine? What's allowed for me? What does God want me to do now? What doesn't He want?

A little before he willed you to be at leisure, to talk with yourself, to write about these things, to read, to hear, to prepare yourself.

Earlier, He wanted you to have leisure, to talk with yourself, to write about these things, to read, to listen, to prepare yourself.

You had sufficient time for this.

You had enough time for this.

Now he says to you: Come now to the contest, show us what you have learned, how you have practiced the athletic art.

Now He says to you: Come to the contest, show us what you've learned, how you've practiced the art of living.

How long will you be exercised alone?

How long will you keep training alone?

Now is the opportunity for you to learn whether you are an athlete worthy of victory, or one of those who go about the world and are defeated.

Now is the chance to find out if you're an athlete worthy of victory, or just someone who wanders around getting defeated.

Why then are you vexed?

So why are you upset?

No contest is without confusion.

No contest is without some chaos.

There must be many who exercise themselves for the contest, many who call out to those who exercise themselves, many masters, many spectators.

There will be many who train for the contest, many who shout at those who train, many coaches, many spectators.

"But my wish is to live quietly."

"But I want to live quietly."

Lament then and groan as you deserve to do.

Then go ahead and complain and groan, as you deserve to.

For what other is a greater punishment than this to the untaught man and to him who disobeys the divine commands: to be grieved, to lament, to envy, in a word to be disappointed and to be unhappy?

What greater punishment is there for an ignorant person or someone who disobeys the divine commands than to be sad, to complain, to envy, in short, to be disappointed and unhappy?

Would you not release yourself from these things?

Don't you want to free yourself from these things?

"And how shall I release myself?"

"How can I free myself?"

Have you not often heard that you ought to remove entirely desire, apply aversion (turning away) to those things only which are within your power, that you ought to give up everything: body, property, fame, books, tumult, power, private station?

Haven't you often heard that you should get rid of all desires, that you should only turn away from things within your control, and that you should give up everything: your body, property, reputation, books, chaos, power, and your social status?

For whatever way you turn, you are a slave, you are subjected, you are hindered, you are compelled, you are entirely in the power of others.

No matter where you turn, you're a slave, you're controlled, you're blocked, you're forced, you're completely at the mercy of others.

But keep the words of Cleanthes in readiness:

But keep these words of Cleanthes ready:

Lead me, O Zeus, and thou necessity. —Iliad vi 490.

"Lead me, O Zeus, and Destiny."

Is it your will that I should go to Rome? I will go to Rome.

Do you want me to go to Rome? I'll go to Rome.

To Gyara? I will go to Gyara.

To Gyara? I'll go to Gyara.

To Athens? I will go to Athens.

To Athens? I'll go to Athens.

To prison? I will go to prison.

To prison? I'll go to prison.

If you should once say, "When shall a man go to Athens?" you are undone.

If you ever say, "When can I go to Athens?" you're already lost.

It is a necessary consequence that this desire, if it is not accomplished, must make you unhappy;

Because if this desire isn't fulfilled, it will make you unhappy;

and if it is accomplished, it must make you vain, since you are elated at things at which you ought not to be elated;

and if it is fulfilled, it will make you vain, because you'll be happy about things you shouldn't be happy about;

and on the other hand, if you are impeded, it must make you wretched because you fall into that which you would not fall into.

and on the other hand, if you're blocked, it will make you miserable because you'll end up in situations you didn't want to be in.

Give up then all these things.

So give up all these things.

"Athens is a good place."

"Athens is a nice place."

But happiness is much better; and to be free from passions, free from disturbance, for your affairs not to depend on any man.

But happiness is much better; and being free from passions, free from disturbances, and not depending on anyone else for your well-being.

"There is tumult at Rome and visits of salutation."

"There's chaos in Rome and people visiting each other."

But happiness is an equivalent for all troublesome things.

But happiness makes up for all the trouble.

If then the time comes for these things, why do you not take away the wish to avoid them?

So when the time comes for these things, why don't you just let go of the desire to avoid them?

What necessity is there to carry a burden like an ass, and to be beaten with a stick?

Why do you need to carry a burden like a donkey and get beaten with a stick?

But if you do not so, consider that you must always be a slave to him who has it in his power to effect your release, and also to impede you, and you must serve him as an evil genius.

But if you don't do this, remember that you'll always be a slave to whoever has the power to either free you or block you, and you'll serve him as if he were a wicked spirit.

There is only one way to happiness, and let this rule be ready both in the morning and during the day and by night: the rule is not to look towards things which are out of the power of our will, to think that nothing is our own, to give up all things to the Divinity, to Fortune;

There's only one path to happiness, and keep this rule in mind morning, noon, and night: don't focus on things outside of your control, don't think that anything belongs to you, and give everything up to God and Fate;

to make them the superintendents of these things, whom Zeus also has made so;

let them manage these things, just as Zeus has made them managers;

for a man to observe that only which is his own, that which cannot be hindered;

focus only on what's yours, what can't be stopped;

and when we read, to refer our reading to this only, and our writing and our listening.

and when we read, let it be for this purpose only, and the same goes for writing and listening.

For this reason I cannot call the man industrious if I hear this only: that he reads and writes;

That's why I can't call someone hardworking just because they read and write;

and even if a man adds that he reads all night, I cannot say so, if he knows not to what he should refer his reading.

and even if they say they read all night, I still can't say they're hardworking if they don't know why they're reading.

For neither do you say that a man is industrious if he keeps awake for a girl; nor do I.

Because you wouldn't call someone hardworking if they stay up all night for a girl, and neither would I.

But if he does it (reads and writes) for reputation, I say that he is a lover of reputation.

But if someone reads and writes for fame, I'd say they're just a lover of fame.

And if he does it for money, I say that he is a lover of money, not a lover of labor;

And if they do it for money, I'd say they're a lover of money, not of hard work;

and if he does it through love of learning, I say that he is a lover of learning.

and if they do it because they love learning, I'd say they're a lover of learning.

But if he refers his labor to his own ruling power, that he may keep it in a state conformable to nature and pass his life in that state, then only do I say that he is industrious.

But if they direct their work towards maintaining their mind in line with nature and living their life in that state, then I'd say they're truly hardworking.

For never commend a man on account of these things which are common to all, but on account of his opinions (principles);

Because you should never praise someone for things everyone does, but for their principles;

for these are the things which belong to each man, which make his actions bad or good.

because these are what belong to each person, and these make their actions good or bad.

Remembering these rules, rejoice in that which is present, and be content with the things which come in season.

By keeping these rules in mind, enjoy what's happening now, and be content with things that come at the right time.

If you see anything which you have learned and inquired about occurring to you in your course of life, be delighted at it.

If you notice something happening in your life that you've learned about, be happy about it.

If you have laid aside or have lessened bad disposition and a habit of reviling; if you have done so with rash temper, obscene words, hastiness, sluggishness;

If you've managed to reduce or get rid of a bad attitude or a habit of complaining, if you've done the same with anger, cursing, impatience, or laziness;

if you are not moved by what you formerly were, and not in the same way as you once were, you can celebrate a festival daily, today because you have behaved well in one act, and tomorrow because you have behaved well in another.

if you're no longer affected by the things that used to bother you, and not in the same way as before, then you can celebrate every day— today because you acted well in one way, and tomorrow because you did well in another.

How much greater is this a reason for making sacrifices than a consulship or the government of a province?

Isn't this a much better reason to be thankful than getting a high office or governing a province?

These things come to you from yourself and from the gods.

These things come from both yourself and the gods.

Remember this: who gives these things and to whom, and for what purpose.

Remember who gives these things, to whom, and why.

If you cherish yourself in these thoughts, do you still think that it makes any difference where you shall be happy, where you shall please God?

If you hold on to these thoughts, do you still think it matters where you'll be happy or where you'll please God?

Are not the gods equally distant from all places?

Aren't the gods just as close to all places?

Do they not see from all places alike that which is going on?

Don't they see everything equally from all places?

Chapter 5
To Those That are Contentious and Brutal

A wise and good person never fights with anyone, and as much as possible, they prevent others from fighting too. We see a great example of this in the life of Socrates. He not only avoided fights himself but also stopped others from quarreling when he could. Look at Xenophon's Symposium to see how many arguments Socrates settled, how he handled people like Thrasymachus, Polus, and Callicles, and how he managed to deal with his wife and son when they were difficult or tried to argue with him.

Socrates understood that no one can control what another person thinks or decides. He only cared about controlling what was in his power. And what was that? It wasn't about making others act a certain way because that's beyond his control. Instead, it was about making sure he lived according to nature, doing what was right, no matter what others did. This is what a wise and good person always aims for. It's not about being the commander of an army or getting married, but if these things happen, the goal is to keep your inner peace and integrity.

If you wish that your son or wife wouldn't make mistakes, you're wishing for something that's out of your control. Learning what you can control and what you can't is the key. So, if you understand this, how can there be any room for quarrels? Are you surprised when bad things happen or when people act badly? Shouldn't you expect bad people to act even worse than they do? If someone insults you, be thankful they didn't hit you. If they hit you, be thankful they didn't wound you. And if they wound you, be thankful they didn't kill you.

Why should someone who hasn't learned that people should love each other act differently? Your neighbor might throw stones, but does that mean you did something wrong? If your belongings are broken, remember that you are not your possessions—you are a free mind. If you're like a wolf, you'll want to bite back and throw more stones. But if you're a person, you should look inside yourself to see what kind of person you are.

Just like a horse is unhappy when it can't run, a person is unhappy when they lose their integrity and honesty. We should pity a person who loses these things, not for losing their belongings or land, because those aren't truly theirs—they belong to others. We should care about the character and principles with which a person was born, just like we care about the stamp on a coin. If the stamp is that of Trajan, we accept it, but if it's Nero's, we reject it as counterfeit. The same goes for people: if a person has qualities like kindness, sociability, and tolerance, we accept them as a fellow citizen and neighbor. But if they are full of anger and resentment, then they are not truly a person.

Should you worry about being despised by those who don't know you? What does their opinion matter? No true craftsman cares about the opinion of someone who doesn't understand their craft. And if people are more hostile to you because of your good nature, why does that bother you? Can they harm your will or prevent you from seeing things as they truly are? No, they can't. So why be disturbed or show fear? Instead, show them that you are at peace with everyone, no matter what they do, and laugh at those who think they can harm you. They don't know who you really are or where your true good and evil lie, because they can't touch what's really yours.

In the same way, people who are safe in a strong city mock those who try to attack it, saying, "Look at all the effort they're wasting! Our walls are strong, and we have enough supplies for a long time." In the same way, nothing can truly harm you if your beliefs are strong. No wall or body is as strong as a person's beliefs, and nothing outside of you can truly harm you if you don't let it.

If you choose to protect the things that truly matter—like your beliefs and principles—then you will remain safe. Remember that it's not the things that happen to you that hurt you, but your opinions about those things. This is the real battle, the real civil war within yourself. What made Eteocles and Polynices enemies was nothing else than their opinions about royal power and exile—thinking one was the worst evil and the other the greatest good.

This understanding is what helped Socrates manage his household and deal with a difficult wife and son. He didn't care when his wife poured water on his head or trampled on a cake sent to him because he knew these things didn't truly matter. He remained in control of his will, knowing that no one could truly harm him unless he allowed it.

These beliefs bring love in a household, harmony in a state, peace between nations, and gratitude to God. They make a person cheerful and confident in all circumstances, knowing that external things are beyond their control and not truly important. We can write and talk about these ideas, but often we don't truly believe in them. We're like the Spartans who are brave at home but cunning and deceitful when they go abroad. We are lions in the classroom, but foxes outside of it.

Chapter 6
To Those Who are Distressed at Being Pitied

Someone might say, "It makes me sad when people pity me." But ask yourself, is it really your problem if someone else pities you, or is it their problem? Can you actually stop them from feeling pity? You might think, "I can show them that I don't need their pity." But are you sure you don't deserve pity, or are you just pretending? You might believe you don't need pity, but people don't pity you for the reasons you think. They pity you because you're poor, don't hold important jobs, or because of sickness and death.

Now, are you ready to convince everyone that none of these things are really bad and that a poor person without a fancy job can still be happy? Or are you going to try to show off that you're rich and powerful? The second option is something a boastful or foolish person would do. Think about what it would take to keep up that appearance. You'd need to hire servants, buy fancy dishes, and display them publicly, even if it's always the same set. You'd need to wear fancy clothes and try to look more handsome and noble than you really are. You'd need to show that you're friends with important people and try to get invited to their homes or at least make people think you dine with them.

If you choose this path just to avoid being pitied, you'll have to do all these things. But the first path, trying to change everyone's mind about what is truly good or bad, is impossible and would take forever. Even Zeus hasn't convinced everyone about what is truly good or bad. Do you think you can do it? The only person you can truly convince is yourself. But if you haven't even convinced yourself, how can you hope to convince others?

How long have you lived with yourself? How much power do you have to convince yourself? Who is closer to you or more interested in your well-being than you are? Yet, you still haven't fully convinced yourself. Are things not upside down right now? Haven't you been trying to learn how to be free from grief, to avoid being disturbed, to avoid feeling low, and to be free?

Haven't you heard that there's only one way to achieve this? You need to give up worrying about things that are not within your control, admit that they belong to others, and not let them trouble you. What others think about you—whether they pity you or not—is not something you can control. So why let it bother you?

Won't you stop worrying about others and focus on being your own student and teacher? Other people will decide for themselves whether they want to live in a way that goes against nature. But for you, no one is closer to you than yourself. Why do you listen to philosophers, agree with them, but still feel no relief? Are you really so foolish? In other areas, you've learned quickly—whether it's reading, wrestling, or solving problems. Has reason not convinced you?

From the beginning, you've chosen what's rational, and you read, listen, and write about these things. You haven't found any stronger reason than living according to nature. So what's missing? Have you not completely gotten rid of your wrong opinions? Have you not practiced applying the right opinions to real-life actions, but instead let them rust like unused armor?

You don't just settle for learning in exercises or in reading and writing. You analyze logical arguments and even create your own. But when it comes to the teachings that can actually free you from grief, fear, and passion, you don't practice them. You care more about what others think of you and whether they see you as someone worth noticing or someone who is happy.

Wretched man, look at what you're saying about yourself. What do you think you are, in your opinions, desires, and actions? Do you care more about what others think of you than about how you see yourself? Are you pained because people don't pity you in the way you think they should? If you're pained by pity, don't you make yourself deserving of it? If you care about being pitied, how are you not an object of pity?

Remember what Antisthenes said: "It's a royal thing, O Cyrus, to do right and be spoken of poorly." —Iliad vi 490. If your head is healthy, but people think you have a headache, what does it matter? If you're free from fever, but people pity you as if you had one, does it affect you? You could even say with a sad face, "Yes, I've been ill for a long time," while secretly laughing at their pity.

Why can't you do the same when people pity you for being poor? If you have the right opinion about poverty, why should their pity bother you? If you're not in power but have the right opinion about power, why care if others pity you? Let them look after themselves. You're not hungry or cold, but because they might be, they think you are too. Should you go around announcing, "Don't be mistaken, I'm fine. I don't worry about poverty or power, I only care about having the right opinions. That's what I care about."

What foolish talk this is. How can you claim to have the right opinions when you're not content with what you are, but are bothered by how others see you?

You might say, "But others will get more and be preferred to me." Isn't it reasonable for those who work hard to get more in the areas they've worked on? They've worked for power, and you've worked on your opinions. They've worked for wealth, and you've worked on using the right perspectives. See if they are better at what you've worked on. Are they less disappointed in their desires? Do they avoid things better than you do? Are they better at aiming their actions, at behaving properly as men, sons, parents, or in other roles?

If they have power and you don't, remind yourself that you didn't work for power, while they did. It's unreasonable to think that you should have more of what you haven't worked for.

"But since I care about right opinions, it's more reasonable for me to have power," you might say. Yes, in the area of opinions, you should have more. But in the area where they've worked harder, they should have more. It's like thinking that because you have the right opinions, you should be better at archery than an archer, or better at metalwork than a smith. If you want power, focus on it, and then lament if you don't get it.

Right now, you're saying you focus on one thing, but you actually want another. You can't mix these different pursuits. Each day, some people wake up thinking about who to flatter, who to please, and how to gain favor. They might lie or deceive to achieve their goals. But if you've focused on using the right opinions, then each morning, ask yourself, "What do I need to do today to be free from passion and disturbance? What am I? A body? A piece of property? No, I'm a rational being."

Reflect on your actions. Have you done anything unfriendly or unsocial? Have you done everything you should have done? There's a big difference in what people desire, what they do, and what they wish for. Yet you still expect to share equally in things you haven't worked for while they have. And you're surprised when they pity you? But they don't mind if you pity them because they believe they have what's good, and you don't. That's why you're not satisfied with what you have and want what they have.

If you were truly convinced that you possess what is truly good, you wouldn't care what others say about you.

Chapter 7
On Freedom From Fear

What makes a tyrant so scary? You might say it's the guards, their swords, the people who stay close to him, and those who keep others out. But why isn't a child scared if you bring them to the tyrant, even when he's surrounded by his guards? Is it because the child doesn't understand what's happening? So, if someone does understand what guards are and that they carry swords, but goes to the tyrant because they want to die and think it will be easier if someone else kills them, are they still afraid of the guards? No, because they actually want what the guards can do.

Now, if someone doesn't want to die or live at all costs, but only lives as long as they're allowed, what stops them from approaching the tyrant without fear? Nothing. If someone feels the same way about their possessions as that person felt about their body, or feels the same way about their children and spouse, and if they are so upset or hopeless that they don't care whether they own these things or not, like kids who play with toys and fight over the game but don't care about the toys themselves, then this person doesn't care about the stuff (possessions) but only about enjoying and using them. So, what tyrant or guards or swords can scare this person?

If someone can become so indifferent to these things because of madness or the Galilaeans can become like this out of habit, is it possible that no one can learn from reason and understanding that God made everything in the universe perfect and free from obstacles, and that every part of it works for the good of the whole? While other animals can't understand how the world works, human beings, who are rational, have the ability to think about these things and

279

understand their place in the universe, and that it's right for the parts to serve the whole. And besides being naturally noble, big-hearted, and free, humans see that some things around them are within their control and free from obstacles, while other things are beyond their control and can be blocked by others. The things that are free from obstacles are within our will, while those that can be blocked are beyond our control.

For this reason, if someone believes that their happiness and well-being come from things that are free from obstacles and under their control, they will be free, successful, happy, safe, big-hearted, pious, and grateful to God for everything. They won't complain about or blame the things that are beyond their control. But if someone thinks their happiness and well-being depend on external things that are beyond their control, they will inevitably be blocked, hindered, and become a slave to those who control the things they desire and fear. Such a person must inevitably become irreligious because they think God is harming them, unjust because they always demand more than what's fair, and cowardly and weak.

What stops a person who understands these things clearly from living with a light heart, easily handling life, quietly waiting for whatever happens, and calmly dealing with what has already happened? Would you ask me to endure poverty? Come and see what poverty is like when it finds someone who knows how to handle it well. Do you want me to have power? Give me power, and I'll take the trouble that comes with it too. How about exile? Wherever I go, I'll be fine because it wasn't the place that made me happy, but my beliefs, which I'll take with me wherever I go. No one can take them from me; they're mine alone, and as long as I have them, I'm content, no matter where I am or what I'm doing. But now, it's time to die. Why do you say "to die" like it's a tragic event? Just say what it really is: it's time for the body to break down into the things it was made from. And what's so scary about that? What's going to disappear from the universe? What new or amazing thing is going to happen? Is this why a tyrant is scary? Is this why guards with big, sharp swords seem intimidating? Tell this to others, but I've thought about all these things. No one has power over me. I've been set free; I know what's right, and no one can make me a slave. I know who I am, and I know who my real judges are. You think you control my body? What does that matter to me? You think you control my property? What does that matter to me? You think you control my exile or my chains? Well, I'll leave all of that and even my poor body when you say so. Test your power, and you'll see how far it goes.

So, who am I supposed to fear now? Those who guard the tyrant's bedchamber? Are they supposed to do something to me? Lock me out? If they find out I want to get in, then let them lock me out. Why do I go to the door then? Because I think it's my role, while the play lasts, to take part in it. So how do I avoid getting locked out? Because unless someone lets me in, I choose not to go in. I'm always content with what happens because I believe that what God chooses is better than what I choose. I'll follow Him as a servant and a follower. I have the same goals as He does, the same desires. In other words, I want what He wants. There's no way to lock me out, but there is for those who try to force their way in. Why don't I try to force my way in? Because I know nothing good is being handed out inside to those who get in. But when I hear someone called lucky because Caesar honors them, I ask, what exactly did they get? A province to govern? Did they also get the right opinion on how to govern? The office of a Prefect? Did they also get the ability to do the job well? Why do I still try to get inside Caesar's chamber? A man throws out dried figs and nuts, and the children grab them and fight each other for them. Adults don't, because they think it's a small thing. But if a man threw out shells, even the children wouldn't grab them. Provinces are given out: let the children worry about that. Money is given out: let the children worry about that. Praetorships and consulships are given out: let the children scramble for them, let them be shut out, beaten, and kiss the hands of the giver, of the slaves. But to me, these are just dried figs and nuts. So what? If you don't get them while Caesar is tossing them around, don't be upset. If a dried fig falls into your lap, take it and eat it; that's how much value it has. But if I have to bend down and turn one over, or get turned over by someone else, and flatter those who got inside Caesar's chamber, then a dried fig isn't worth the trouble, nor is anything else that's not really good, which the philosophers have taught me not to value.

Show me the guards' swords. Look how big they are and how sharp. So what do these big and sharp swords do? They kill. And what does a fever do? The same thing. And what does a falling tile do? The same thing. Should I be amazed at these things, worship them, and walk around as a slave to all of them? I hope not. But when I've learned that everything that comes into existence must also disappear, so the universe doesn't stop or get stuck, I no longer care whether a fever, a tile, or a soldier ends my life. But if I have to choose between them, I know the soldier will do it with less trouble and faster. So, when I neither fear what a tyrant can do to me nor want anything he can give, why am I still amazed? Why am I still confused? Why do I fear the guards? Why am I happy if he talks to me nicely and receives me? Why do I tell others how he talked to me? Is he a Socrates? Is he a Diogenes that his praise should prove my worth? Have I been eager to copy his morals? But I keep playing along and go to him, and serve him as long as he doesn't ask me to do something foolish or unreasonable. But if he says to me, "Go and bring Leon of Salamis," I say to him, "Find someone else because I'm not playing anymore." (The tyrant says): "Take him to prison." I go; that's part of the game. "But your head will be cut off!" Does the tyrant's head always stay in place, and the heads of those who obey him? "But you will be thrown out unburied." If the corpse is me, I'll be thrown out; but if I'm different from the corpse, then speak more accurately according to the truth, and don't try to scare me. These things are scary to children and fools. But if someone has entered a philosopher's school and still doesn't know what they are, they deserve to be full of fear and to flatter those they used to flatter. If they haven't learned yet that they're not just flesh, bones, or muscles, but the mind that uses these body parts and controls them and understands the world, then they deserve to be afraid.

"Yes, but this kind of talk makes us despise the laws." And what kind of talk makes people more obedient to the laws? Things that are under the control of a fool aren't laws. And yet, see how this kind of talk makes us act the way we should, even towards these foolish people; because it teaches us not to seek the things they can surpass us in. This talk teaches us to give up our bodies, our property, our children, parents, and siblings, and to let go of everything except our opinions, which even Zeus has willed to be each person's private property. Where is the disobedience to the law here? Where is the foolishness? Where you are stronger, I let you win; but where I am stronger, you should let me win, because I've studied this, and you haven't. It's your study to live in houses with fancy floors, to have servants at your beck and call, to wear fine clothes, to have many hunters, musicians, and actors. Do I want any of these things? Have you studied opinions and your own rational mind? Do you know what it's made of, how it's put together, how it works, and what powers it has? Then why are you upset if someone who has studied these things better than you has the advantage? But these things are the most important. And who stops you from working on these things and taking care of them? Who has a better supply of books, more free time, and more people to help you? Just turn your attention to these things at last, even if only for a little while, to your own mind. Think about what it is that you have, where it came from, this thing that uses all your other abilities, tests them, chooses, and rejects. But as long as you focus on external things, you'll have those things better than anyone else, but you'll have your mind just as you choose to have it: neglected and filthy.

Chapter 8
To Those Who Hastily Assume the Character of Philosophers

Never praise or blame someone just because they do something that most people do. Don't assume they are skilled or unskilled because of it. By doing this, you will avoid being too quick to judge or being unfair. For example, if someone bathes very quickly, is that wrong? No, it's not. But what does it mean? It just means they bathe quickly. Does it mean everything they do is done well? Not at all. Only actions that come from good thinking are done well; those that come from bad thinking are done poorly. So, until you understand why a person does something, don't praise or blame them for it. But it's hard to know a person's thoughts just by looking at their actions.

If you see someone using a hammer, do you automatically assume they're a carpenter? No. What about someone who sings—do you assume they're a musician? Not necessarily. Now, if you see someone wearing a philosopher's cloak and growing a beard, do you assume they're a philosopher? Just because they dress like one doesn't mean they are one. So, if you see someone who looks like a philosopher acting foolishly, don't say, "Look at what that philosopher is doing!" Instead, you should say, "This person isn't really a philosopher." If we did this in other professions, we would never say, "Carpenters are bad at their job," just because we saw one person using a hammer poorly. We'd say, "This person isn't a good carpenter."

But when it comes to philosophy, people do the opposite. If they see someone acting against what a philosopher teaches, they don't take away the title of philosopher. Instead, they assume that person is a philosopher and conclude that philosophy itself must be useless.

Why does this happen? Because we value the skills of a carpenter or musician and judge them based on their actions, but we don't value philosophy the same way. We judge philosophers only by their appearance, which leads to confusion. Other professions don't take their name from what they wear but from their skills and the tools they use. What is the tool of a philosopher? Is it a cloak? No, it's reason. What is the goal of a philosopher? Is it to wear a cloak? No, it's to have correct thinking.

Before you judge a philosopher for acting wrongly, first see if they are doing what they profess. But now, when you see someone acting inappropriately, you say, "Look at the philosopher," as if the name "philosopher" belongs to someone who behaves badly. But you wouldn't say, "Look at the carpenter," if you knew a carpenter was cheating or overeating. You understand, to some degree, what a philosopher should be, but you get confused and don't pay attention.

Even those who call themselves philosophers often start by focusing on things that don't really matter. As soon as they put on the cloak and grow a beard, they say, "I am a philosopher." But no one says, "I am a musician," just because they've bought a guitar, and no one says, "I am a blacksmith," just because they've put on an apron. The tools are made for the art, and the name comes from the art, not the tools.

Euphrates said it well: "I tried for a long time to be a philosopher without anyone knowing it. And this helped me because when I did something good, I knew I did it for myself, not for an audience. I ate well, composed myself well, walked properly—all for myself and God.

If I did something wrong, I didn't endanger philosophy or hurt others by my actions. For this reason, people who didn't know me were surprised that I spent so much time with philosophers but wasn't one myself. What harm was there in being known as a philosopher by my actions and not by outward signs?"

See how I eat, drink, sleep, and deal with challenges. See how I control my desires, how I avoid things I shouldn't want, how I handle my relationships, both natural and acquired. See how I live free from confusion and obstacles. Judge me by these things if you can. But if you're so blind that you can't recognize a good blacksmith unless you see him with a hammer, then what does it matter if I'm not recognized by such a foolish judge?

Socrates wasn't known as a philosopher by most people. They would come to him and ask to be introduced to philosophers. Was Socrates upset about this? Did he say, "Don't you know that I'm a philosopher?" No, he would take them to meet other philosophers, satisfied with simply being a philosopher himself. He didn't need to be seen as one. He didn't care if people didn't think he was a philosopher because he focused on what really mattered to him.

What is the job of a good and honorable person? Is it to have many students? Not at all. Those who care about that can focus on it. Was Socrates' job to study difficult ideas? Others can handle that. So, what was Socrates focused on? He was focused on what could harm or benefit him. If anyone could harm him, he wasn't doing anything. If he was waiting for someone else to help him, he was nothing. If he wanted something and didn't get it, he was unlucky. He challenged anyone to this contest, and I don't think he would have refused a challenge from anyone.

What do you think? Did Socrates go around saying, "I'm a great man"? Not at all. That would be the act of a fool, saying, "I'm free from worry and disturbance. My friends, while you're all anxious and upset about trivial things, I'm the only one free from all troubles." Is it not enough for you to be free from pain unless you announce it to everyone? Do you need to gather those suffering from headaches, fevers, and other ailments and say, "Look at me! I'm free from all pain"? This is empty boasting unless you can immediately show them how to be free from pain too and offer your own health as an example.

That's the true Cynic, honored by Zeus with the scepter and crown, who says, "Look, people, you're searching for happiness and peace in the wrong places. I'm sent by God to show you by example. I have no property, house, wife, children, bed, coat, or tools, and yet I'm healthy and happy. Test me, and if you see that I'm free from trouble, I'll tell you how I've been cured." This is noble and kind. But it's the job of Zeus or someone he chooses to serve this purpose, to always act in a way that supports the truth of virtue and doesn't undermine it.

But now, some people are drawn to philosophy as someone with a bad stomach might be drawn to food they can't digest. They rush towards the symbols of philosophy, like the cloak and beard, and argue with anyone who crosses their path. If they see someone in a warm coat, they'll pick a fight with them. Man, first, learn to handle the cold. Make sure your desires are not like those of a sick person or a pregnant woman. First, try to keep your philosophy to yourself for a while. Just as fruit needs time to grow and ripen, you need time to develop before you're ready to show yourself. If a plant sprouts too soon, it will wither and die in the cold. You, too, are like a plant that has grown too quickly. The cold will kill you because you've rushed into fame too soon. You think you're something special, but you're just a fool among fools. You've been harmed by the cold, even if you think you're still thriving.

Let us grow naturally. Why do you expose us before we're ready? Why do you force us? We're not yet strong enough to face the world. Let the roots grow, then the first joint, then the second, and then the third. Only then will the fruit naturally appear, even if I don't choose for it to happen. Who, having developed such great principles, doesn't recognize their own power and move towards the right actions? A bull doesn't need anyone to tell him to fight when he sees a predator. A dog doesn't need to be told to chase a wild animal. If I have the qualities of a good person, why should I wait for someone else to push me to act? Right now, I don't have those qualities, believe me. So why do you want me to wither before my time, as you have?

Chapter 9
To Someone Who Has Lost Their Sense of Shame

When you see someone else with power, remember that you don't have the desire for power. When you see someone who is rich, think about what you have instead of money. If you have nothing in place of riches, you might feel unhappy. But if you don't want riches, understand that you have something more valuable than wealth. If someone else has a beautiful wife, remember that you're lucky not to crave a beautiful wife. Do these things seem small to you? Think about how much those who are rich, powerful, or with beautiful spouses would give to be able to not care about wealth, power, or even those they love.

Do you understand how a thirsty person with a fever feels? It's nothing like how a healthy person feels thirst. A healthy person stops being thirsty after drinking, but a sick person feels nauseated after drinking, may vomit, and ends up even thirstier. Wanting and having wealth, power, or a beautiful spouse can be like that—leading to jealousy, fear, indecent thoughts, and bad behavior.

You might ask, "What have I lost?" My friend, you used to be modest, and now you're not. Haven't you lost something? Instead of reading wise philosophers like Chrysippus and Zeno, you're now interested in stories of people who seduce women. Haven't you lost something? Instead of admiring Socrates and Diogenes, you admire someone who can attract and corrupt the most women. You want to appear handsome and make efforts to look good, even though you aren't. You like to show off fancy clothes to attract women, and you think finding some fancy hair oil makes you happy. But before, you didn't care about any of this. You were more interested in good conversation, noble people, and high-minded ideas. You used to sleep, walk, and dress like a good man. Now, can you really say you've lost nothing?

Do people only lose money? Isn't losing modesty a loss? Isn't losing decent behavior a loss? If someone has lost these things, haven't they suffered a loss? Maybe you don't think these things matter. But there was a time when you believed losing these was the only real loss, and you were determined not to be disturbed from living a good life.

Now, nobody is disturbing you from living well except yourself. Fight with yourself, bring yourself back to decency, modesty, and freedom. If someone had told you that I was forced to become an adulterer, dress like you do, or use perfumed oils, wouldn't you have been outraged and wanted to defend me? Now, will you not defend yourself? And how much easier is it to help yourself? There's no need to hurt anyone, chain anyone up, insult anyone, or go to court. All you need to do is talk to yourself, the person who's easiest to persuade. Nobody has more power over you than you do.

First, condemn what you're doing. Then, after you've condemned it, don't give up on yourself. Don't be like weak-spirited people who, after giving in once, completely give up and let themselves be swept away like they're caught in a flood. Look at what trainers do with boys. If a boy falls, they say, "Get up and try again until you're strong." Do the same with yourself. Be assured that nothing is more adaptable than the human soul. You just need to exercise your will, and it can be corrected. On the other hand, if you're careless, you'll ruin everything. Ruin and help both come from within.

You might ask, "What do I gain?" What greater gain is there than this? You'll go from being shameless to modest, from being disorderly to orderly, from being untrustworthy to faithful, from being reckless to self-controlled. If you seek anything more than this, keep doing what you're doing—but not even a god can help you now.

Chapter 10
What We Should Disregard and What We Should Value

People's difficulties mostly come from things outside their control. They feel helpless about these external things. They ask questions like, "What should I do?" or "How will this turn out?" or "Will this happen?" or "Will that happen?" These are the kinds of questions people ask when they focus on things they can't control.

But who ever asks, "How can I make sure I don't believe something that's false?" or "How can I keep myself from turning away from what's true?" If someone is good enough to worry about these kinds of things, I would tell him, "Why are you worried? These things are within your control. Be confident; don't rush into agreeing with something before you've thought it through properly."

On the other hand, if someone is anxious about wanting something but afraid he won't get it, or if he fears ending up with something he's trying to avoid, I would first give him a big hug because he's thinking about his own life and actions instead of worrying about things outside of himself that others usually fuss over.

Then I would say to him, "If you don't want to end up wanting something you can't have or trying to avoid something but failing, then don't desire things that belong to others or try to avoid things that aren't under your control. If you don't follow this rule, you're going to end up frustrated by not getting what you want and stuck with what you don't."

What's so hard about this? Where is there any reason to ask, "How will this turn out?" or "What will happen next?"

Isn't what happens outside your control? Yes, it is. And isn't the nature of good and bad based on things that are within your control? Yes, it is. So, can anyone stop you from handling things the right way, according to nature? No, they can't. So, stop asking, "How will it be?" No matter how it turns out, you'll handle it well, and the outcome will be good for you.

Imagine if Hercules said, "How can I make sure I don't run into a big lion?" or "How can I avoid meeting a wild boar?" or "How can I keep from running into bad people?" Why would he care about that? If a big boar shows up, he'll have a bigger challenge to overcome. If bad people show up, he'll get rid of them and make the world a better place.

You might say, "But what if I die in the process?" Then you'll die doing something noble. Since everyone has to die someday, isn't it better to be found doing something worthwhile, like helping others or being kind?

But if I can't be found doing great things, at least let me be found doing something within my control, like improving myself, practicing using my thoughts wisely, working on staying calm, and treating people the right way. If I succeed in these areas, then I'll move on to the next goal: making sure my judgments about things are correct.

If death finds me while I'm busy doing these things, that's enough for me. I can stretch out my hands to God and say, "I've used the tools you gave me to understand your plan and follow it. I haven't disrespected you with my actions. See how I've used my thoughts and beliefs? Have I ever blamed you? Have I ever been unhappy with what happens, or wished things were different? Have I ever tried to go against the natural order of things? I'm thankful that you gave me life, and I'm grateful for everything you've given me. I'm content with the time I've had, and now I return everything to you."

Isn't this a good way to live? And isn't it a good way to die?

But to be able to say these things, you have to let go of some other things. You can't want to be a powerful leader and also be able to live this way. If you want things that belong to others, you lose what's truly yours. That's just how things work—nothing is free.

And where's the surprise in that? If you want to be a leader, you'll have to stay awake at night, run around pleasing people, flatter everyone, exhaust yourself by standing at the doors of important people, say and do things that don't suit a free person, and give gifts to many people. And what do you get in return? You get a position where you can give orders a few times, host some games, and throw fancy dinners. Or if you disagree, show me what else there is besides these things.

On the other hand, if you want peace of mind, freedom from worry, a good night's sleep, to be truly awake when you're awake, and to fear nothing, then you'll need to give something up and put in some effort. But if you lose something while focusing on these things, or if something you value is wasted or someone else gets what you thought you deserved, will you immediately get upset? Or will you consider what you've gained in return and realize how much you've received in exchange?

Do you expect to get something so valuable for nothing? And how could you? You can't focus on both external things and your inner self. If you want external things, you'll have to give up working on your inner self. If you don't, you'll lose both because you're trying to do two things at once.

You might spill oil or break household items. So what? But you'll remain calm. A fire might destroy your books, but you'll still treat situations the right way. "But I'll have nothing to eat," you might say. If you're that unfortunate, then death is like a safe harbor where you can find refuge. Death is a safe harbor for everyone, which is why life isn't so hard. Whenever you choose, you can leave, and you won't have to endure any more suffering.

So why worry? Why lose sleep over things? After thinking about what's truly good and bad, you should say, "These are within my power, and no one can take them from me or force bad things on me against my will."

Then you can rest easy, knowing that what truly matters is safe. As for the things that belong to others, let those who get them worry about them. I can only control what's mine, and I'll do my best with that. Everything else is up to the one who controls everything.

When a person understands this, they don't toss and turn at night worrying about what might happen. They don't regret losing a friend like Patroclus or Antilochus or Menelaus, because they knew from the beginning that no friend is immortal. They didn't fool themselves into thinking their friend would outlive them and take care of their children. If you did think that, you were foolish. Why blame yourself or cry like a child?

You might say, "But my friend used to serve my meals." Well, he did that because he was alive. But now he's gone, so someone else will serve you. If that person dies, you'll find another.

If the pot you cook your meals in breaks, does that mean you'll starve because you lost your favorite pot? No, you'll go out and buy a new one.

And if you say, "No greater ill than this could happen to me," like it says in the Iliad, remember that it's not the loss that hurts you. You just need to stop blaming your situation and realize that these things happen to everyone.

Do you think Homer wrote these stories to show us that even the strongest, richest, and most handsome people, when they don't have the right mindset, can still be miserable?

Chapter 11
On Cleanliness

Some people wonder whether caring for others is part of human nature. But I think those same people would have no doubt that a love for cleanliness is definitely part of human nature. If humans are different from animals in any way, it's this. When we see an animal cleaning itself, we often say with surprise, "That animal is acting like a human!" On the other hand, if a person criticizes an animal for being dirty, we immediately excuse the animal by saying, "Well, it's not a human." So we believe there's something special in humans, something we first received from the Gods. Because the Gods are naturally pure and free from corruption, the more humans use their reason, the more they are drawn to cleanliness and purity. But since it's impossible for human nature to be completely pure, because we are made up of different materials, reason is used to make us love cleanliness as much as possible.

The first and highest form of cleanliness is in the soul, and the same goes for impurity. You can't see the impurity of the soul the way you can see dirt on the body. But when it comes to the soul, what could make it dirty except for its own bad judgments? The actions of the soul include moving toward or away from something, feeling desire or aversion, preparing, planning, and agreeing to something. So, what makes these actions dirty and impure? Nothing else but the soul's bad judgments. Therefore, the impurity of the soul is its bad opinions, and to purify the soul, we must plant good opinions in it. A soul is pure when it has good opinions because only then is it free from disturbance and pollution in its actions.

We should try to do the same with our bodies, as much as we can. It's natural for mucus to flow from the nose, given how the human body is made. That's why nature provided us with hands and nostrils to remove it. If someone doesn't wipe away the mucus, they aren't behaving like a human. It's also natural for our feet to get muddy and dirty when we walk through dirty places. That's why nature provided us with water and hands. It's impossible to eat without leaving some food stuck in the teeth, so nature tells us to clean our teeth. Why? So that you behave like a human and not like a wild animal or a pig. It's also natural for sweat and tight clothing to leave dirt on the body that needs to be cleaned off. That's why we have water, oil, hands, towels, scrapers, and other tools to clean our bodies. But if you don't act this way, think about it: even a blacksmith will remove rust from his tools, and you would clean a plate before eating if you weren't completely impure and dirty. So, why wouldn't you wash your body and keep it clean? Why not? I'll tell you: first, to act like a human being; and second, so that you won't be unpleasant to those around you. You do something similar in this matter, and you don't even realize it: you think you deserve to stink. Fine, go ahead and stink. But do you think those who sit beside you, those who eat with you, or those who kiss you deserve the same? Either go live in a desert, where you belong, or live by yourself and smell yourself. It's only fair that you alone should have to deal with your own filth. But when you're in a city, behaving so thoughtlessly and foolishly, what kind of person do you think you're being? If nature had given you a horse, would you neglect it? Now think that you've been entrusted with your own body as if it were a horse. Wash it, wipe it down, and take care that no one turns away from you or avoids you. But who wouldn't avoid a dirty, smelly person whose skin is filthy more than they would avoid someone covered in muck? That smell is from outside; it's put on him. But the other smell is from neglect, coming from within, almost as if the body is rotting.

"But Socrates rarely washed." Yes, but his body was clean and beautiful, so much so that the most handsome and noble people loved him and preferred to be near him rather than those with the best physical appearance. He could choose not to bathe or wash himself if he wanted, yet even using water rarely had an effect. "—The Clouds," line 102. But Aristophanes says: "Those who are pale, unshod, 'tis those I mean." For Aristophanes claimed that Socrates walked on air and stole clothes from the gym. However, all who have written about Socrates provide the exact opposite testimony: they say he was not only pleasant to listen to but also pleasant to look at. The same was written about Diogenes. For we shouldn't let the appearance of the body discourage people from philosophy. Just as a philosopher should show that he is cheerful and calm, he should also show that in matters related to the body: "See, people, that I have nothing, that I want nothing. See how I live without a home, without a city, and if it happens that I am an exile and without a hearth, I live more freely and happily than all those of noble birth and the rich. But look at my poor body too and observe that it isn't harmed by my tough way of living." But if someone like this says to me, with the appearance and face of a condemned person, "What God would persuade me to take up philosophy if it makes people like this?" Far from it; I wouldn't choose to do so, even if I were to become wise. I would rather a young person just starting out in philosophy come to me with their hair neatly trimmed than dirty and scruffy because this shows a certain sense of beauty and a desire for what is proper. Where they think beauty lies, they strive to find it. All they need is to be shown where true beauty is and told: "Young person, you seek beauty, and that's good. You must know that it grows in the part of you where your rational mind is. Look for it where your desires and aversions are because that's where your higher nature resides. The body is just earth, so why waste time on it? If you learn nothing else, time will teach you that the body is nothing." But if someone comes to me covered in filth, dirty, with a mustache down to their knees, what can I say to them? What can I use to change their mind? What resemblance can I use to guide them? Can I tell them that beauty isn't about being covered in muck but lies in the rational mind? Does this person even care about beauty? Does he have any idea of it in his mind? Go and talk to a pig, and tell it not to roll in the mud.

For this reason, Xenocrates' words also affected Polemon, since he was a lover of beauty. Polemon had some inclination towards beauty, but he was looking for it in the wrong place. Even animals that live with humans aren't dirty. Does a horse ever roll in the mud? Does a well-bred dog? No, but pigs, dirty geese, worms, and spiders do, creatures that are banished farthest from human society. Do you, as a human, want to be like a worm or a spider? Will you never wash yourself, even just a little? Will you not clean off the dirt from your body? Will you not be clean so that those who are with you will enjoy your company? But do you enter temples with us in this state, where it's not even allowed to spit or blow your nose, while you are a heap of spit and snot?

Does anyone demand that you decorate yourself? Far from it; the only decoration needed is the natural one—your rational mind, your opinions, your actions. As for your body, it only needs to be clean enough not to offend others. But if someone tells you that you shouldn't wear clothes dyed with purple, would you then smear dirt on your cloak or tear it? "But how can I keep a clean cloak?" you ask. Man, you have water—wash it. Here is a youth worthy of love, here is an old man worthy of loving and being loved in return, someone trustworthy enough to teach your children. Would you want this teacher to give lessons while sitting on a dung heap? Let this not be so: every mistake comes from something in human nature; but this (neglect of cleanliness) is close to being something against human nature.

Chapter 12
On Attention

When you have let your attention slip for a short time, do not think that you can regain it whenever you choose. Instead, keep in mind that because of the mistake you made today, your situation will be worse for everything that follows. First, and what is most troubling, is that you develop a habit of not paying attention; then you form a habit of postponing your attention. By continually postponing it, you keep pushing away the happiness of life, proper behavior, and living according to nature. If delaying attention is useful, then completely abandoning attention would be even more useful; but if it's not useful, then why don't you keep your attention steady?

"Today I choose to play." Well then, shouldn't you play with attention? "I choose to sing." What stops you from singing with attention? Is there any part of life where attention isn't needed? Will you do anything in life worse by paying attention to it, or better by not paying attention at all? What in life is done better by those who do not use attention? Does a carpenter work better by not paying attention to what he's doing? Does a ship's captain manage his ship better by ignoring it? Is any smaller task done better by inattention?

Don't you see that once you've let your mind go, it's no longer within your power to bring it back to proper behavior, modesty, or moderation? You end up doing whatever comes into your mind, following your impulses.

So, to what things should I pay attention? First, focus on the general principles and always have them ready. Without these principles, do not sleep, do not get up, do not drink, do not eat, and do not interact with others. Remember that no one has control over another person's will; only your own will contains good and bad. No one else has the power to bring me good or to cause me harm—only I have control over myself in these matters. Once these things are secured, why should I be worried about external things? What tyrant should I fear, what disease, what poverty, or what offense from another person?

Well, I did not please a certain person. Is it my job to please them, to be judged by them? No. So why should I worry about them? But this person is considered important. Let them concern themselves with that, as will those who think so. But I have someone I should please, someone I should obey—God, and those who are closest to Him. He has placed me in charge of myself and has given me control over my own will, along with rules for how to use it correctly. When I follow these rules in reasoning, I don't care about what anyone else says. In tricky arguments, I do not care about anyone else's opinion. So why, in more important matters, do I get annoyed by those who criticize me? What causes this disturbance? Nothing but the fact that I haven't been disciplined in this area. All knowledge looks down on ignorance and the ignorant. This applies not only to sciences but even to the arts. Bring forth any shoemaker you like, and he will mock those who don't know his craft. The same goes for any carpenter.

First, we should have these rules ready and never act without them. We should keep our minds focused on this goal: not to pursue anything external or anything that belongs to others or is under their control, but to act according to the rules of the one who has the power. We should pursue only what is within the power of our will, and everything else as allowed. Next, we should remember who we are and what our name is, and strive to direct our actions according to the roles we play in life. For example, when is it the right time to sing, when is it the right time to play, and in whose presence? What will be the outcome of our actions? Will our companions lose respect for us? Will we lose respect for them? When should we joke, and whom should we tease? On what occasion should we agree with others, and with whom? And finally, how can we maintain our own character while agreeing with others? But whenever you stray from these rules, there is immediate damage—not from anything external, but from the action itself.

So, is it possible to be completely free of faults if you do all this? It is not possible, but it is possible to aim constantly at being free of faults. We should be satisfied if, by never neglecting our attention, we can at least avoid some mistakes. But when you say, "Tomorrow I will start paying attention," you must realize that you are really saying, "Today I will be shameless, careless about time and place, and mean-spirited. Today, others will have the power to hurt me. Today, I will be angry and jealous." Look at all the bad things you allow yourself to do. If it is good to pay attention tomorrow, how much better is it to do so today? If it is in your interest to pay attention tomorrow, it is even more important to do so today, so that you'll be able to do it tomorrow as well, and not put it off again until the day after tomorrow.

Chapter 13
To Those Who Easily Share Their Secrets

When someone seems to talk openly and honestly about their own affairs, why do we often feel compelled to share our own secrets with them? It might seem unfair to listen to someone else's affairs without sharing our own in return. We might also think that if we don't share our own stories, we won't seem honest or open. People often say, "I've told you all about myself; why won't you tell me something about yourself? Is that fair?" We also tend to believe that we can safely trust someone who has already shared their secrets with us. We think that this person wouldn't reveal our secrets because they wouldn't want us to reveal theirs. This is how careless people often get trapped by soldiers in Rome. A soldier might sit next to you in plain clothes and start speaking badly about Caesar. Then, thinking that the soldier is trustworthy because he started the criticism, you share your own thoughts. After that, you get arrested and taken away in chains.

Something similar happens to us in other situations. If someone confidently shares their affairs with me, does that mean I should share mine with anyone I meet? No, because if I'm the kind of person who knows how to keep quiet, I won't tell anyone else what I've heard. But the other person might go out and tell everyone what I shared. If I find out about this, and if I'm the same type of person, I might want to get revenge by revealing what they told me, causing trouble for both of us. But if I remember that no one can truly harm another, and that everyone's actions affect themselves, then I won't act like them. Even so, I still suffer because of my own foolishness in talking too much.

"True, but it's unfair if you've heard someone's secrets and don't share your own in return." Did I ask you for your secrets? Did you share your affairs with me on the condition that I must share mine too? If you're a chatterbox who thinks everyone is your friend, should I be like that too? Why should I be reckless just because you were? It's like if I had a barrel that was watertight, and you had one with a hole in it. You come to me and ask to store your wine in my barrel, but then you complain that I didn't store my wine in yours. How is that fair? You trusted your affairs to someone who is trustworthy and discreet, someone who understands that only their own actions can harm or benefit them, and that external things don't matter. Should I then trust my affairs to you, someone who has no control over their own will and might even betray me for a bit of money or some small favor, like Medea who would kill her own children? How is that fair? But if you show me that you are trustworthy, discreet, and steady, and that you have good principles, then I won't wait for you to ask—I will come to you myself and ask you to hear my affairs. After all, who wouldn't want to use a good barrel? Who wouldn't value a kind and trustworthy advisor? Who wouldn't be happy to have someone who is willing to share the burden of their troubles and help lighten the load?

"True, but I trust you; you don't trust me." First of all, you don't really trust me; you're just a chatterbox who can't keep anything to yourself. If you truly trusted me, you would only tell me your affairs. But instead, whenever you see someone who seems available, you sit down and say, "Brother, I have no better or dearer friend than you; please listen to my affairs." And you do this even with people you barely know. But if you really trusted me, it would be clear that you trust me because I'm trustworthy and discreet, not because I've shared my affairs with you. Let me have the same opinion about you. Show me that sharing your affairs makes you trustworthy and discreet. If that were true, I'd go around telling my affairs to everyone if that would make me trustworthy and discreet. But that's not how it works, and this situation requires a special set of principles. If you see someone who is focused on things outside their control and lets those things dictate their will, you must understand that this person is easily influenced by thousands of things. They don't need physical torture

302

to force them to reveal what they know. Even a slight nod from a girl, the flattery of someone connected to Caesar's court, the desire for a government position, or an inheritance—any of these things could sway them. So, remember as a general rule that discussions about secret matters require trust and matching principles. But where can we easily find that nowadays? If you can't answer that, let someone show me a person who can say, "I care only about the things that are truly mine, the things that cannot be taken away, the things that are naturally free. This is what I believe is good; as for everything else, let them be as they are. I do not concern myself."

Excerpt from the Perfect Discourse (Asclepius 21-29)

"If you want to understand this mystery, Asclepius, think about what happens when a man and woman come together. When a man releases his seed at the highest moment, the woman receives his energy, and at the same time, the man also receives strength from the woman. The seed is the way this exchange happens.

"This act is done in private so that men and women aren't embarrassed in front of people who don't understand. Both man and woman share in the creation of new life. But if someone who doesn't understand sees it, they may laugh or not take it seriously. These are sacred acts—not just things we talk about, but things we do. They aren't meant for everyone to see or hear.

"That's why people who laugh at or reject these mysteries show no respect for what is holy. Most people don't honor them, because they don't learn the truth that was meant to guide them. But true learning and wisdom can heal the soul from harmful thoughts and desires.

"If someone doesn't learn or try to understand, then these harmful desires stay inside them. These turn into deep pain and suffering, like a sore that never heals. It slowly eats away at the soul. But this isn't God's fault—he gave people the ability to learn and know the truth so they could be free from this."

Asclepius asked, "Did God give this ability only to people?"

"Yes," I said. "God gave it only to people. Let me explain why. God, the Father and Lord of everything, made people after He made the gods. He used material from the physical world to create us.

Because of that, humans are affected by emotions and desires. These feelings always affect our bodies. We need food, and we're not immortal, so we're more likely to struggle with temptation. But the gods were made from pure matter, so they don't need to learn. Their immortality is like their knowledge—it comes naturally. But for humans, God set a boundary. We need learning and understanding to grow.

"That's why God gave us knowledge and learning—to help us fight off sin and harmful urges. With it, even though we are mortal, we can live better and become more like the gods—good and spiritually alive forever. God gave us two natures: one part that is mortal, and another that is immortal.

"In fact, God made humans greater than the gods in one way. The gods are only immortal, but humans are both mortal and immortal. That's why humans can understand divine things. We can know what the gods know, and they can know us too. But I'm only talking about people who truly seek knowledge and have understanding. We shouldn't speak badly of those who don't. We are spiritual beings, and this is a holy conversation.

"Now let's talk about how people and gods are connected. Asclepius, listen carefully. Just as God creates gods, humans—though we are mortal—also create gods. We don't just receive power; we also give it. We are not only like gods—we help bring gods into being.

"Does that surprise you, Asclepius? Are you starting to doubt like most people?"

"No," Asclepius replied. "I believe what you say. I'm just amazed by it. I think people are truly blessed to have this kind of power."

"There's something even more amazing," I said. "Everyone agrees that the gods came from pure matter and that their bodies are just heads. But the gods that humans make look like full people. They have all the body parts, just like us. Just as God made the inner person in His image, people on earth make gods that look like themselves."

Asclepius asked, "You don't mean statues or idols, do you?"

"You're the one who said idols," I replied. "See, Asclepius, you're doubting again. You're calling idols those who are full of spirit— beings that cause powerful things to happen. You're calling idols those who give prophecies, bring healing, or even cause illness.

"Don't you know that Egypt is a reflection of heaven? It holds the power of heaven. If I'm allowed to say this truth, I'll tell you— our land is the temple of the world. And you should know something important: a time will come when it will seem like the Egyptians worshipped God for nothing. People will laugh at their devotion. All that is holy will leave Egypt and rise back to heaven. The gods will leave.

"Strangers will take over our land and stop Egyptians from worshiping. Those who try to stay faithful will suffer—especially anyone caught praying or showing honor to God."

"In the future, the land that once followed God more than any other will completely turn away from Him. It won't be filled with temples anymore—just tombs. It won't be known for honoring gods, only for holding the dead. Egypt will become like a story people forgot. Its sacred treasures and miracles will be gone. Even the stories about Egypt will seem odd or unbelievable. People from other lands—like the Scythians, Indians, and others—will respect their gods more than the Egyptians do.

"But Egyptians won't leave their land. When the gods leave Egypt and return to heaven, many Egyptians will die. Their land will become empty, abandoned by both the gods and the people. The Nile River will carry more blood than water, and dead bodies will stack up higher than the riverbanks. The living won't even cry for the dead because staying alive will be more painful. People will still speak the Egyptian language, but their ways will no longer feel truly Egyptian. Asclepius, I see you crying—but even worse things are coming. Holy Egypt, once loved by God and filled with temples and knowledge, will become known for turning away from faith.

"At that time, people won't care about how amazing the world is. They won't value life or eternal truth. The world will feel broken and heavy. People will ignore the beauty of God's creation. They will choose darkness instead of light, and death instead of life. No one will lift their eyes to heaven. Believers will be seen as crazy, while those who reject God will be praised as wise. Cowards will be called brave. Good people will be treated like criminals.

"And people like you—Tat, Asclepius, and Ammon—who believe in the soul and life after death, will be laughed at and mocked. But those who mock are in real danger. Their souls are at risk. A new kind of law will lead people away from what is right. Evil spirits will stay with them and push them into sin, disbelief, war, and destruction. These spirits will teach them to live in unnatural and harmful ways.

"The earth will become unstable. People will stop sailing. They won't understand the stars anymore. God's voice will no longer be heard. Even the air will become sick. This is how the world will fall apart—through disbelief, disrespect, and ignoring the truth.

"When this happens, Asclepius, God—the Father, the true Creator—will step in. He will act against the chaos. He will remove lies and destroy evil. Sometimes He will send great floods. Other times fire, war, or disease. These will clean the world. This is how the world was created—and how it will be restored.

"The people who lived faithfully will return to their proper place. This return has no beginning because God's will has no beginning. God's nature and His will are the same—and they are always good."

"Trismegistus, is God's purpose the same as His will?"

"Yes, Asclepius. His will comes from perfect wisdom. He doesn't want things because He lacks them—He already has everything good. Whatever He wants, He already has. And the world is a reflection of His goodness."

"Trismegistus, is the world good?"

"Yes, Asclepius, it is. Let me explain. Everything—from the human soul to the changing seasons and the ripening of fruit—shows God's goodness. God rules over everything, from the sky to the earth. He isn't limited to one place—He exists everywhere, beyond the stars and even beyond the physical world.

"God has control over the space between heaven and earth. People call Him 'Zeus,' which means 'Life.' Another spirit, Plutonius Zeus, rules the land and sea, but he doesn't feed all living things— that's Kore's job, the one who brings fruit. These powers work through the earth, but they all come from the One who truly exists.

"When the gods leave the earth, they will gather in a city at the far western edge of Egypt. People will come there from land and sea."

"Trismegistus, where exactly will that city be?"

"Asclepius, it will be a great city on the Libyan mountain. Some people will be afraid of what happens there because they don't understand. Death will come—it's when the body can no longer hold itself together. Death happens when the body is no longer strong enough to carry the person. It's when the body breaks apart and loses its senses. But we shouldn't fear death itself—we should fear what we don't understand or believe in."

"What are the things we don't understand or believe?"

"Listen, Asclepius. There's a powerful spirit that God put in charge of judging souls. He waits in the space between earth and heaven. When someone dies, their soul meets this spirit. He looks at how the person lived. If they lived faithfully and did what they were meant to do, the spirit lets them pass. But if they lived badly, he grabs them and throws them down. They are left hanging between heaven and earth, full of pain and without hope.

"These souls don't reach heaven or return to earth. They float in a wild place filled with fire, water, and chaos. Their bodies are burned or broken in many ways. I won't say their souls die—but they are judged and sentenced. They're no longer part of this world, but they suffer greatly.

"Believe what I tell you, Asclepius. Fear these things so we can avoid them. People who don't believe in them are not only disrespectful—they also sin. But later, they'll be forced to believe—not just by hearing, but by living through it. They think it won't happen to them—but it will.

"Everyone on earth will die. Those who lived wicked lives will be punished. People who live on earth won't be like those who lived rightly in other places. The evil spirits who rule over the wicked will be punished every day.

"Trismegistus, what kinds of sins are there in that place?"

"Asclepius, you think stealing from a temple is terrible—and it is. That person is a thief. But don't compare earthly sins with what happens after death. I'll tell you something private—most won't believe it. Souls full of great evil don't float freely. They're thrown into places filled with pain, blood, and suffering. Their only food is people's cries, sadness, and pain."

"Trismegistus, who are these spirits?"

"They're called 'stranglers.' They pull souls down to the ground. They beat them, throw them into fire or water, and cause suffering.

These spirits aren't from God. They aren't part of a human soul either. They come from a deep and terrible kind of evil."

Thank You for Reading

Dear Reader,

We hope this timeless classic has sparked your imagination and enriched your literary journey. Now that you've turned the final page, we want to share a vision for the future of reading—one where every classic you've ever wanted to explore is at your fingertips, in a format that best suits your life.

We'd like to invite you to gain immediate, unlimited digital & audiobook access to hundreds of the most treasured literary classics ever written—along with the option to secure deluxe paperback, hardcover & box set editions at printing cost. Together, we can spark a new global literary renaissance alongside our small, independent publishing house called "The Library of Alexandria."

Thousands of years ago, the Library of Alexandria stood as a beacon of knowledge—until it was lost to history. We aim to reignite that spirit of preservation and discovery right now, in the modern age— only this time, it's accessible to all, in every language and every format.

Picture a world where every timeless classic, novel, poem, or philosophical treatise is not only available to read but also updated for today's readers—modernized, translated into any language or dialect, and ready to enjoy in any format you choose, whether that is in an eBook, audiobook, paperback, or deluxe hardcover & box set version a printing cost.

By joining our movement to rebuild the modern Library of Alexandria, you become part of an unprecedented mission to offer:

- **Unlimited Audiobook & eBook Access to the Greatest Classics of All Time**

  Instantly explore thousands of legendary works, from Plato and Shakespeare to Jane Austen and Leo Tolstoy. All are instantly ready to read or listen to, giving you a complete literary universe at your fingertips.

- **Paperback & Deluxe Editions at Printing Costs:**

  Purchase any title in a paperback, deluxe hardbound, or deluxe boxset edition at printing costs, shipped right to your doorstep. Curate your personal library of Alexandria with editions worthy of display—crafted to last, designed to captivate, and delivered straight to your door.

- **Modern translations for Contemporary Readers in all languages and dialects**

  Discover a vast selection of classics reimagined in clear, current language—no more struggling with outdated phrases or obscure references. Next to the original versions, we aim to offer translations in as many languages and dialects as possible.

  As we continue our translation efforts and add new languages, readers everywhere can connect with these works as if they were written today. By bridging linguistic divides, you're contributing to ensuring that these timeless stories become more meaningful, accessible, and inspiring for people across the globe.

- **Your Personal Library of Alexandria:**

  Over the months and years, you'll curate a unique physical archive of classics—each volume a testament to your taste, curiosity, and love of knowledge. It's not just about owning books—it's about curating a cultural legacy you'll cherish and pass down for generations to come.

- **Join a Global Literary Renaissance:**

  Your support fuels an ongoing mission: allowing us to reinvest in offering deluxe print editions (including special boxsets) at their true cost, broaden the range of available formats and translations, and extend the reach of these works to new audiences worldwide. By joining today, you're not just preserving a legacy of masterpieces; you set in motion a powerful wave of literary accessibility.

  We are more than a publisher—we're a movement, and we can't do it alone. Your support lets us scale our mission, preserving and reimagining history's greatest works for tomorrow's readers.

Become a Torchbearer of knowledge.

Thank you for picking up this book and allowing us into your literary journey. As you turn the pages, know that you're part of something larger: a global effort to keep these stories alive, share their wisdom across borders and generations, and spark a true cultural revival for the modern era.

If this resonates with you—please consider taking the next step by visiting:

www.libraryofalexandria.com

With gratitude and a shared love of knowledge,

The Modern Library of Alexandria Team

Visit:

www.libraryofalexandria.com

Or scan the code below: